QUEER PALESTINE AND
THE EMPIRE OF CRITIQUE

QUEER PALESTINE AND THE EMPIRE OF CRITIQUE

Sa'ed Atshan

Stanford University Press
Stanford, California

Stanford University Press
Stanford, California

Printed in the United States of America on acid-free, archival-quality paper

Library of Congress Cataloging-in-Publication Data

Names: Atshan, Sa'ed, author.
Title: Queer Palestine and the empire of critique / Sa'ed Atshan.
Description: Stanford : Stanford University Press, 2020. | Includes bibliographical
    references and index.
Identifiers: LCCN 2019037604 (print) | LCCN 2019037605 (ebook) | ISBN 9781503609945
    (cloth) | ISBN 9781503612396 (paperback) | ISBN 9781503612402 (epub)
Subjects: LCSH: Gay liberation movement—Palestine—History. | Sexual minorities—
    Political activity—Palestine. | Sexual minorities—Civil rights—Palestine. | Gay
    rights—Palestine.
Classification: LCC HQ76.8.P19 A78 2020 (print) | LCC HQ76.8.P19 (ebook) |
    DDC 306.76/6095694—dc23
LC record available at https://LCCN.loc.gov/2019037604
LC ebook record available at https://LCCN.loc.gov/2019037605

Cover design: Angela Moody
Cover painting: Nabil Anani, *Nostalgia*, 2016, acrylic on canvas, 120 × 105 cm.
    Courtesy of Zawyeh Gallery and the artist.
Typeset by Motto Publishing Services in 10/14 Minion Pro

Contents

Preface

I TRACE MY QUEER CONSCIOUSNESS to 1999, when I was a fifteen-year-old adolescent. I have vivid memories of the time I spent with my male friends, filled with laughter and joy. But I also experienced bewilderment and disorientation when we looked at pictures of women and when my friends expressed their attraction to them.

"Why do I not desire the same? Why am I finding myself drawn to other boys?" I asked myself. But the mere thought of exploring the answers to my questions led to feelings of deep shame. There was no conceptual tool kit or vocabulary and no words in Arabic that came to mind to help me navigate what was becoming a journey of self-discovery.

"When two men lie together in bed, the throne of God shakes with anger!" After hearing these words from a preacher through the loudspeakers of a local mosque as I walked past it one day, I vowed to never let anyone know about the thoughts raging inside me.

I then became particularly sensitive when strangers and family members commented that my voice was not deep enough, my grip not firm enough, my walk not straight enough, or my posture not bold enough. I felt grateful and relieved that I attended the Ramallah Friends School, a Quaker institution established in Palestine in 1869. Books become my sanctuary, and theater became my escape. I loved taking on roles as Tiresias and King Arthur, because they made me feel as if I could project a more masculine self.

The Second Intifada, or Palestinian uprising against Israeli occupation, was omnipresent in 2001. I remember the visceral malaise in my stomach from eating only lentils while trapped under military curfew. The sounds of helicopters, bulldozers, bombs, funeral processions, and protests all around us were frightening, but eventually I could not fall asleep unless I heard the shooting outside. The soldiers raided our house, targeting the men. They took my grandfather, father, and me for questioning. I trembled with fear. "Be strong; be a man." I could hear my father saying that to me without him even having to utter the words. But he, too, was quivering. I was frozen while attempting to broaden my shoulders.

I pushed myself harder than ever that year, achieving the rank of first in my class and being elected president of the student government. Yet nothing cured the melancholy of realizing that I could not live up to the expectations of hegemonic masculinity placed on men in my society.

I was thrilled to arrive at Swarthmore College in 2002, an institution outside of Philadelphia that was also founded by the Quakers. The violence of the Second Intifada continued back home. I worried about my family every day, and I was consumed with guilt for leaving my people behind for this idyllic campus, all of which is an arboretum. The tragic events of September 11, 2001, were still fresh. "I never knew there was affirmative action for terrorists!" A fellow student exclaimed that after discovering my Palestinian background. I was in shock. I wracked my brain for a response but was frozen in silence.

Being one of a few token Arab students was challenging. But I loved my experience overall. And I was committed to fitting Middle Eastern Studies into my academic pursuits while educating my peers about the region and promising myself to try to never be silent about anything again.

I also read Audre Lorde for the first time. She writes, "For we have been socialized to respect fear more than our own needs for language and definition, and while we wait in silence for that final luxury of fearlessness, the weight of that silence will choke us."[1]

I developed the courage to speak with openly queer students but soon found I could not escape my feelings of alienation. Gripped by my anxiety about coming to terms with who I am given the constant violence back home, I had difficulty relating to queer students. I remember how my sense of isolation deepened when a peer was complaining that his parents were pressuring him to limit himself to a single boyfriend; he wanted to pursue multiple partners. The difference between our concerns at that time was vast. Silence continued its hold on me.

In the summer after my sophomore year, I stepped out of the train station in the Castro District of San Francisco for the first time. I stood at the top of the hill, with the enormous rainbow flag above me and smaller rainbow flags at each stop sign below. Numerous same-sex couples were holding hands or walking all around me. I could not hold back my tears. A stranger saw me, walked over, gave me a hug, and said, "I know. I know. It will be okay."

Through my internship at the American Civil Liberties Union in California that summer, I had unconsciously made a gay pilgrimage to San Francisco. There I discovered the group SWANABAQ (South West Asian and North African Bay Area Queers). It finally dawned on me that I was not the only gay Arab on the planet. I had my first relationship that summer, began to accept myself, and then revealed my sexual orientation to my closest friends. But I remained vigilant about protecting my privacy.

I spent the fall semester of my junior year of college at the American University in Cairo and then the spring semester at the American University of Beirut. Farha Ghannam, my advisor and mentor at Swarthmore and a brilliant Middle East anthropologist, introduced me to anthropology and helped me gain a deep appreciation for the discipline. She also served as my faculty mentor for the Mellon Mays Undergraduate Fellowship, a scholarship program for minority students interested in becoming academics. Ghannam encouraged me to conduct thesis research comparing the LGBTQ communities in Beirut and Cairo. I fell in love with ethnography and found it exhilarating to be immersed in queer social milieus in the Middle East. I spent significant time in Beirut at Helem ("Dream" in Arabic), the first LGBTQ organization in the Arab world. This allowed me to bring together two salient identities: being queer and being Arab. Up until that point, I had experienced these identities only in tension with each other, and it has simply been with time that I have learned to appreciate how connected they are in me.

I was taken with the scholarship of Palestinian academic Joseph Massad, particularly his critiques of what he terms the "gay international" agenda. I drew on that work, particularly his article "Re-Orienting Desire: The Gay International and the Arab World,"[2] and Michel Foucault's *The History of Sexuality* to problematize the universalizing of LGBTQ categories from the West to the Middle East. In my thesis, I described the gay flag in the United States as a form of nationalism and cited Foucault's assertion that the "Western man has become a confessing animal"[3] (which he linked to Catholicism) to delineate the limits of coming out discourses for queer Arabs.

In discovering Massad's work, I was excited to finally see the topic of gay Arabs taken seriously as a scholarly endeavor. That led me to internalize his analysis. It was only later, with more self-confidence, that I realized I needed to consider that analysis more critically. I then questioned the simple binaries between East and West that I had reified in the thesis project. My coming out had taken place in an academic setting; so queerness, scholarship, and academic acceptance have all been tied up for me. I had excelled in academia as a way to compensate for the shame of homosexuality. Personal self-acceptance has subsequently enabled me to embrace a more nuanced academic voice.

I graduated from Swarthmore in the spring of 2006, receiving an award the institution named that year—the Edward Said/Audre Lorde Scholar-Activism Award. It was an honor, but it was also daunting to receive because of my experiences with impostor syndrome in the academy and because of how towering both those figures were in my intellectual and political imagination.

With both apprehension and excitement, I arrived at Harvard University that fall, matriculating at the Kennedy School of Government for the master's in public policy program. I was eager to undergo professional graduate training after my liberal arts undergraduate education. The knots in my stomach I had the first year of college returned to me that fall when I realized that I was the only Palestinian student at the Kennedy School and merely one of a handful of the LGBTQ caucus members there. It was in becoming increasingly open about my Palestinian and queer identities that I grew more secure, self-loving, and at ease at Harvard.

I returned home to Palestine the summer after my first year of graduate school to intern with the unit overseeing high-level Palestinian negotiations with Israel. My family did not yet know about my gay identity, but a number of close friends and colleagues did, and they were supportive. They shared with me that a Palestinian who had recently worked with the same negotiations team in a significant position had been completely forthcoming to everyone—including at the highest levels of the Palestinian political leadership—about the fact that he was gay. They also shared that no one had given him any trouble about his sexuality. That possibility had been unimaginable to me until that point. I had never heard of, let alone met, an openly queer Palestinian.

After completing my master's degree, I immediately began the joint PhD program in anthropology and Middle Eastern studies at Harvard. I chose to study the politics of international humanitarian aid in the Occupied Palestinian Territories. Israel's military offensives in the Gaza Strip, and the unfolding humanitarian crisis there, became increasingly devastating. I channeled my desperation into research about the topic.

During my final pre-fieldwork visit home, I began to anticipate what to expect upon my return the following year for fourteen consecutive months of ethnographic research. I wondered whether I could ever resettle in Palestine and live as an openly gay man. "Is it safe?," I asked myself. I had heard about people being disowned or met with violence from their families due to their sexuality. I had also heard about queer Palestinians being forced by the Israeli occupation forces to serve as collaborators and informants.

I confided in a dear friend about my sexuality, and he became deeply uncomfortable. I had been very close with him and his family in Ramallah. They were devout Palestinian Christians, and his father worked for a local church. The religious traditions of both Christianity and Islam in the Levant have been inhospitable to compassionate reception of homosexuality in the contemporary context. When I went to see my friend and to visit his family the next day, his father opened the door, his face filled with sadness, and then informed me that he was the only one home. He invited me to sit on the rooftop with him and proceeded to say that my friend had revealed to him that I was gay and that this is unacceptable in our society. He said that I could not speak with them anymore unless I sought to change my sexuality through particular church services. It was devastating for me to bear the pain this caused. I looked at the sun as it began to set, felt the breeze of the evening air, mustered every bit of strength I could, and then graciously replied that it was not possible for me to change. No one from that family has spoken to me since.

During my last night at home that summer, as I looked around into the caring eyes of my family members, I imagined them withdrawing their love for me if they discovered my secret. The thought of living in exile as a result of familial homophobia was too much to bear.

In 2010, I established a research base in Bethlehem and began my fieldwork on international aid. Only days after my arrival, one of my straight family members, whom I had never come out to about my sexuality, introduced me to one of his gay friends in the hopes that we would date each other. He succeeded in facilitating this romantic relationship. It came as a complete surprise to me that a relative would not only know about this aspect of my identity but also be so supportive. He shared that he promised to keep his lips sealed but that I should also remember, as he put it, that "we are your family, and we love you, and we just want you to be happy." I have never been able to forget those words. They also planted seeds of confidence for me to come out to my parents two years later, even though I was consumed by dread; one never knew what kind of visceral response to expect.

I discovered that in the years I had been away studying in the United States, a queer Palestinian movement in Israel and the West Bank had emerged. I then joined an LGBTQ Palestinian organization, Al-Qaws (short for *Qaws Quzah*, or "rainbow" in Arabic), and became an activist with the group, co-facilitating a workshop series in the West Bank on queer Palestinian empowerment. Through this work, I saw how the figure of Joseph Massad, whom I had admired as a college student during my thesis writing, loomed over queer activists in the region. They shudder at the prospect of being called "local informants" of the "gay international" by him and his followers. Being immersed in the queer Palestinian movement forced me to revisit my previous embrace of Massad's framework and to understand how East/West binaries, the language we use, and the political projects we espouse are not black and white in the increasingly globalized and transnational world in which we live. I have since aspired to pursue engaged scholarship that makes room for more complexity.

Two Palestinian organizations and initiatives, Al-Qaws and Aswat ("Voices" in Arabic, also known as Palestinian Gay Women), came together in 2011 and worked with prominent queer writer and activist Sarah Schulman to organize the first LGBTQ delegation from the United States to Palestine. I agreed to serve as one of two coleaders of the delegation, which would accompany the sixteen American delegates for the full ten days in Palestine. On the eve of the delegation's start, I decided that it was time to come out to my broader family. My mother's response will be with me forever. Upon sharing that I am gay with her in Arabic, she replied,

> The reason that I am crying is that I cannot believe you have gone through all of this without me. I wish that I had been able to be by your side. But I am now comforted that you have come to me. I am proud of you for how far you have come. I did know deep down inside, like every mother does, but we hold on to the doubt until it is confirmed to us otherwise. I want you to know that my respect for you has only increased. This is something incredibly difficult in our society, but you are my son. I love you, forever and always.

No words of my own have ever been able to communicate the depth of my gratitude for her words.

Buoyed by familial support, I have since become public in my activism in the global queer Palestinian solidarity movement. Trips home to Palestine during Christmas and summer breaks also have kept me connected with the developments on the ground for my community of queer Palestinians. I am now determined to help advance a new generation of scholarship in LGBTQ Middle East/North African studies.

In writing this book, I chose to approach it using a global framework of solidarity with Queer Palestine and to include my autoethnography, which traces my own political and intellectual development as a person, activist, and scholar over the past twenty years. I selected diagnostic events that mark critical junctures in my consciousness as a queer Palestinian. This inclusion also speaks to the coming out genre with which many queer readers are familiar. In my own life thus far, I have been a witness and participant in the Palestinian landscape in three distinct periods: before the emergence of the queer movement in Palestine, after the rise of the movement locally in 2002 and internationally in 2009, and currently in its moment of plateau that began in 2012.

By exploring my own engagement with the global queer Palestinian solidarity movement, I offer an autoethnographic[4] account of how I have come to approach the issues surrounding Queer Palestine as an academic and activist. Carolyn Ellis and Arthur Bochner link autoethnography to autobiographies, defining autoethnographies as works that "self-consciously explore the interplay of the introspective, personally engaged self with cultural descriptions mediated through language, history, and ethnographic explanation."[5] As an anthropologist, I am drawn to a particular form of autoethnography—analytic autoethnography as delineated by Leon Anderson. He explains, "Analytic autoethnography has five key features. It is ethnographic work in which the researcher (a) is a full member in a research group or setting; (b) uses analytic reflexivity; (c) has a visible narrative presence in the written text; (d) engages in dialogue with informants beyond the self; and (e) is committed to an analytic research agenda focused on improving theoretical understandings of broader social phenomena."[6] Finally, this autoethnography demonstrates how my analysis and knowledge production in the domain of Queer Palestine shape and are shaped by my positionality and my deeply close and personal proximity to this material. As Paul Atkinson writes, "The very possibility of social life and of understanding it ethnographically depends on an elementary principle: the homology between the social actors who are being studied and the social actor who is making sense of their actions. It is this principle that generates the ethnographic enterprise."[7]

In this text, I was willing to study myself critically to put myself under the same analytical scrutiny as others, to situate where I am, and to decenter/denaturalize my authorial perspective by situating it. I draw attention to the places that animated my queer consciousness and the trajectory of the global queer Palestinian solidarity movement. And although I certainly cannot speak for all queer Palestinians, I invite readers to join me in reflecting on my deeply personal journey.

Acknowledgments

FIRST, AND MOST IMPORTANTLY, I am forever grateful to the people of Palestine for modeling collective warmth and resilience each and every day. Their tenacity is the primary source of my inspiration to keep moving forward. Although survey data reveals that my society of origin overwhelmingly holds unfavorable views on LGBTQ issues, rendering it impossible for me to live with equality as an openly gay man were I to return to Palestine permanently, my love for my ancestral land and compassion for its people only deepens. That society has shaped me into the person I am today. My LGBTQ rights activism is naturally an extension of the struggle for Palestinian human rights, to which I am also deeply committed. I truly believe that my people, with increased political freedom and exposure to more knowledge on queer struggles, would largely embrace their queer and trans family members, neighbors, and other LGBTQ individuals and communities.

This book project developed from a paper I gave at Brown University in 2013. Their Middle East Studies program hosted the "Knowledge Production, Ethics, Solidarity" Engaged Scholarship Workshop that year. This workshop connected me with scholars from other universities who were thinking through the relationship between the academy, activism, and the contemporary Middle East. I then accepted a fellowship for the following two years at Brown's Watson Institute for International Studies. This enabled me to host a conference there in 2015 on LGBTQ movements across the Middle East/North Africa region. These experiences planted the seeds for my more public and extensive writing on these issues. In particular, I am profoundly thankful to Beshara Doumani and Richard Locke for their mentorship during my time at Brown.

I have since presented parts of this book's material on the LGBTQ Palestinian movement at academic conferences, including at annual meetings of the American Anthropological Association, the American Studies Association, the Middle East Studies Association, and the Peace and Justice Studies Association, as well as at various universities. These lectures have taken place at institutions including Amherst College, Bates College, Boston College, Boston University, Brown University, Columbia University, Davidson College, Earlham College, Emerson College, George Washington University, Gettysburg College, Guilford College, Harvard University, Haverford College, Humboldt University, Institute for Cultural Inquiry (Berlin), Kenyon College, Lehigh University, Loyola University, Macalester College, Marymount Manhattan College, Massachusetts Institute of Technology, New York University, Northeastern University, Occidental College, Princeton University, Providence College, Rutgers University, Sarah Lawrence College, Swarthmore College, Temple University, Tufts University, University of California Los Angeles, University of Chicago, University of Delaware, University of Illinois Urbana Champaign, University of Michigan, University of Pennsylvania, University of Puget Sound, University of Tennessee Knoxville, Vanderbilt University, Villanova University, and Yale University. The comments and questions posed by the students, staff, and faculty at these talks have been tremendously eye-opening and have enriched my arguments.

Over the past two years, a delightful group of interlocutors have generously read parts or all of this manuscript: Rebecca Alpert, Samer Anabtawi, Huda Asfour, Phillip Ayoub, Tareq Baconi, Soha Bayoumi, Kent Brintnall, Sarah Eltantawi, Katherine Franke, Farha Ghannam, Aeyal Gross, Sherine Hamdy, Yaqub Hilal, Rhoda Kanaaneh, Nancy Khalek, Tim McCarthy, Minoo Moallem, Darnell Moore, Saffo Papantonopoulou, Ahmed Ragab, Jonathan Rosa, Omar Sarwar, Sarah Schulman, Jake Silver, Eve Spangler, and Patty White. The fact that these brilliant minds shared their respective insights and feedback on my work means the world to me. I have also benefited from the careful editorial assistance of Matthew Berkman and Eliana Yankelev. I cannot thank them enough.

I am grateful to Rashid Khalidi and the *Journal of Palestine Studies* community for inviting me to join the JPS Editorial Committee. Serving JPS has been an incredible privilege, and I have felt included in our field more than ever before as a result, instilling hope in me that we can continue building bridges between Palestine Studies and Queer Studies.

I also greatly appreciate the time that the two anonymous readers took to review my manuscript for Stanford University Press. At SUP, Michelle Lipinski's encouragement on completion of the first draft was unbelievably kind. I also could not have asked for a better editor than Kate Wahl at all stages thereafter. The Middle East Studies list she has nurtured is breathtaking. I am honored for my book to be the first one that is queer focused in this program.

The remarkable support of Lee Smithey, my colleague here at Swarthmore College, has been a gift, providing me with a role model whose intellectual passion for Peace and Conflict Studies is infectious. A group of my students at Swarthmore volunteered to read this manuscript, and their queries and perspectives as super bright undergraduates were very helpful. They include Hanan Ahmed, Mohammed Bappe, Marissa Cohen, Isabel Cristo, Vinita Davey, Omri Gal, Zackary Lash, Cindy Lopez, Nora Shao, Therese Ton, Lily Tyson, Nate Urban, and Lila Weitzner. Their reflections made my ideas more clear and my writing more accessible.

The moral support of dear friends has also been invaluable—thanks to Najib Abualetham, Naira Der Kiureghian, Sarah Goldberg, Husam Hammad, Weeam Hammoudeh, Harb Harb, Maram Jafar, Kira Jumet, Reem Kassis, Rashad Nimr, Jayanti Owens, Maliheh Paryavi, and Hannah Schafer. They are beautiful souls, and I hope I am able to reciprocate their friendship. Finally, this project would not have been possible without the love of my family and the spirits of my ancestors.

QUEER PALESTINE AND
THE EMPIRE OF CRITIQUE

Introduction

"there is no hierarchy of oppressions"

THE CONTEMPORARY global queer Palestinian solidarity movement began to visibly surface in 2002. Courageous LGBTQ activists broke formidable taboos and defied deeply entrenched social norms of gender and sexuality to give a public face and voice to queer Palestinians. The movement then experienced significant growth in Palestine until it reached a plateau in 2012. Since then, the movement has neither grown nor retreated.

The foundation of the movement was built by queer Palestinians in Israel/Palestine (also known as Israel and the Occupied Palestinian Territories or as historic Palestine) working with or under or being supported by Israeli LGBTQ organizations. Inspired by the Palestinian feminist movement that argued simultaneously for the liberation of the nation and the liberation of women, the queer Palestinian movement articulated the need for a similar cause that is not dependent on Israeli institutions. As a result, queer Palestinian citizens of Israel, and lesbian women in particular, catalyzed the rise of the Palestinian LGBTQ social and political sphere. Thus, in many ways, the queer Palestinian movement was a by-product of the feminist movement, and many queer activists consider themselves feminists as well. These queer Palestinian feminist activists in Israel then reached out to queer Palestinians in the Occupied Palestinian Territories and built connections among Palestinians across Israeli-imposed divides. At the same time, the differences between Palestinians with Israeli citizenship and stateless Palestinians under military occupation have sharpened an asymmetry in power within the queer Palestinian movement.

1

Queer Jewish Israelis, in showing solidarity with queer Palestinians, became some of the most vigorous and vocal among non-Palestinians in the struggle against homophobia, anti-Arab racism, and the Israeli state. Queer Jewish North Americans and Europeans now play a disproportionately large role in the global queer Palestinian solidarity movement, particularly as the left—and the peace movement—has diminished in Israel in recent years. Furthermore, diaspora Palestinians and non-Palestinians who are solidarity activists work to support the queer movement in Palestine through campaigns in local contexts, particularly in Europe and North America, which has led to the global reach of the movement.

In recent years, those within the global queer Palestinian solidarity movement and their allies have increasingly turned against one another, resulting in deep divisions and contestation that have inhibited the movement from reaching its full potential. Activists and members are being worn down by the enduring nature of different and intersecting systems of oppression. There have also been shifts favoring a subset of activists whom I describe as "radical purists." Their competition over moral purity, debates on representation, limits on institutional capacities, rigid policies on international aid, criticism of those to whom they are closest, and other factors have led to the fragmentation of the movement. Nonetheless, queer Palestinian activism persists on the ground in Israel/Palestine. Solidarity with Palestine remains one of the most dynamic and salient domains of global queer politics today.

Pinkwashing and Pinkwatching

Palestinians have long engaged in a nationalist struggle to maintain a strong Palestinian identity in the face of military occupation by Israel. They live under Israeli domination, with virtually every aspect of their lives ultimately controlled by this foreign power. For decades, Israeli intelligence and security services have targeted queer Palestinians and used homophobia as a weapon, threatening to out them to their families and communities if they do not serve as informants and collaborators. At the same time, some Zionist institutions have worked over the past decade to co-opt queer Palestinian voices in order to attempt to justify Israel's military occupation of Palestine to global audiences. It is in this context that queer Palestinian activists built a movement to respond and resist.

The queer Palestinian movement extended internationally to respond to the Israeli state's efforts to flatten queer Palestinian sexualities. Like many states, Israel has long been concerned with its global image, devoting substantial resources to diplomacy and public affairs. Israel is particularly invested in establishing its legitimacy on the world stage *in spite of* the occupation of the Palestinian Territories and its illegal practices under international law.[1] The global nation-branding consulting firm East West, in its index ranking of two hundred countries based on their reputations in international media, has consistently found that Israel has been ranked near the bottom.[2] Although there have been some improvements in Israel's image, the country remains far from the point the state aspires to in terms of global public relations. Israeli governments have increasingly invested in "Brand Israel" campaigns done in the name of security, self-defense, and Israel's reputation for having a world-leading technology scene, expanding entrepreneurship, and what it describes as "the only democracy in the Middle East." Sarah Schulman writes that the Brand Israel campaign seeks to depict Israel as "relevant and modern."[3] Of particular note in these efforts to achieve liberal recognition of modernity is the Israeli state's incentivizing of LGBTQ discourse—what queer Palestinian activists have termed "pinkwashing." Schulman adds, "The government later expanded this marketing plan by harnessing the gay community to reposition its international image."[4]

Pinkwashing is defined as a discourse on Israeli LGBTQ rights aimed at detracting attention from violations of Palestinian human rights.[5] The term has become salient in queer activist and academic circles around the world. The dynamic that this term signifies is as follows: rather than improve its global standing by providing Palestinians with basic human rights, the Israeli state and its supporters, increasingly moving to the right, seek to market Israel as a state that supports LGBTQ individuals and communities.

In 2005 the Israeli government launched its Brand Israel campaign, and Palestinian civil society launched its Boycott, Divestment, and Sanctions (BDS) movement. The BDS movement demands boycotts against institutions complicit in Israel's system of oppression and has motivated queer Palestinian activists to cultivate transnational solidarity networks. Its genesis marked a turning point for queer Palestinian activists, connecting their activism not only to Palestinian and Israeli audiences but also to people around the world.[6]

The LGBTQ dimension of Brand Israel became a phenomenon in 2009, after Ron Huldai, the straight mayor of Tel Aviv, developed a strategy to market Tel Aviv for gay tourism. Journalist Itay Hod elaborated on how this emerged: "A study commissioned by the mayor's office showed gay tourists were more inclined to go to cities like Barcelona or Berlin rather than Israel, a country they associated with religion and war. So the mayor had an idea: brand Tel Aviv as its own separate entity."[7] As a result, promoters of gay tourism often focus on branding Tel Aviv separately from Israel more generally. This strategy is in line with the words of Yaniv Waizman, the Tel Aviv mayor's adviser on gay community affairs, who said, "So we made a switch. We no longer talked about Israel, but Tel Aviv."[8] In 2013, Waizman boasted about the amount Israel spent on global gay marketing: "We now spend a quarter of a million dollars a year on gay tourism, a fortune by Israeli standards."[9]

Responding to pinkwashing galvanized queer activists within and outside of Palestine, who identified patterns in the ways LGBTQ discourses were marshaled to justify backing the Israeli state. These patterns include a bifurcation of Israel and Palestine and a failure to recognize Israel/Palestine as a de facto single state with Israel as the ultimate sovereign throughout for all Israelis and Palestinians who reside there. Pinkwashers characterize Israel as a space in which homosexuals can be safe and Palestine as a space in which homophobia is endemic. This obfuscates the range of queer subjectivities and experiences in Israeli and Palestinian societies while disavowing an intersectional framing of sexuality. Israeli gay pride parades then become largely emblematic of the queer subject in Israel, as though all Israelis live as comfortably as wealthy white European, Ashkenazi Jewish cisgender gay men in Tel Aviv.

It would be simplistic to argue that the transnational queer Palestinian solidarity networks have been solely a response to pinkwashing. Before the advent of pinkwashing, queer solidarity organizing was practiced in 2001 by a San Francisco–based group, Queers Undermining Israeli Terrorism (QUIT), as well as by the queer Israeli group Black Laundry. In 2008 (one year before the introduction of the LGBTQ dimension to the Brand Israel campaign) the rise of Queers Against Israeli Apartheid (QuAIA) in Toronto was "followed by a number of other groups under the name QuAIA forming in cities across North America, most notably in New York, Seattle and Vancouver, among others."[10]

In response to the calls from both Brand Israel and BDS, queer Palestinians—led by their two existing major organizations, Aswat (Palestinian Gay Women) and Al-Qaws (Rainbow)—launched two additional initiatives that helped catalyze the queer Palestinian movement in becoming transnational: Palestinian Queers for Boycott, Divestment, and Sanctions (PQBDS) in 2010 and then Pinkwatching Israel in 2011. These two organizations collaborated with audiences abroad, primarily in Europe and North America, on the response to pinkwashing and BDS, further building these queer Palestinian and Arab collectives. Although there were core committed queer Palestinian activists running PQBDS and Pinkwatching Israel, both of these initiatives were intended to be largely virtual, with their websites attracting thousands of people around the world looking for resources on how to engage with Israel/Palestine through a queer Palestinian solidarity lens.

Pinkwatching also quickly emerged as a salient term to describe the process of deconstructing and debunking pinkwashing. The online nature of so much of this activism has enabled queer activists outside of Israel/Palestine to feel that they can contribute to Palestinian solidarity with their own forms of pinkwatching: promoting counterpinkwashing messages to their publics. PQBDS propelled the voices of queer Palestinians in the global sphere as the BDS movement gained momentum and became more controversial. The thought of boycotting Israeli institutions was new for many populations around the world, especially in Western contexts, and as they were introduced to arguments for and against it, they were also introduced to the existence of queer Palestinians through PQBDS statements. While the primary focus of PQBDS's online activism was to engage queer activists globally, their messaging also reached increasing numbers of individuals and institutions within civil society in Palestine. Because so many Palestinian organizations issued and cosigned the BDS call, having queer Palestinian organizations also endorse BDS so strongly helped to positively reconfigure local civil society understandings of the queer Palestinian subject.

The Israeli intelligence services' history of entrapment of LGBTQ Palestinians from the West Bank and Gaza Strip has contributed to the further stigmatization of queerness in Palestinian society because of the subsequent association of homosexuality with betrayal and collaboration with Israel. PQBDS provided queer Palestinians with an opportunity to challenge this stereotype and to counter homophobic prejudices; they introduced a more nuanced discourse on queerness in Palestine, portraying it as not always a sign of fragility, weakness, and immorality. More individuals within Palestinian society began to see homosexuals as not necessarily alienated from the nation. PQBDS demonstrated a commitment to the struggle for liberation for all Palestinians, a visible and vocal display of strength, a clear agenda that coupled sexual liberation with resistance of the Israeli regime, and an unapologetic assertion that queer Palestinians are an integral part of the broader Palestinian social fabric. Queer Palestinian activists like to remind their audiences that they swim in the same river as their straight counterparts. A critical moment in the broader recognition by Palestinians of their queer compatriots' role in society and politics was in April 2011 when Omar Barghouti, cofounder of the BDS movement, acknowledged PQBDS in a media interview alongside the queer Palestinian solidarity activist Sarah Schulman. He demonstrated that queer Palestinians are entitled to "equal rights" and that they are integrally linked to the Palestinian national movement.[11]

Despite these developments, the mainstream narrative persists in many Western circles that Israel is not only the most gay-friendly country in the Middle East but among the friendliest gay destinations in the world. In that way, the Brand Israel campaign has largely succeeded. For instance, GayCities .com and American Airlines named Tel Aviv the world's "Best Gay City."[12] This corporate branding helped obfuscate Israeli homophobia, particularly the significant role that familial, religious, regional, personal, and affective details play in relation to sexuality and feelings of belonging. It also highlights the confluence of state-sponsored branding, neoliberal logics, and the distinctions—as well as shared features—between city and nation. At the same time, queer Palestinians have advanced formidable challenges to Brand Israel efforts globally. The movement's activists have been able to claim their share of successes, particularly in forming alliances with progressive movements around the world and undermining the standing of the Israeli state among leftist queer activist communities.

Ethnoheteronormativity

What has remained consistent since the queer Palestinian movement's inception is the notion among many queer Palestinian activists and individuals that the two systems that they are primarily resisting are Zionism and homophobia. How the term *Zionism* is referenced in this text reflects the language that the queer Palestinian movement invokes in its own work and on the ground. Although queer Palestinians are heterogeneous and disagree on almost every matter imaginable, they have reached near consensus on resistance to Zionism as a contemporary ideology and political project. Zionism is rooted in ethnocracy. Here, I draw on Israeli political geographer Oren Yiftachel's description of Israel/Palestine as an "ethnocracy," namely, when a "regime facilitates the *expansion*, *ethnicization*, and *control* of a dominant ethnic nation . . . over contested territory and polity."[13] Yiftachel elaborates, saying,

"Ethnocracy manifests in the Israeli case with the long-term Zionist strategy of Judaizing the homeland—constructed during the last century as the Land of Israel, between the Jordan River and the Mediterranean Sea."[14] Because Palestinians identify with the same land, the term *Zionist* has become the very antonym to Palestinian identity. The movement I study is committed to an emancipation from Zionism as mediated through Palestinians' experiences of being among its primary targets and, often, its victims.

There are debates about the different early visions for Zionism, a number of which would have, in theory, enabled Palestinian Christian or Muslim subjects to exist equally within the Zionist political imaginary. Queer Palestinians look at these debates not as the delineation of real political plans but as intellectual exercises that obfuscate Palestinian realities and experiences. Many of the early strands of Zionism—such as cultural and spiritual Zionism, which envisioned binationalism with Palestinians—are now relics of the past. The Labor Party in Israel eventually embraced many of Russian political leader Ze'ev Jabotinsky's revisionist Zionist ideologies, pulling Israel toward right-wing politics and militarism. This was catastrophic for Palestinians.

Whereas some Zionists are committed to excavating and building a future Zionist ideology and political project that incorporates Palestinians as first-class citizens, Jewish thought leaders, such as queer theorist Judith Butler, envision Jewish anti-Zionism as the ethical and requisite path forward for the sake of Israelis and Palestinians.[15] Butler is joined by public figures such as *New York Times* columnist Michelle Goldberg who take issue with the knee-jerk "conflation of anti-Zionism with anti-Semitism."[16] Although there can be overlap between anti-Semitism and opposition to Zionism, distinguishing between them is essential, and acknowledging that distinction is necessary in order to recognize when anti-Semitism has actually become manifest.

From the Palestinian vantage point, what matters is not how Zionism is romanticized but how it is practiced. Since the founding of the state of Israel in 1948, the Zionist reality has been established as a discriminatory regime in Israel/Palestine. There is not a Palestinian in Israel, the Occupied Territories, or the Diaspora who has not been adversely affected in some way by the hierarchies and the distribution of power that relegates Palestinians to the realm of second-class citizenship, statelessness, or exile. The Zionism that ultimately prevailed in Israel/Palestine has been profoundly alienating to the Palestinian inhabitants who struggle to remain in their ancestral homeland. The queer Palestinian movement regards the struggle against Zionism, and the ethnoreligious privileges it denies to Palestinians, as a fundamental organizing principle. Although there are many queer Palestinians who do not identify with the queer Palestinian movement, their disagreements on this issue are largely related to the strategies, timing, and resource allocation needed to resist Zionism.

Israel continues to apply pressure on the Palestinian people and their leaders to recognize Israel as an indigenous nation with the right to self-determination, the right to a "Jewish state," the right to maintain a Jewish demographic majority, the right to fully enfranchise only one ethnoreligious group, the right to expand its conquest of land and natural resources in the Occupied Palestinian Territories, and the right to deploy state and settler violence to maintain this system. Under no circumstances do the prevailing logics and practices of Zionism today permit an equal distribution of land, resources, or socioeconomic and civic-political rights for Palestinians.

I am certainly sympathetic to the need for Israel/Palestine to be a homeland for Jewish Israelis (alongside Palestinian Christians and Muslims) after centuries of global anti-Semitism, persecution, and horrific violence led to genocide against Jewish victims in Europe. I support Israel/Palestine becoming a binational country that is a shared homeland for Jews and Palestinians and that honors self-determination for historically oppressed Jewish communities from around the world. Yet the Israeli state does not need to continue its current status as an ethnocracy, lauding one ethnoreligious group over others, in order to realize the understandable goal of establishing a haven for Jewish Israelis. In fact, perpetual conflict with the Palestinian people on the same territory makes Israel/Palestine a land of strife rather than a haven for all. Israel's 2018 Nation-State Law codified Israel's exercise of national self-determination as "unique to the Jewish people"; therefore it excluded indigenous Palestinians from recognition. Anti-Arab racism often underlies the notion that coexistence with Palestinians is impossible due to a falsely assumed endemic and permanent Arab proclivity toward violence against Israelis. Many Palestinians view the expectation that they should normalize Zionism, the very political project that has been driving their oppression for over seven decades now, to be a form of cruelty.

Queer Palestinians, along with the rest of the Palestinian population, are languishing under the pseudotheocratic and intensely militaristic Israeli system that exists today. They experience Zionism as the relegation of Palestinian fears, dreams, and material and psychological conditions to oblivion, neglect, or suppression. This subordination is to the whims of an Israeli state that purports to represent all global Jewish communities. The Israeli state defines those Jewish populations in opposition to the Palestinian people. Israel then maintains control over both queer and straight Palestinian lives and livelihoods.

Gil Z. Hochberg, a leading scholar of Israel/Palestine, notes that "a key organizing principle of Zionism was the remasculinization of Jewish national identity, a need to regenerate a Jewish masculinity and to redeem it from its historical ties to effeminacy."[17] American Israeli historian of religion Daniel Boyarin traces the ideas of Jewish effeminacy to European masculinity and anti-Semitism, reclaiming the "gentle male" as integral to the Jewish tradition.[18] The Israeli scholar Orna Sasson-Levy argues that dominant masculinity in Israel is "identified with the masculinity of the Jewish combat soldier and is perceived as the emblem of good citizenship."[19] And queer Jewish American researcher Brandon Davis writes:

> This desire for masculinity is often touted as a precondition for the Zionist enterprise—which would later evolve into a sometimes violent, militaristic culture. The settler frontier culture of the early kibbutzim, with its focus on both agriculture and the military, served to remake the Jewish male as a masculine figure. And as the Jew had been both feminized and Orientalized in Europe, the Zionist culture similarly feminized and Orientalized the indigenous Palestinian Arabs, who were also seen as inadequate.[20]

As the contemporary Israeli state aims to appease homophobic supporters of Israel in certain Western religious fundamentalist contexts while representing Israel as a gay haven to supporters and potential allies in certain Western secular contexts, the relationship between masculinity and Zionism has become more fraught.

Many Israelis and their supporters perceive the Palestinian subject as either overly feminine or overly masculine. Such a Palestinian is represented only either as a victim of internal Palestinian homophobia or as a violent perpetrator of homophobia among Palestinians and terrorism against Israelis. The Israeli subject is meant to have transcended European effeminacy and is so securely masculine that he can accommodate masculine homosexuals into the political imaginary as well as, in some cases, effeminate homosexuals in his midst. Women are expected to contribute to the cultivation of the masculinity of the men in their local and national worlds.[21] The conflicts within Israeli discourse between heteronormativity and gay friendliness and between Zionists and Palestinians all focus on male experiences and stand silent on questions of Palestinian women's sexuality. The queer Palestinian movement, led disproportionately by women, has attempted to address that silence.

As readers will see, the struggle against Palestinian homophobia and toxic masculinity is equally important as that against Zionism, and the potency of this homophobia and masculinity in queer Palestinian lives can be just as devastating. The compulsion of heteronormativity in Palestinian society is the expectation that citizens will contribute to the normalization of gender binaries and gender norms—with gender and sexual orientation being neatly mapped onto one another according to reproductive organs—and to the disavowal of gender and sexual pluralism. The intensity of heteronormativity in Palestine places unimaginable pressure on young people to enter into heterosexual marriages, to produce offspring, and to abide by strict gender and sexual norms that are consistent with pervasive norms connecting religion and nationality. This is tremendously suffocating for the vast majority of queer, trans, and gender-nonconforming Palestinians.

Meanwhile, in their everyday existence in Palestine, queer Palestinians face what I call "ethnoheteronormativity." This reality is the result of life as racialized queer subjects experiencing intertwined oppression from dual systems of ethnocracy on one hand and heteronormativity and toxic masculinity on the other. As for the global queer Palestinian solidarity movement, it undermines Israeli state efforts in diplomacy and public relations on an international scale. The movement models resistance to the confluence of gendered and sexualized settler-colonial nationalism.[22]

The queer Palestinian solidarity movement is under scrutiny from Zionist critics across the political spectrum who, drawing on dehumanizing racialized discourses, insist on characterizing Palestinians as uniformly and viciously homophobic. Simultaneously, some leftist critics demand that queer Palestinians subordinate resistance to Palestinian homophobia to a Palestinian nationalist struggle that fails to acknowledge them. And there is a cadre of international intellectuals who accuses them of enacting their Palestinianness in ways that are not affirming of radical purist activists and theorizing professors.

Certain actors in the global queer Palestinian solidarity movement have subsequently prioritized the struggle against Zionism over that against systems of oppression internal to Palestinian society. Because the radical purist focus is on anti-imperialism, resistance to Zionism emerges as the priority of these actors given the association between Zionism and imperialism. In some circles, the issue of Palestinian homophobia is neglected as a result, and a form of what I have termed "discursive disenfranchisement" is in force. The languages of certain social movements—here, ones challenging Palestinian homophobia—are under discursive assault from a subset of vocal radical leftists who take issue with the naming of Palestinian homophobia. These radical purists often attribute the mere articulation of the term *homophobia* to imperialist origins and agendas. Since the most fundamental concepts at the heart of the queer Palestinian movement are associated with anti-imperialism, members of this movement find it demoralizing to be subjected to charges of complicity with imperialism. This criticism denies queer Palestinians the right to name their own experiences or to be citizens of the world who can choose dialogue partners according to their own desires.

Queer Palestinians thus experience a naturally resulting voicelessness because of queer Zionist activists who aim to prevent the naming of Israeli oppression. Queer Palestinians then find themselves under surveillance for daring to use terms for self-identification or for articulation of their struggle, including *Zionism, occupation, apartheid, lesbian, gay, bisexual, transgender, queer,* and even *homophobia.* This discursive disenfranchisement reaches academics like me who subsequently find it challenging to identify and describe the "social facts"[23] influencing the lives of queer Palestinians. Although social facts are socially constructed, they remain important for shaping people's subjectivities. This book, then, is a response, in our own voices, to the constraints on the representation of queer Palestinians.

As they navigate their political and social milieu, queer Palestinians face systems from all directions of marginalization, policing, and repression of both Zionism and homophobia. The structure of ethnoheteronormativity attempts to recast queer Palestinian political subjectivity in terms of patriarchal and state logics. This makes spaces for radical hybridity invisible; if queer Palestinians combine critiques of homophobia *and* Zionism, their critiques become invisible because the terms they are using (*gay* and *lesbian*) to critique homophobia are seen as by-products of Israel and the West's colonial agenda. Compounding the force of ethnoheteronormativity is the fact that critiques against it can lose efficacy. Despite this reality, the body, voice, and resilience of the queer Palestinian subject persists in challenging the hegemonic disciplines of ethnoheteronormativity.

Although queer Palestinian activists adopted a deeply intersectional articulation of Palestinian homophobia and resistance to Zionism, particularly after the movement's inception, some leaders of the movement have continued acquiescing to pulls toward radical purity and prioritization of anti-Zionism. Yet ethnoheteronormativity in Israel/Palestine highlights Zionism's relationship to toxic masculinity, along with Palestinian nationalism's reliance on heightened masculinity. This includes not only the fundamental link between gender, sexuality, racism, and nationalism[24] but also the interdependence of Israeli and Palestinian political subjectivities. Although the gaps between queer Israelis and Palestinians are widening, largely as a result of a form of apartheid segregating the populations, I put forward a vision of queer Israeli-Palestinian solidarity in contesting ethnoheteronormativity and the Israeli-Palestinian toxic masculinity that is interwoven in these societies.[25] This project thus grapples with historical legacies and delineates present dynamics but also looks ahead to future possibilities of sexual and national liberation.

It is possible for scholarship to recognize the particular context that Palestine presents to the global stage while also deexceptionalizing Palestine. Just as ethnocracy and heteronormativity are not limited to Israel but can be found across the world, ethnoheteronormativity shapes the lives of queer Palestinians in a manner parallel to the experiences of racialized queer subjects elsewhere. As far-right, populist, ultranationalist movements gain power internationally, with their combination of ethnic chauvinism, religious nationalism, toxic masculinity, and homophobia, queer subjects and LGBTQ activism and social movements are increasingly under siege. As Israeli state leaders deepen Israel's strategic alliances with forces such as Jair Bolsonaro in Brazil, Victor Orban in Hungary, Matteo Salvini in Italy, and Donald Trump in the United States, among others, we see the global reach of ethnoheteronormativity. Although such political currents undermine queer civil society in palpable ways, they also present opportunities for queer Palestinian activists to further cultivate transnational queer resistance and solidarity with their counterparts living under ethnoheteronormativity in other contexts.

Intellectual Foundation

This book is ultimately concerned with how transnational progressive social movements are able (or not) to balance struggles for liberation along more than one axis at a time. The underlying goal of my focus on the case of the global queer Palestinian solidarity movement is to empower queer Palestinians to achieve national and sexual freedom. Activists around the world celebrate that over the past eighteen years, this LGBTQ social movement has arisen in Palestine and has become a transnational queer Palestinian solidarity movement. The global networks and reach of the Queer Palestine sphere are now formidable. But like many movements on the left, a vanguard of radical purists has taken hold of the leadership, attempting to maintain ideological conformity among its ranks. The political currents of radical purism have subsequently helped transform the critique of empire into an "empire of critique" in which queer Palestinians—and to a large extent, many of their allies—find themselves under numerous overlapping regimes of surveillance, suspicion, and control. They face the same sets of conditions as their queer counterparts in the broader Arab region and other regions, but they must also navigate the particularities of their local context. Whether from Israeli state, society, and security bodies; from pro-Israel activists; from Palestinian political, armed, religious, social, and familial institutions; from international academics, journalists, and filmmakers; and even internally from the movement itself, queer Palestinians are regularly being met with critiques that span a wide range of seemingly insurmountable concerns and criticisms.

My formulation of the empire of critique as a theoretical framework also reveals its three major consequences. First, queer and trans Palestinians face discursive disenfranchisement from many directions, with their ability to articulate a sense of self and to employ conceptual tools to define their identities and their movement increasingly coming into question. Second, despite the concomitant forces of ethnoheteronormativity, what was initially a queer Palestinian struggle for both national and sexual liberation has in more recent years prioritized resistance to Zionism over resistance to homophobia. Third, the global queer Palestinian solidarity movement is no longer experiencing growth; while its activism and influence are not decreasing, it is currently at a plateau. As my next chapter will examine, the intensification of the empire of critique has led to alienation, implosion, and the loss of family, community, and even life for queer Palestinians.

Although the movement is no longer ascending as it was during its first decade, when the empire of critique was not as vast and totalizing as it is now, it has nonetheless continued its advocacy in Palestine and around the world. This activism has survived as a result of capturing leftist camps of global queer movements. Its current strategies are not conducive to engaging queer activists and organizations outside of the most radical ends of the political spectrum. Nonetheless, the survival of the queer Palestinian movement is a testament to extraordinary achievements; the queer Palestinian spirit of agency, defiance, and creativity is especially formidable, despite the daunting pressures and forces working to constrict it.

This study and its anthropological foundation serve as both an ethnography of the movement and a documentation of its history. Although my investigation is by no means comprehensive, I have selected critical junctures from 2001 to 2018 that illustrate how different global actors and contingents have entered this story through time, introducing new rubrics for gauging, judging, and critiquing the words and intentions of queer Palestinians and their allies. I synthesize not only public debates that I have followed for a decade in the press and on social media but also my activism, ethnographic research, and sixty-five formal and informal interviews in the Middle East, Europe, North America, and Latin America. This is in addition to the autoethnography featured in this book. Beyond this study's personal and political relevance, it serves as a contribution to knowledge production and theorization in studies of the Middle East, Israel/Palestine, anthropology, queer theory, peace and conflict studies, and literature on social movements.

I am interested in queering scholarship on Palestine and going further than that. "Queering" has emerged as a common academic trend to point out homophobias in various forms. But with major queer Palestinian solidarity activists in Europe and North America making a significant impact by utilizing queering methodology, allegations of a gay international Western imperialist agenda in the Middle East have effectively been resuscitated. Such allegations are problematic for the discursive disenfranchisement that underlies them. Queering Palestine has plateaued because it has not sufficiently inter-articulated critiques of heteropatriarchy, Zionism, and coloniality, but I aim to introduce a new valence into the discourse on Queer Palestine. I hope that academics and activists who are interested in contemporary progressive social movements beyond Palestine will also identify resonances and useful insights for their own contexts.

A watershed moment for the global queer Palestinian solidarity movement was the publication of the October 2010 special issue of the *GLQ: A Journal of Lesbian and Gay Studies*, which was titled "Queer Politics and the Question of Palestine/Israel." Edited by Gil Z. Hochberg, the issue was a critically important discursive and political event because it brought queer Palestinians into the academic spotlight in a manner that was unprecedented. The material presented by the issue's contributors continues to resonate today.[26]

An equally critical moment came with the appearance of "Queering Palestine," the spring 2018 special issue of the *Journal of Palestine Studies*,[27] edited by three remarkable Palestinian women scholars, Leila Farsakh, Rhoda Kanaaneh, and Sherene Seikaly. They solicited ten pieces on the relationship between Palestinian studies and queer theory—three stand-alone articles and a roundtable featuring seven contributors, including me. Seeing queer Palestinians and those who care about them brought to the forefront of scholarly work in the leading journal in Palestine studies was encouraging. The publication of this series was an invaluable first step toward opening the door for potential future engagement on the empirical realities of homophobia and queer agency in Palestine and beyond.

Fortunately, a nascent subfield of queer Arab studies is coalescing, and this anthropological book on Queer Palestine will have arrived after the intellectual contributions of anthropologist Sofian Merabet. Merabet's *Queer Beirut* (2014) has been described as the "first ethnographic study of queer lives in the Middle East."[28] Preceding texts have addressed queer themes in the region, such as Orientalist writings on travel and homosexual encounters in the Arab world, but it is rare to find rigorous, analytical, fieldwork-based scholarship on queerness in the region. Merabet's book on the lives of young gay men in Beirut is an exception. Merabet reminds his readers of Judith Butler's conception of queer as "a site of collective contestation."[29] He defines queerness with regard to the etymology of the word *queer*, namely the German word *quer*, or "transverse, cross, oblique."[30] The queer subject is one who "thinks and translates outside the normative box and against the dominant paradigms . . . whose very habitus is to invest in the countless ramifications of ever-shifting epistemological intersections," and who is a "prisoner of love whose captivity is ever entangled with the very object of his desire."[31] I adopt this understanding of queerness as it relates to the queer Palestinian movement, particularly with regard to "dissident sexuality."[32]

Queer Beirut emphasizes space and how queer Lebanese men contest and appropriate that space in the city, even with the "always looming potential of violence."[33] Merabet identifies the emergence of queer space in Beirut, designating "the geographical, along with the socio-cultural and mental, fields in which various homoerotic practices take place and are being integrated into the respective lives of different individuals."[34] Even while these queer spaces "challenge and rupture"[35] heteronormativity, they "are perpetually contested by a multiplicity of subjects and subject matters."[36] A "homosexual sphere"[37] in Beirut emerges with "zones of queer encounter."[38] Merabet's ethnography traces the "intricate social processes of ascertaining a queer presence in Lebanon."[39] Although space does not feature as centrally in my book, Merabet's example nonetheless provided a framework for my recognition of the homosexual sphere with zones of queer encounter in Palestine and the social processes that have subsequently shaped the queer presence in the global Palestinian solidarity community.

A critical distinction between *Queer Beirut* and this book is my representation of queer women as well as the ethnographic accounts of queer activism and individual lives. Merabet writes that his scholarship "is not on organized activism, but the ethical practice that is at work through the politics of what [he] like[s] to call a 'queer habitus.' It is a politics that amounts to the individual challenge directed toward social norms, on one hand, and the embodiment of alternative identity formations on the other."[40] I see value in academic work that extends such conceptions of queer habitus to the realm of local and transnational activism. Furthermore, queerness is where we can expand, rather than limit, the spaces of possibility for self and collective expression and engagement with the world.

This ethnography of the Queer Palestine sphere includes the domains of queer Palestinians, the queer Palestinian social movement, the ways homophobia and Zionism reinforce one another, and the ways queer Palestinians are talked about in global contexts. The Queer Palestine sphere is therefore both local and global. Queer Palestinians, whether or not they are part of the movement, are part of this sphere, and many non-Palestinians are as well. Because queer Palestinian bodies in this sphere face ethnoheteronormativity, this book focuses on queer Palestinian voices and experiences in this context. It also includes nonqueer Palestinian actors who are central to the queer Palestinian experience because of the movement reaching Israel/Palestine and other geographies, mainly in North America and Europe. Global queer Palestinian activism is largely a response to transnational discourses on queer Palestinians, whether from locals or those abroad who are with them in solidarity or even antisolidarity.

Critique of Critique

Anthropologist Didier Fassin's essay "The Endurance of Critique" has been an inspiration, shaping my definition of *critique* and my conceptualization of the empire of critique (hence the subtitle of this book).[41] Fassin makes a powerful case for the enduring nature of critique in anthropology as well as for the necessity of critique to our discipline and practice. Fassin lauds Edward Said's critique of Orientalism for exemplifying how critique requires explication, reaffirmation, openness, and consistency in the face of misunderstandings and misappropriations.[42]

Fassin cautions against automatically disqualifying and dismissing critiques as anti-intellectual, passé, or "mere mantra."[43] In fact, he argues that critique can challenge the "unbearable lightness of being that paradoxically characterizes certain forms of alleged radicalism as well as certain retreats in an ivory tower."[44] He makes a case for ethnography as critique and delineates how it can lead to "emancipation" by "removing the ideological veil imposed on people so as to allow them to realize the deception that renders their domination possible" and by "contesting the self-evident representations of the world they hold true while acknowledging the possibility of other representations."[45] By invoking the work of Judith Butler, Fassin reconciles critique's search for a "hidden truth" alongside the "regimes of truth."[46] Fassin writes, "The ethnographer must therefore acknowledge his debt toward his interlocutors, and part of his activity consists in transcribing and arranging the invaluable knowledge he has received from them. However, he is not only a cultural broker between the world he studies and his various publics. He translates but he also interprets."[47]

The critique of critique that I present should not be mistaken for a disavowal of critique; in fact, I largely share Fassin's commitment to critique as he has delineated in his essay. My work follows Fassin and attempts to move further. Ethnography is a form of practice, and my own reveals how actors deploy critique to "remove the ideological veil imposed on people." Yet sometimes critique does not remove the *entire* veil because certain types of critique are (wrongly) believed to be at odds with one another. I want to move away from critique as a generalized abstract practice and center critique on the material lives of people and the struggles they encounter. This book is not simply ethnography as critique but ethnography as lived critique.

Too often, unconstructive criticism is masked as critique. The Israeli legal scholar Aeyal Gross draws on the writing of another French theorist, Didier Eribon, to caution against "the transformation of critical thinking into policing of thought."[48] Gross explicates that critical thought "is not merely about the denunciation of our opponents' positions, which would only amount to *criticism*. *Critique* also entails questioning the imposition of the very terms of debate."[49]

In the case of the global queer Palestinian solidarity movement, the increased radical purism has led to an ethos of "ultimate judgment" rather than to "a critical analysis of the complex consequences of the production of distinct truths."[50] As a member of the movement, I am sympathetic to its anti-imperialist impulse, but my concern is that this activism will elevate anti-imperialism above the struggle against homophobia or see the two as disparate. This is in line with Audre Lorde's recognition that "there is no hierarchy of oppressions."[51]

Absolving oneself from relations to imperial powers does not necessarily mean that one can be absolved from other relations of oppression. The pervasiveness of critiques in the name of anti-imperialism, alongside all the other regimes of critique to which queer Palestinians and their allies are subjected, is what has led to the empire of critique. In many ways, it is the charge of imperialism leveled from the left against a fundamentally anti-imperialist movement that is most debilitating. The queer Palestinian movement is subjected to the disciplinary power of this discursive empire even as it helps sustain it.

Fassin's writing reveals the intimate connections between critique and anti-imperialism in the case of anthropology in particular. He elaborates that "the critique of imperialism [became] inseparable from the critique of anthropology since both were regarded as ideologically linked."[52] Anthropological critiques of empire were in many ways born after the discipline itself was critiqued for "accompanying and even giving scientific backing"[53] to colonialism and "maintaining the structure of power represented by the colonial system."[54]

Fassin writes that "astonishment and indignation are, indeed, the two driving forces of anthropology and, to some degree, of other social sciences. They are what motivate critical inquiry."[55] Even in the face of Israeli oppression and Palestinian homophobia, it is my hope that queer Palestinians can augment rightful indignation with a constant sense of astonishment. We need to reinsert the anthropological aspects of critique into our everyday lives. Critique, as called for by Fassin, is not always the result of reading up on and learning about things; in many cases, critique involves uncanny experiences and encounters, a sense of astonishment that shatters previous assumptions. Ethnographic work attunes us to the ways that even our previous critiques can become reified assumptions by laying bare the everyday struggles of those to which these critiques purport to apply.

I also deeply appreciate Fassin's attention to the place of public anthropology when leveling critique. He writes,

> The encounter with publics is a source of enrichment for critique. It is a way to test, amend, strengthen, develop and even abandon interpretations through the confrontation with alternate views, concrete concerns, and productive misunderstandings. . . . The work of the ethnographer cannot be limited to academic circles. The voices it renders audible as well as the material and interpretations it produces have their place in the public sphere, where it is destined to be appropriated, transformed, or contested. In the end, the public presence of anthropology . . . may be regarded as an expansion of critique into society.[56]

In producing this ethnography on the global queer Palestinian solidarity movement, I have been mindful of the need for multiple publics and audiences. I wonder how we, as anthropologists and nonanthropologists alike, can deploy our critiques with sensitivity, with proportionality to the power that actors wield, and with attention to how our critiques interact with those leveled by others in different domains. Many progressive movements are confronting what I see as critique fatigue among their activists. If everyone's critique was a constructive form of critical engagement, then that would pose one less obstacle for social movements to overcome. I recognize that solidarity with social movements requires leveling critique at certain times and withholding both criticism and critique at others.

Plateau

My experience within the global queer Palestinian solidarity movement as an academic and activist in Palestine and the United States has solidified my realization that the movement is currently at a plateau. This book follows my tracing of the movement's rise in Palestine and its subsequent global emergence as a result of transnational queer solidarity networks focused on pinkwatching and BDS activism. The empire of critique, which I also account for, has contributed to a period that began in 2012 and continues today in which the movement is neither growing nor receding. In discussing the idea that social movements hit plateaus, I distinguish between naturally occurring plateaus and toxic ones. Natural plateaus are the result of the movement having reached its natural market share in terms of audience and capacity, having caught the attention of most of those who would be interested in its work. Toxic plateaus are those in which the normal forward motion of a movement is cut off, which occurs when activists find themselves besieged on all sides so that they no longer know to whom they are accountable or how to construct a progressive agenda. The plateauing that results from trying to construct an effective agenda at the confluence of so many sometimes ill-considered or disingenuous critiques can be described as toxic.

The "retirement" of Queers Against Israeli Apartheid (QuAIA) in 2015 is one example of this toxic plateauing. The best explanation the public got for the QuAIA retirement was from their press release, including this statement:

> Over the past year, however, the deteriorating situation in the Middle East, Canada's involvement in attempts to suppress the movement for Boycott, Divestment and Sanctions against Israel and other pressing issues have pulled activist energies in many directions. Most of the original members who came together during QuAIA's formative years are now working within a variety of fields and organizations within Toronto and internationally, stretching the small group's resources to continue in its current form.[57]

Several individuals with knowledge of the decision to dismantle QuAIA informed me that internal divisions and interpersonal conflict within the group also played a role in the leadership's decision for activists to work in other ways outside of the group. That being said, no group is expected to last forever. But the retirement of QuAIA, together with the dissolving of another queer Palestinian solidarity group—PQBDS—and other examples referenced in this text, led to the plateau in which the global queer Palestinian solidarity movement now finds itself.

In 2011, Benjamin Doherty, a vocal queer Palestinian solidarity activist, published an article that foreshadowed the plateauing of the movement. Doherty traced pinkwashing's duration from 2008 to 2011, declared the Israeli state strategy was discredited, and hence wrote what he called its "obituary."[58] Drawing on Sarah Schulman's work and other sources of queer Palestinian solidarity activism, he wrote that pinkwashing had been exposed and undermined. This was a premature and ambitious prognosis, considering the persistence of pinkwashing campaigns and that pinkwatching campaigns do not always succeed, as we will see throughout this book. Nonetheless, pinkwatching activism continues as long as pinkwashing campaigns have not desisted. One factor that contributed to the loss of the movement's momentum was the sense among some queer Palestinian solidarity activists that their discourse on pinkwashing was all-encompassing and therefore that the need for their future activism was increasingly obsolete. This factor reveals the potential for activism to exist within echo chambers. Although pinkwatching activism has been far-reaching, and many LGBTQ individuals around the world have become familiar with this queer Palestinian solidarity strategy, the logic of queer pro-Israel campaigns remains hegemonic in many Western spaces. Formidable pro-Israel advocates have also gained experience in defeating queer Palestinian solidarity activism.

For instance, in October 2016, some pro-Israel activists organized to defeat a pinkwatching resolution put forward by the Queer Arabs of Halifax group at the Halifax Pride Society in Canada. Reflecting on the experience of being present during the contentious debate on the resolution, in which reports revealed that LGBTQ people of color there were—by and large—supporting the motions for queer Palestinian solidarity and the removal of Israeli pinkwashing from Halifax Pride space, El Jones writes, "It was impossible to be a woman and person of colour in that room and not feel the intense hostility. White men literally shoved their hands in my face and told me to shut up at this meeting."[59] Jones also described how these queer people of color walked out of the room during the deliberations and that the meeting felt "violent and harmful" to them.[60] Increasingly, global queer Palestinian solidarity activists, in describing their struggles against pinkwashing, have linked this issue to the larger struggle against global white supremacy.

Even if pinkwashing was completely discredited, as some queer Palestinian solidarity activists have argued, and even if pinkwashing ceased and pinkwatching was no longer necessary, the queer Palestinian solidarity movement remains important. This is because queer Palestinians in Israel/Palestine continue to face dual forms of marginalization under ethnoheteronormativity and therefore call for international support and solidarity. The global queer Palestinian solidarity movement often—though not always—places queer Palestinian voices and experiences front and center in its pinkwatching activism.

For every queer Palestinian or non-Palestinian who joins the queer movement in Palestine or its related global solidarity movement, one has chosen not to engage in activism in recent years. Existing activists have also ceased their work with queer Palestinian organizing as a result of the overwhelming weight that activists in this struggle must carry. The forces of Zionism and homophobia are now accompanied by forces of the empire of critique and the myriad forms of alienation within the movement. These forces are not identical in power, but they all pose obstacles to the movement. There are now factions in the world of queer Palestinian organizing that disagree on how the relationship between these forces should be understood and engaged with.

The internal critiques within the movement have led to a certain form of debilitation, and in certain circumstances, queer Palestinian activists mirror the surveillance, policing, and excommunication that is practiced against them by parties external to the movement. With the confrontation of Zionism and homophobia being so daunting and with their inability to reach the epicenters of power, queer Palestinian activists have, at times, turned to leveling critiques against other queer Palestinians. There are moments in which those critiques address an external audience, whether to prove to a Western-based academic that this activism is indeed radical, or to a straight Palestinian that this activism is indeed nationalist, or to another activist that this activism is morally pure. It can be puzzling to watch as Al-Qaws, the largest queer Palestinian organization, exerts its political capital in order to launch numerous public critiques against queer Palestinians or allies in the local and global queer Palestinian solidarity movement. I have seen how these critiques can be animated by an underlying hope that voicing them will shield oneself from critique. Considering the nature of the empire of critique, this works only to further scrutiny, suspicion, and stigmatization of queer Palestinians, who are already so deeply suspect. The pervasive sense that one could be shamed or shunned anywhere at any time has contributed to the demoralization of queer Palestinians and the plateauing of the queer Palestinian movement.

In this text, I have aimed to strike a difficult balance between honoring the responsibility to give the leading queer Palestinian organizations the respect and acknowledgment they deserve for their invaluable contributions and recognizing that this progressive movement has room to grow. Even as these activists experience critique fatigue themselves, they play a role in helping sustain the empire of critique. These dynamics are not unique to this movement but can be found among movements on the left in many domains in many parts of the world.

The momentum-slowing nature of internal critiques becomes evident when considering anthropologist Sherine Hamdy's delineation of the affect and politics motivating *muzayada*. Hamdy writes,

My friend and colleague Soha Bayoumi taught me the Arabic word *muzayada* that is commonly evoked in Egyptian leftist activist circles, for which there is no ready English equivalent. People who engage in *muzayada* are constantly upping the ante, asserting that they are even more morally pure and politically committed than their comrades. In addition to describing a form of political and moral competition, the term *muzayada* also suggests a cynical skepticism, an anticipation that what is to come is further oppression that must be condemned. Those who engage in *muzayada* are judgmental and suspicious of others' levels of commitment, and they are always *more* committed, *more* dedicated than everyone else. If one expresses joy or a sense of accomplishment over a battle won, those practicing *muzayada* are suspicious that one could ever feel victory and still be a morally and politically committed subject who has not naively capitulated to the ploys of the oppressor.[61]

Hamdy adds that *muzayada* can leave critics "with no other choice than to simply talk amongst themselves, preaching to choirs. Engagement requires messiness in that meeting space between speaker and audience. Those who practice *muzayada* are intolerant of the contamination that both precedes and follows engagement with others who do not share their same moral highground."[62] Hamdy also links *muzayada* to political impotence, arguing that "*muzayada* privileges the purity of an ideological position over recognizing a good. When we practice *muzayada*, we refuse to celebrate any small gain as long as larger structural inequality persists."[63] Hamdy expands: "I understand *muzayada* to both contribute to political impotence, and to result from it. Shunted from effective significant change, participants turn on one another and attempt to claim the pleasures of being the most radical and ideologically pure."[64]

While witnessing one queer Palestinian activist lambaste another on social media and observing another queer Palestinian activist critique a long list of progressive Palestinian social movement leaders for not being morally pure enough, it appeared to me that *muzayada* is also exacerbated by the temporal and spatial distance that lies between now and the time when the structures of Israeli occupation and Palestinian homophobia can be dismantled. When anti-imperialism becomes the dominant focus of such activism, the pervasiveness of empire makes it so that no one can ever truly be pure, even as the most radical activists and academics claim that pure moral high ground.

Activism at the intersection of LGBTQ and Palestinian rights can reveal the potential of what sociologist Eve Spangler calls the "more Mao than thou" trend in many leftist circles.[65] Because progressives see themselves as challenging power and oppressive forces, they can become self-righteous to some degree and thus think they have a monopoly on truth and morality. They can aim to enlighten others without being genuinely open to learning from others, as though they have figured out what there is to know due to self-authorized expertise. They grow accustomed to being on the margins and then cherish the purity of their positions, but when a compatriot in their movement aims to enact social change in the world, which requires compromise, they chastise them for that compromise. Because truly reaching the most powerful and relevant institutions to directly challenge them is difficult, they turn on one another due to proximity. They have often mastered the ability to deconstruct ideas, institutions, and mobilizations with their words, but they are less vocal in delineating what can be built instead. They sometimes excommunicate those who imagine transcending the periphery by engaging the mainstream.

A social movement can grow and nurture its members when it helps enact progressive values in interpersonal relations. Peace and justice start within us, when we treat the people closest to us with kindness and compassion. Social justice work requires humility, openness, and empathy for others regarding the ethical decisions they make when resources and avenues for change are constrained. The empire of critique reveals how easily the politics of solidarity can be replaced with the politics of suspicion, thereby impacting the growth of a social movement. With each additional critique they face, internal divisions are accentuated as activists struggle with whether to respond and in what manner. This can lead to movement plateau and paralysis. As a movement shifts increasingly in the direction of radical purity, nihilistic elements can begin to emerge. When the distance to realizing the ultimate goals of the movement is unknown and as the criticism they face from countless directions is amplified, activists struggle to remain cohesive and instead police their boundaries for moral purity. It is then possible for ideological stances to become both the means and the end of the movement.

Beyond the White Gaze

Progressives around the world are becoming increasingly introspective about the propensity for turning against one another and about the politics of excommunication in their circles of activism and the social movements they build. On social media, resources such as Frances Lee's article "Why I've

Started to Fear My Fellow Social Justice Activists" have been circulating to catalyze much-needed reflection.[66] My book also serves to echo calls for progressive academics and activists to treat each other with compassion and inclusivity whenever possible. The overlapping systems of oppression that we face are real, and many of us are in these struggles for the long haul. We have no other choice because so much is at stake for our communities. In the meantime, it is imperative that we not reproduce the harm we face among ourselves and others along the way.

If we return our gaze to Queer Palestine, we remember that this movement is not ultimately about Toronto, New York, or London but is part of a struggle to ensure that all queer and trans Palestinians can one day lead their lives with dignity in their ancestral homeland. Queer Palestinian activism continues to confront critiques revolving around different political and racial contexts: morality, civility, liberalism, coloniality, and the "gay international." A group of queer Palestinian activists have triumphed in building this local and transnational movement. I foreground the valiant accomplishments of this social movement in Israel/Palestine, but I am also interested in what its future may be in the wake of the empire of critique.

In finding my voice and vision, I have been inspired by the work of feminist Black American writer Toni Morrison, who once reflected, "If there's a book that you want to read, but it hasn't been written yet, then you must write it." Morrison has also spoken of the "white gaze" that she has had to face in her work: "Our lives have no meaning, no depth without the white gaze. And I have spent my entire writing life trying to make sure that the white gaze was not the dominant one in any of my books."[67] These reflections have resonated deeply with me, because in addition to the white gaze I must also contend with the Zionist gaze, the heteronormative gaze, and the radical purist gaze. One cannot overstate the politically fraught nature of this field. Zionism, homophobia, Palestinian nationalism, and transnational activism from the left and right are all interconnected, and this can be suffocating for Palestinian queers. There are countless individuals around the world who feel strongly and passionately about how this population and movement should be represented.

Because I am a queer Palestinian who is also entrapped in forms of external surveillance, the development of my own consciousness in some ways mirrors the development of this movement at large. In this context, I am most concerned with the politics of survival of a sexual-national subaltern subject and the case for the necessary entanglement of queer and anticolonial struggles. My vision is one in which radical purism does not prevail as the only form of radicalism and in which the empire of critique can be replaced with pluralism of thought and practice as well as genuine transnational reciprocal solidarity.

1   LGBTQ Palestinians and the Politics of the Ordinary

IN JUNE 2015, after the United States Supreme Court ruling that legalized same-sex marriage, Palestinian artist Khaled Jarrar painted a rainbow on a part of the Israeli wall in the West Bank. He said that "his art was meant as a reminder of Israeli occupation, at a time when gay rights are in the news" and "to put a spotlight on Palestinian issues."[1] A few hours later, a group of young Palestinian men responded angrily, painting over the rainbow in white. One of the individuals who whitewashed the rainbow told the *Associated Press* that he did so because "we cannot promote gay rights." The young men also quoted Muhammad al-Amleh, a forty-six-year-old Palestinian lawyer who supported the painting-over. He stated, "It would be shameful to have the flag of gays in our refugee camp." Khaled Jarrar added that the painting-over of his rainbow "reflects the absence of tolerance and freedoms in the Palestinian society" and that "people don't accept different thinking in our society."[2] Palestinians such as Jarrar who care about personal freedoms in Palestinian society, including those in the realms of gender and sexuality, connect the lack of freedom to the Israeli occupation and the resulting denial of political freedoms. The controversy over the rainbow and its whitewashing was debated intensely on social media among Palestinians, and it was heartening for me to see, alongside the homophobic responses, numerous Palestinians expressing support both for the US Supreme Court decision and Jarrar's rainbow. I found it ironic that the Palestinians who painted over the rainbow took such ownership of the Israeli wall and what should or should not be on it—forgetting, at that moment, the oppression of the Israeli occupation that the gray concrete represents in the first place.

Public queer resistance to oppressive Palestinian gender and sexual norms does exist, though such resistance to homophobia in Palestine is often met with different forms of rejection. Instances of the Palestinian public's critical engagement with gender- and sexuality-related symbols, norms, and practices and of resistance to patriarchy and heteronormativity among queer Palestinians are occurring largely at the private, local level. Although these instances are sometimes linked to spaces made possible by queer Palestinian organizations such as Al-Qaws and Aswat, the queer Palestinian movement has, in many ways, highlighted resistance at the hands of organization-affiliated queer Palestinians more than it has the ordinary forms of resistance outside of formal organizations. I reflect on this certainly not in order to diminish the work of queer Palestinian organizations; they are valuable and essential. It is possible, and indeed imperative, to lift simultaneously the voices of formally organized queer Palestinian activists and of queer Palestinians who move in the world independently from queer NGOs and activist groups. All of them contribute to the movement in invaluable ways.

This chapter traces the rise of the LGBTQ Palestinian movement in Israel/Palestine. The first section delineates an ethnographic approach to social movement theory as the conceptual framework to analyze this movement. The second section outlines the heterogeneity of queer Palestinian subjects, and the third provides an overview of Palestinian homophobia. In the fourth section I account for the emergence of the LGBTQ movement in Palestine, in the fifth I discuss queer Palestinian epistemologies, and in the sixth I cover the rise of radical purists in the movement. Finally, I conclude in the seventh section with examples of queer Palestinian subjectivities. I argue that queer Palestinian life and resistance derive their power from ordinary acts in extraordinary contexts under ethnoheteronormativity. This chapter furthers the case for attention to affect and more pluralism and inclusivity within the movement.

Ethnography and Social Movements

My ethnographic focus on queer Palestinians in Israel/Palestine serves as a contribution to a broader understanding of social movement theory. The scholarship of sociologist Sharon Kurtz has anchored my thinking about social movements adopting identity politics. Kurtz demonstrates how social movements navigate pressure to simultaneously unite their members based on a common factor and address categories of identification that are salient to their diverse constituents. Kurtz does not disavow identity politics but calls for "multi-identity politics"[3] instead, alongside what she terms "identity practices" or a movement's "demands, framing and ideology, culture, leadership, organizational structure, and support resources."[4] Particularly striking is Kurtz's recognition of the importance of informal and unofficial methods of identity practices so that movements can reflect the subidentities of their members. Otherwise, as Kurtz argues, movements risk schisms. We can clearly see that schisms exist in the queer Palestinian solidarity movement between those who primarily champion the anti-imperialist identity of anti-Zionism and those who engage in identity practices and multi-identity politics to integrate resistance to both Zionism and homophobia in the queer Palestinian struggle.

Collective action among queer Palestinians often stems from submerged participation in everyday life experiences. This constitutes a "latent network," a "system of individuals or small groups that exist[s] out of the public eye and out of the visible membership of NGOs and organizations" and thereby disseminates "new cultural codes."[5] The queer movement in Israel/Palestine does not mirror movements elsewhere; public displays of queer solidarity in Western and democratic contexts can be salient. The queer Palestinian movement in Israel/Palestine includes NGOs but is mostly submerged and latent as a result of Israeli subjugation of Palestinians and Palestinian patriarchy and homophobia. Public and private forms of queer Palestinian contestation and mobilization exist in Israel and the Occupied Territories, and I argue that everyday expressions and embodiments of queer resistance have come to constitute an aggregate of contexts, networks, and practices that comprises a social movement.

Joel Beinin and Frederic Vairel's research on social movement theory's neglect of the Middle East has motivated their call for a "more processual, dynamic, and historicized approach" to the study of social movements, accounting for mobilization, contestation, and the "emergence and development of collective action in hostile and repressive contexts."[6] The queer Palestinian movement reveals the importance of Beinin and Vairel's model of integrating an analysis of contexts ("the historical dimension in understanding social and political processes"),[7] networks (formal and informal), and practices ("repertoires of contentious action").[8]

The latent network of queer Palestinians is largely invisible to the Palestinian public, but the internet and social media are changing that in powerful ways. Queer Palestinians who engage on a micro level in ordinary acts of queer Palestinian resistance are part of a network connecting them to other social and political actors. Whether those actors are working within or outside of queer Palestinian organizations, the proliferation of persistent consciousness and resistance at an individual, local, and personal level ultimately does lead to social change at a larger level and to the coalescence of the queer social movement in Palestine.

With increased scholarship on queer social movements around the world, political scientist Phillip Ayoub addresses the relationship between visibility, norms, and movement building in a manner that resonates with the findings presented in this chapter on the queer movement in Palestine. Ayoub distinguishes between "interpersonal visibility" ("brings individuals into interaction with people identifying as LGBT") and "public visibility" ("the collective coming out of a group to engage and be seen by society and state").[9] I appreciate Ayoub's delineation of both forms of visibility and how they build queer movements. Ayoub argues that when there is homophobic opposition as a result of that visibility, it is because some queer movements cannot overcome the association of this queer visibility with values that are external to the local religion and nationality, while other movements are able to contextualize that queerness with local frames. The local queer Palestinian movement's relationship to the global queer Palestinian solidarity movement fits well within Ayoub's delineation of the transnational flow of norms on LGBTQ rights. His recognition of the power—as well as the debilitating potential—of visibility is consistent with queer Palestinian activists' practices. They are cognizant of what level of visibility can be met with a backlash that is manageable and even productive and what level will result in a backlash that is too debilitating, driving them to retreat to more latent networks. The arrival of interpersonal and public visibility of queerness to Palestine is undeniable and has been essential for the development of the queer Palestinian movement.

As an anthropologist, I recognize the importance of ethnography as an intellectual mode of inquiry and method that reveals the social dynamics of latent social movements. In her ethnographic research among Palestinian refugees, anthropologist Diana Allan raises concerns about the "politics of solidarity" and its relationship to the "politics of nationalism."[10] Allan writes, "The ethical obligation that those of us in sympathy with the aims of Palestinian nationalism may feel does not entitle us to speak politically for those whose lives have been determined by these events."[11] Furthermore, she says that "refugees have been reduced to symbols of a historical and political grievance awaiting redress, and their political and legal claims are almost always discussed with reference exclusively to Israel."[12] Given the tendency to understand Palestinian refugee experiences through the prism of nationalist slogans and orthodoxies, such as their commitment to the "right of return [to historic Palestine]," Allan finds that what is often missing from this analysis is the "material pragmatism" that she observed in the refugee camps. One example of such pragmatism was the securing of electricity for homes given the lack of social services in Lebanon's Palestinian refugee camps. Material pragmatism "keeps these communities going against all odds and is producing new forms of subjectivity and belonging."[13] I extend Allan's frame of reference to queer Palestinians whose relationships to nationalist orthodoxies are varied and who also must engage in practices of material pragmatism for survival. Queer Palestinian material pragmatism and resistance to ethnoheteronormativity is varied.

Analysis of the queer movement in Palestine is strengthened and nuanced in accounting for this landscape of queer Palestinian material pragmatism and quotidian life. Anthropologist Jason Ritchie, whose work on queer Palestinian activists has revealed "the politics of the ordinary" in this context,[14] provides a theoretical and methodological example for how this can be done. In his critique of the theory of homonationalism, Ritchie "suggests a political and analytical shift away from the *totalizing* theory of homonationalism" (emphasis added).[15] *Homonationalism* is a term coined by queer theorist Jasbir Puar to describe the phenomenon by which certain nation-states incorporate some queer subjects while disavowing other subjects (such as Arabs, Muslims, Sikhs, and South Asians). There is a homonormativity that then emerges—maintaining racial, class, and gender dynamics in service of hegemonic national projects. Homonationalism becomes evident in Puar's analysis as applied to the United States, particularly in the context of the war on terror there, and its relationship to sexuality. Puar also extends her analysis to Israel's homonationalism. She argues that "American exceptionalism feeds off of other exceptionalisms, particularly that of Israel, its closest ally in the Middle East," leading to the "collusion of American and Israeli state interests, defined through a joint oppositional posture towards Muslims."[16] In combating what they consider to be terrorist threats, both the United States and Israel now recruit LGBTQ soldiers in their missions.

Jason Ritchie calls for our analysis to move toward "a more complex and contextualized focus on the ways in which ordinary bodies are regulated in their movements through time and space."[17] In the examination of bodies in

Palestine in this manner, the Israeli occupation and its connections to Israeli homonationalism inevitably feature prominently. The Israeli state certainly appropriates queer bodies and subjects to reinforce nationalist ideologies and practices of Zionism, with harmful impacts on queer Israelis and Palestinians. Nonetheless, I share Ritchie's concern that such frameworks should not be totalizing in our analysis. Attention to ordinary queer Palestinians from an ethnographic vantage point demonstrates the complexities at play among such a heterogeneous population that is confronting an empire of critique with so many layers of surveillance, criticism, and policing. In elaborating on the politics of the ordinary, Ritchie recognizes that it "will not boost the popular appeal of absolutist dogmas that do not require serious thought or self-reflection, but it does hold the potential to offer a more empirically convincing framework for understanding how and why queerness emerges—and the meanings and values it takes on—in particular times and places."[18]

Similarly, anthropologist Veena Das writes, "The suspicion of the ordinary seems to me to be rooted in the fact that relationships require a repeated attention to the most ordinary of objects and events, but our theoretical impulse is often to think of agency in terms of escaping the ordinary rather than as a descent into it."[19] In her ethnographic work among vulnerable Hindu and Muslim women who had been kidnapped and abused by men from other sectarian groups during the India/Pakistan partition, Das describes the "poisonous knowledge" that these women must carry based on their experience. For many of them, "none of the metaphors used to describe the self that had become the repository of poisonous knowledge emphasized the need to give expression to this hidden knowledge. Or rather, containing it was itself the expression of it."[20] Das's ethnography demonstrates that "in the delicate task of finding voice and withholding it in order to protect it, they show the possibilities of a turn to the ordinary."[21] Queer Palestinians also carry poisonous knowledge from their experiences of ethnoheteronormativity, and they hide or express this in ways that my ethnographic research reveals in this chapter. As readers will see, this poisonous knowledge is revealed at the quotidian level.

Heterogeneity of Queer Palestinians

Today, the queer Palestinian subject is perpetually under the gaze of forces near and far. For many queer Palestinians, discovering oneself is the primary struggle. One may seek recognition from a confidante, support from an ally, a sexual encounter with a stranger, love from a partner, acceptance from a family member, encouragement from a coworker, or an alliance with a civil society member. At the same time, the fear of being outed in these domains is also real. And in a number of cases that I have witnessed, those with whom queer Palestinians have had the most intimate relationships, such as a disgruntled roommate or an ex-lover seeking revenge, can be the ones to level such a threat. This fear is exacerbated by the knowledge that queer Palestinians are under the surveillance of larger institutions and individuals, including the security services of Israel, Hamas, and the Palestinian Authority. The risk of being arrested, interrogated, tortured, or trapped into becoming an informant is ever present; in plenty of incidents, families as well as armed groups have inflicted violence against queer people.

Many queer Palestinians are also cognizant of the fact that there are now queer Palestinian activists who want to recruit them as fellow activists, beneficiaries of social services, or members of their personal and social networks. There are internationals seeking to identify queer Palestinians, whether they are global solidarity activists eager to connect LGBTQ Palestinian rights to their own platforms and agendas, critics of Israel who want to highlight the Israeli oppression of queer Palestinians, or right-wing and Islamophobic groups eager to highlight Palestinian homophobia. This also includes Israeli civil society organizations willing to support queer Palestinians, international journalists and human rights workers seeking queer Palestinian narratives to publish, foreign tourists in Israel/Palestine excited to explore the queer Palestinian scene, and academics and researchers aspiring to turn queer Palestinians into the subjects of their analysis. Although the search for queer Palestinians can at times be productive to their own self-actualization, the saturated gaze on such a small population has inevitably led to layers of surveillance. As feminist scholar Minoo Moallem has noted, violence is often "intrinsic to the fixation of the gaze" and protection against violence itself can "become a site of violence."[22]

Within the queer Palestinian landscape, desire, actions, and categories of gender- and sexuality-based identities often do not necessarily map onto subjectivities in the same ways that they do in other parts of the world. Even within the Palestinian context, there is tremendous heterogeneity of experience and self-identification. Half of the world's Palestinian population lives in exile or the Diaspora, what Palestinians call the *shataat*[23] (or "scattering"). Within Israel, 1.9 million Palestinians live as second-class citizens, while 2.8 million reside in the West Bank (including East Jerusalem), mainly as stateless noncitizens, and 1.9 million noncitizen Palestinians are in the Gaza Strip. According the American Friends Service Committee (a Quaker organization that first provided humanitarian aid to Palestinian refugees in 1948), there are now over seven million Palestinian refugees worldwide (in the West Bank, Gaza Strip, and Diaspora).[24]

The political and national context within which queer Palestinians exist shape their relationship to sexuality, with differences between a Palestinian in a Lebanese refugee camp and someone who is a third-generation resident of Paris or Santiago. One's geographic location—whether Gaza City, Tel Aviv, or Jenin, for example—also plays a fundamental role in one's experience of queerness. Palestinians are cisgender and transgender, feminist and misogynist, religious and secular, Christian and Muslim, rich and poor, able-bodied and disabled, rural and urban, traditional and cosmopolitan, homebound and itinerant, politically left and right, without regular access to a computer and online throughout the day, from stable families and broken families, and everything in between all these seemingly dichotomous spheres. These circumstances either expand or constrain the queer Palestinian's journey to realizing their sexual orientation.

There are many individuals who are not conscious of their same-sex desires, while others repress that consciousness, and yet others actively work to deny and purge those desires through abstinence or a focus on heterosexuality. A villager from a farming family might live her entire life without ever hearing the term *almithliyyeh aljinsiyyeh* ("homosexuality") in Arabic, English, or any other language. Then there are queer Palestinians who are conscious of their homosexual desires and who engage in same-sex behaviors, whether in fleeting exchanges or in more permanent relationships. Many of those individuals may never consider that the label homosexual or bisexual applies to them, while others reject these labels entirely. A man could be married to a woman, with or without genuine attraction to her and with or without sustained sexual activity with her, and simultaneously have private sexual relations with other men while repudiating any connection to homosexuals. If such men are active and not passive sexual partners with their male lovers, then they can argue to themselves and others that it is merely their partners who are homosexual. Some queer Palestinians see themselves as homosexuals but keep it to themselves, while others share this part of themselves with a few trusted individuals, and still others are willing to be public about it. And again, one can find everything in between.

It is a small minority of queer Palestinians who commit themselves to long-term monogamous relationships with a person of the same sex. An even smaller minority of queer Palestinians become LGBTQ activists. Some queer Palestinians believe that acting on their homosexual desire is a sin or that the mere desire itself is from the whisper of the devil. Some religious individuals, both Muslim and Christian, believe that their homosexuality is a challenge from God and that they must choose abstinence. Others are sexually active but are consumed with guilt for their supposed sins, while others repress that guilt or struggle to reconcile their faith and homosexuality. Still others entirely reject the validity of theology for their lives. Many queer Palestinians experience changes in their self-definitions and spiritual and sexual journeys over a lifetime. Some are supported by their families, but others are rejected, and many others never share this part of themselves with their families at all.

Some gay men and lesbian women marry each other to fulfill familial and societal expectations in marriages of convenience. Some of those couples have partners on the side, while others remain monogamous, are sexually active with each other, or are not sexually active. Some inform others of this arrangement, whereas others safeguard this secret. Some Palestinians avoid specific sexual acts with their partners, such as anal sex, while others maintain a purely emotional relationship with their same-sex partners. I have met queer Palestinians who find themselves along many points of these continuums.

More Palestinians are taking on the categories of lesbian, gay, bisexual, or transgender (LGBT), while activists often prefer the term *queer*. I use *LGBT* and *queer* interchangeably, with a preference for *LGBTQ* to be as inclusive as possible.[25] The number of LGBTQ Palestinians who have participated in one way or another in queer Palestinian spaces or events with at least several other queer Palestinians has increased over the past eighteen years in historic Palestine, namely in present-day Israel and the Occupied Palestinian Territories. This is largely a result of the emergence of the queer Palestinian movement, which has the herculean task of forging a political agenda from a constituency diverse in virtually every dimension of its existence and of doing so under the shadow of the empire of critique.

Homophobia in Palestinian Society

Homophobia is not unique to Palestinian society; it is intimately linked to a nearly universal combination of fears: of sex, of the feminine, and of the other around the world. Queer Palestinian activists struggle with how to confront homophobia in Palestine. They must determine to what extent and how robustly they will name and resist the very real violence, threats, and intimidation that many queer Palestinians face from their society and families if their sexuality is discovered. This struggle stems partly from a fear of reinforcing dehumanizing narratives about their people and society, although another salient factor is the fear of homophobic backlashes if queer rights are publicly discussed in Palestine.

While conducting fieldwork in the West Bank, I exchanged a series of panicked Facebook messages with "Tamer,"[26] a self-identified gay Palestinian (out only to his close friends) who had found himself in a terrifying and desperate situation. Tamer had recently returned to the West Bank after completing higher education abroad only to realize that his brother had been monitoring his cell phone usage since his arrival. The brother discovered that Tamer was in a relationship with another male and that the two were exchanging text messages in which they expressed sexual and romantic affection toward each other. Horrified by the thought that Tamer could have homosexual tendencies, the brother informed their parents, expressing his concern about—and revulsion for—the content and implications of the text messages. The parents proceeded to detain Tamer at home. Taking turns policing him, the brother, father, and mother took away his money, Palestinian identification card, cell phone, and laptop and forbade him to look for work or leave the house for any reason until the matter was "resolved." After sneaking onto his brother's computer without his family's knowledge, Tamer narrated to me the humiliation to which he was subjected. He expressed relief that his family was not employing physical violence against him, but he was nonetheless devastated by the psychological violence that they had inflicted. When Tamer refused to promise his parents that he would purge himself of any homosexual desires through prayer and instead attempted to explain to them that these were instincts he could not control, they proceeded to spit in his face. In the messages he sent me, Tamer stated that being spat on by his mother and father in this manner and enduring the words they continuously repeated ("You are a disgrace to our family, to Christianity, and to Arabs") were profound forms of degradation and pain, moving him close to "collapse." Nonetheless, he refused to succumb to his parents' demands, even at the risk of losing his independence. Tamer managed to leave the country several years later.

I then received even more alarming messages from "Salma,"[27] a self-identified queer woman in the West Bank who was out to her closest friends and was enduring an experience similar to Tamer's. Salma, like Tamer, reached out to me for moral support and counsel. Salma was also in a relationship with a person of the same gender. After her girlfriend gave her a ride home one day, the two exchanged kisses on the lips as they said goodbye while sitting in the car, which was parked in front of Salma's house. She was not aware that her father was looking through the window and that he witnessed this act. He then severely beat Salma after she entered the house, to the point that she lost consciousness. The father announced that she would not be permitted to leave the house under any circumstance. Salma explained to me that her mother was ill and unable to comprehend what was transpiring, while the father declared that Salma had two choices: either marry a man or be killed by her family. From another room, Salma's younger sisters would hear her father and uncle beating her on a regular basis, with Salma's mother too ill and helpless to intervene. While this case is particularly severe, it reflects the emphasis on marriage, hegemony of heteronormativity, sharp distinctions between men and women in Palestinian society, and the use of violence to police gender norms. Salma succumbed to her father's demand to marry a man, ultimately entering into a marriage of convenience with a gay male Palestinian friend of hers so that they both could placate their families and the larger society.

Many queer Palestinian activists are concerned about the sensationalizing of such narratives of homophobia and queer life in Palestine and their exploitation by those who support the Israeli occupation. They problematize how tolerance of homosexuality can become a marker of a people's humanity, whereas homophobia can become a symbol of an uncivilized people. Homophobia as backwardness then becomes a hermeneutic to attempt to rationalize the subjugation of Palestinians under the Israeli regime. It is possible for scholars and activists to recognize the problematic nature of such dehumanizing discourse while acknowledging the reality that Palestinians fear that their families will discover the poisonous knowledge about their homosexuality.

Queer Palestinians also largely reject the widespread notions that Israel is a gay haven for queer Palestinians from the Occupied Territories and that it is even possible for them to receive asylum and protection in Tel Aviv. There are documented cases in which gay Palestinian men from the West Bank have made it to Tel Aviv to escape threats from their families or to become laborers in the informal Israeli economy. But these Palestinians do not receive asylum or any semblance of security from Israel. It is difficult for queer Palestinians to move freely within the Occupied Territories, let alone within Israel. Queer Palestinian activists often humorously point to the nonexistence of a pink gate to the Israeli wall that is supposed to magically appear when queer Palestinians approach this barrier. Neither is there a separate pink line that appears at Israeli checkpoints for queer Palestinians to pass, with the soldiers creating a VIP lane for LGBTQ Palestinians. Queer Palestinians face the same sets of conditions as straight Palestinians living under Israeli military occupation.

And the few from the West Bank who are able to relocate to Tel Aviv often have difficulties there. One such example is "Basil,"[28] who worked as a prostitute, sleeping with gay Israeli men for money, and was sent back to his village in the West Bank by the Israeli authorities. He was then outed as gay, as a former prostitute, and as someone who had sex with the "colonists." I never heard back from him ultimately, but it is safe to assume that his situation did not end well, particularly given the threats of violence from his family. As for gay Palestinians who are citizens of Israel, queer Palestinian activists such as Ghadir Shafie have spoken of the racism and discrimination they experience in Tel Aviv and other Israeli cities from Jewish Israelis.[29] The situation for queer Palestinians from the Occupied Territories trying to survive in Israel is even more devastating, with the harsh labor conditions of the Israeli black market; the fear of being surveilled, targeted, or made to become an Israeli informant; and the omnipresent threat of deportation.

Queer Palestinians are cognizant of the hegemonic critiques of homosexuality in Palestine, and queer Palestinian activists are also aware of the threats they face from Palestinian society if they cross particular thresholds in public discourse on this issue. A 2019 BBC News–Arab Barometer survey found that 95 percent of respondents from the Palestinian Territories did not find homosexuality "acceptable."[30] The disapproval rates of homosexuality in the Occupied Palestinian Territories are among the very highest globally, and this has remained relatively consistent. For instance, a 2014 Pew survey found that 94 percent of Palestinian respondents viewed homosexuality as morally unacceptable. The plateauing of the queer Palestinian movement in 2012 means that the movement has not been able to increase overall acceptance for queerness in broader Palestinian society. The 2014 Pew survey also revealed that 43 percent of Israelis characterized homosexuality as morally unacceptable.[31] The Israeli newspaper *Haaretz* reported that an average of 59 percent of the global population disapproved of homosexuality and that this number was a marker of Israelis being "more open than most of the world."[32] Although queer Palestinian activists aspire to change Palestinian understanding of homosexuality, most believe it is impossible to do so radically without an end to the Israeli military occupation. As long as Palestinians are collectively denied freedom from Israeli captivity and domination, they cannot realize collective queer liberation within their society, considering that political and sexual freedom cannot be divorced. Queer Palestinian activists also are concerned that the invocation of figures related to Palestinian homophobia without context is problematic, especially when it is cited as further justification for the Israeli occupation. They are wary of essentializing Israeli and Palestinian attitudes on this issue and are worried that the juxtaposition can reinforce colonial logics. The facts nonetheless remain that the overwhelming majority of Palestinians do condemn homosexuality in moral terms and that this is the climate in which queer Palestinian activists must operate.

In July 2017, Palestinian writer Abbad Yahya was threatened with murder and later had to flee Palestine for a life in exile after the publication of his novel *Crime in Ramallah*. In it, he addressed themes of Palestinian corruption and included a gay main character who is portrayed as having oral sex with a man. The Palestinian Authority banned the book and stated that it "contained indecent texts and terms that threaten morality and public decency."[33] Yahya had to deal with threats by Palestinians to burn down bookstores that carried it. Bookstore owners are still detained by the Palestinian Authority police for merely searching for the book. In reflecting on this ordeal and what it reveals about censorship and conservativism in the Arab world, journalist Joumana Haddad writes, "As for gay sex, it is the ultimate transgression. Never mind that Abu Nawas, one of the greatest Arab poets of all times, had written, back in the eighth and ninth centuries, countless erotic poems about his gay sexual encounters."[34] It is important to note that internal Palestinian violence is not outside the context of the military occupation but gets essentialized as "culture" in many Israeli and Western discourses on Palestinian society. All of these forms of violence must be acknowledged, and the Palestinian perpetrators should be held accountable. The broader conditions of structural and physical violence that result from the Israeli occupation must also be considered for their role in exacerbating internal forms of Palestinian violence and oppression.

Queer Palestinians view the possibility of a public gay pride parade in a West Bank or Gaza Strip city to be completely out of the question anytime soon. Although such a parade does not resonate for many queer Palestinians in the first place, it does for others, especially when they participate in such events outside of the country and are able to enjoy the opportunity for public expression. This demonstrates how diverse symbols can belong to people differently as well as express different desires. Palestinian gay pride marchers have not been attacked by homophobic vigilantes in Palestine because there has never been such a march. Queer Palestinians share the realistic expectation that such vigilantes and attacks would surface were they to dare to proceed with a parade. Although there is no coordinated widespread campaign in the West Bank by Palestinians to physically target queer Palestinians in a systematic fashion, the community does hear about instances of families attacking their own children or of Palestinian Authority security officials using homosexuality against a gay Palestinian civilian. It is not common for Palestinians in the Occupied Territories to blur gender norms openly and visibly in public, but when it does happen it often results in verbal harassment or even physical attacks. A gay Palestinian man who left the West Bank and then married a Canadian man in Ottawa lamented to me that they could not even conceive of holding their wedding ceremony in the West Bank and that they expected to be immediately killed and the entire venue being burned down if they dared to do so. The situation in the Gaza Strip for queer people is becoming increasingly described as "hellish," with devastating reports of harassment and torture.[35] Hamas members are threatening anyone who dares to come out, and LGBTQ individuals face intense surveillance from Islamist groups.

While openly advocating for their rights and for protection, queer Palestinians are challenging the fundamental linguistic foundation of their society, which is based on Arabic's strict feminine-masculine binary of words and concepts. Both Palestinian Christian and Muslim clergy condemn homosexuality in the strongest terms. Palestinian nationalism has reified a neat association of gender, sexuality, and the norms of contribution with the struggle for national liberation. Palestinians, by and large, continue to see homosexuality as a Western phenomenon that comes with Western domination through cultural imperialism and a foreign conspiratorial erosion of morality.

Palestinian public discourse on sexuality in general, let alone on homosexuality, is limited, which is also at least partially a result of the overwhelming majority of Palestinians who are not addressing these taboos. Challenging the hegemonic gender- and sexual-based norms in Palestine is a cause for repercussion, and queer Palestinian activists display formidable courage in being visible and speaking openly on these issues. Although queer Palestinian activists are contributing to the public discourse on gender and sexual pluralism—for example, with initiatives to engage young Palestinians in educational institutions in Israel and the West Bank on these matters—the response of Palestinian society to queer Palestinian activism has been slow, gradual, limited, strategic, and selective. Queer Palestinian activists prefer more localized outreach to other queer Palestinians as well as to potential allies within Palestinian civil society. They cultivate these strategic alliances with internal constituencies whose attitudes on homosexuality reflect a willingness for more nuanced engagement with LGBTQ issues.

By and large, Palestinian society as a whole does not acknowledge the existence of homosexuals in their midst, unless it is in the form of haphazard characterizations of queer and trans Palestinians as immoral or mentally ill. As a result, queer Palestinian communities do not provoke repression from patriarchal authorities. It is an exceptional moment when a Palestinian authority openly targets queer Palestinians in a sustained manner, and it is equally rare that queer Palestinian activists challenge homophobia vociferously in the public domain. One example of the latter is a June 2015 statement released in Arabic by fifteen Palestinian organizations in Israel, including Aswat and Al-Qaws, condemning an article by Sheikh Kamal Khatib, the deputy head of the Islamic Movement for Palestinians in Israel. The signatories made a critical distinction between "difference of opinions" and "discourse of hatred and incitement."[36] Khatib had used deeply hurtful and homophobic language to describe LGBTQ individuals as repulsive and to say that they made him "sick." He wrote, "It is noteworthy that suspicious local organizations, tabloids and biased writers have been advocating this perversion. To all those, I say not 'may you be well and have boys' but rather 'may you be miserable and suffer plagues and AIDS, you perverts!'"[37] The statement responding to Khatib reflected increasing sensitivity to homosexuality within Palestinian civil society in Israel. Balad, the Arab nationalist party in Israel, also issued a statement, equating its opposition to homophobia with its opposition to the "colonialist Israeli regime."[38] It is challenging to find survey data of attitudes toward homosexuality among Palestinian citizens of Israel, but it would not be surprising if rates of acceptance among this population were confirmed to be higher than for the Occupied Territories.

One of the most challenging critiques that queer Palestinians must confront from other Palestinians is the notion that queerness, whether manifested as desire, practice, or identity, is not only a foreign concept in an Arab and Muslim context but also a vehicle through which Palestinian society is colonized, dominated, and politically and morally corrupted. For instance, in June 2016, a Gaza-based news agency published images of the Tel Aviv Pride parade on its Facebook page with homophobic commentary in Arabic. The text told of "a march with hundreds of thousands of perverts in the settlement of 'Tel Aviv' with the participation of members of the Zionist parliament and political and military figures. This activity happens annually in the place that has one of the highest rates of homosexuality in the world."[39] The average Palestinian looking at this post felt a sense of loss that Israel captured this area of historic Palestine, frustration that they are denied access to this part of their ancestral homeland, and revulsion that homosexuals were marching so openly on this land and are part of the colonial project. The perception that Israelis are likely to have more homosexuals than other societies is meant to serve as evidence of Israeli moral inferiority and their illegitimate presence in the Holy Land. Queer Palestinians must then grapple with how to repress and conceal the poisonous reality of their homosexuality so as not to be discovered and associated with these "inferior" Israelis.

The linking of homosexuality with the degradation of Palestinian society and the undermining of resistance to Israeli domination also became apparent in 2007. Hamas took control of Gaza from Fatah, the secular Palestinian political group, that year. Before the takeover, Hamas leaders made homophobic statements such as Mahmoud Zahar's characterization of homosexuals as "a minority of perverts and the mentally and morally sick." When Hamas took Fatah's place in Gaza, they accused Fatah of "corruption, collaboration with Israel, and a total lack of morals, including homosexual relations between officials."[40] Hamas viewed the homosexual acts between members of their rival political group as evidence of Fatah's moral and political inferiority and as another reason to justify the need for Hamas to purify governance and society in Gaza. Homosexuality among Fatah members also further bolstered Hamas's depiction of Fatah as "little more than a gang of kleptocratic narcissists bent on sacrificing the future of the Palestinian people for their own self-enrichment. Homosexuality is just another indication of their corruption."[41]

In March 2016, the *New York Times* published a story titled "Hamas Commander, Accused of Theft and Gay Sex, Is Killed by His Own." Thirty-four-year-old Mahmoud Ishtiwi, a commander in Hamas's armed wing, was executed by the group. The article reported,

> A dragnet investigation began, drawing in Mr. Ishtiwi's soldiers. Qassam officials found a man who claimed he had had sex with Mr. Ishtiwi and provided dates and locations. They concluded that the missing money had been used either to pay for sex or to keep the man quiet. If Israeli intelligence officials knew Mr. Ishtiwi was gay, the officials surmised, perhaps he had given them information in exchange for keeping a secret that, if uncovered, would have made him an outcast in his society.[42]

Human Rights Watch investigated the extrajudicial execution, finding that Ishtiwi had been detained in different locations for a year and tortured by Hamas's Izz al-Din al-Qassam Brigades. This included "beatings and suspension from the ceiling. He said his commander had beaten him about 500 times with a hose, ordering him to confess."[43] Human Rights Watch also reported that "upon viewing the body, [his relatives] saw that scarred into his arms and legs was the Arabic word "wronged [مظلوم]," which [Ishtiwi] had apparently cut into his body with a sharp implement."[44] Hamas accused Ishtiwi of "moral violations" as a result of the allegations of homosexual acts; this was initially linked to the accusations of collaboration with Israel and financial embezzlement. After being cleared of the latter two allegations, he was ultimately executed for the former. This case demonstrates the association of homosexuality in Palestinian society with moral deprivation, political corruption, and betrayal of national, social, and religious norms.

Fatah members can also subscribe to homophobic logic and discourse. For instance, before a Jerusalem Pride parade, Sheikh Abu Sneineh and Azmi Shiukhi, "prominent Fatah activists" in Hebron, spoke against it at a press conference. They were alarmed that it was further "defiling Jerusalem" and that it constituted a "moral massacre" in Jerusalem.[45] Thus, the mere presence of a queer body declaring itself as such is considered by many Palestinians to be an assault on their homeland. The Fatah activists added, "The occupation hurts al-Aqsa and us but gives foreign anarchists defense and protection to march in the streets of the city. This is a cancer whose objective is to destroy the Islamic nation through humiliating Jerusalem by demonstrating the perversions of gays and lesbians. The world must unite against this ugly, unprecedented crime."[46] For the most conservative segments of Palestinian society, the discovery of homosexuals in their midst is tremendously disconcerting, revealing what is seen as an erosion of the proper masculine, moral nation that can ultimately prevail in the struggle against Israel. During Palestinian political contestations, the open presence of homosexuals in the opposing group—whether it is Israel or a rival Palestinian group—can be used by Palestinian actors as a tool for delegitimization in the eyes of the Palestinian public. The fact that Israel also utilizes Palestinian homosexual bodies for Israeli state projects puts queer Palestinians in an even more precarious position.

There have been some reports that the Fatah-dominated Palestinian Authority in the West Bank is also employing, to a limited extent, certain methods of surveillance against gay Palestinians that are similar to those used by the Israeli security services. For instance, *Vice* journalist Nigel O'Connor recounts the story of "Saif," a gay Palestinian who reported the following:

> Saif is wondering what would happen if his homosexuality was made public. As a gay guy in the Palestinian West Bank, such information could see him murdered. While his sexuality remains hidden from his direct family, Saif said local Palestinian Authority police are aware and keep files on him and other homosexuals, blackmailing them into working as spies and informants.[47]

Queer Palestinian activists have explicitly addressed the issue of blackmailing by Israeli occupation forces but not by the Palestinian Authority to the same extent.

There are queer Palestinians who feel strongly that meaningful social change and protections for LGBTQ Palestinians cannot be realized unless the struggle against homophobia is waged in the public domain and on a much larger scale. They remain in the minority. Queer Palestinian activism is constantly being calibrated to avoid reaching the critical threshold at which activists and others would fear for their physical safety as a result of nascent campaigns against homosexuals. It is in the Gaza Strip where such homophobic campaigns can be found either in practice or on the horizon, with Hamas authorities policing what they deem to be moral and immoral. This has included combating what they call "the masculinization of women and the feminization of men," which they see as signs from God, according to their view of the Islamic tradition, that the end of times and the Day of Judgment are near. Gays and lesbians, as well as those who cross-dress and those who adopt nontraditional gender roles, are seen by many Palestinians, through their interpretation of Islamic theology, as literally helping precipitate the end of the world. This belief was repeated to me multiple times during my fieldwork.

Since Hamas points to gay pride parades in Israel as further signifiers of the foreignness of Israelis and their illegitimate presence on the land of historic Palestine, Palestinians openly marking their queerness in Palestinian society and publicly calling for an end to homophobia can be associated with a colonial subjectivity. Queer Palestinian activists are pressured to distance themselves from their queer Israeli counterparts to maintain their links to the Palestinian social fabric. And in othering homosexuals and gender-non-conforming individuals and in considering the very real risks of putting their voices and bodies on the line for queer liberation, these queer Palestinian activists find it convenient to shield themselves behind arguments such as, "Coming out and gay pride are Western." Although there are important reasons to distinguish LGBTQ rights agendas in Western contexts from those in a Palestinian context, the severe repression of displays of gender and sexual defiance of Palestinian social norms dramatically limits the ability of queer Palestinian self-realization and self-actualization. There are queer Palestinians who want to break down East-West binaries and create more spaces for queer Palestinians to lead their lives in ways that honor both their commitment to the national struggle and their desire to cultivate their personal relationships and networks. With the dominant social forces attempting to describe queerness and Palestinianness as mutually exclusive, queer Palestinian activists do feel pressure to render queerness as subordinate to Palestinianness so that they can feel safe, legitimate, and understood in their own society. Only privately, with trusted allies, can queer Palestinians explicate their queerness without omnipresent homophobia, and even then, internalized homophobia is often latent.

There are queer Palestinian activists and their allies who choose to challenge use of the term *homophobia* in the Palestinian context. Geographer Walaa Alqaisiya draws on her research and activist experience in Al-Qaws to problematize the applicability of the concept of homophobia in Palestine several times in one article.[48] I agree with some aspects of such analyses, especially on the necessity of combining conceptions of queerness with those of anticoloniality. Yet I also question why all of Alqaisiya's references to homophobia seem to have the purpose of undermining its salience as an analytical category in relation to Palestine. My concern is that such an approach could contribute to the denial of the social fact of homophobia as a system of oppression. One cannot completely erase the very real embodied experiences of homophobia that queer Palestinians must negotiate regularly, even as important interventions (such as some of those in Alqaisiya's article) are advanced about the limits of *homophobia* as a term. There is no concept that is free from all epistemic impurities.

Furthermore, Alqaisiya justifies not naming homophobia in Palestine with the argument from some queer Palestinian activists that they "live in a society that does not publicly discuss sexuality."[49] Although robust discourses on sexuality can be found in the private sphere, it is true that robust public discourse on sexuality is generally lacking in Palestinian society. Many queer Palestinians do not believe that this should continue forever or that their culture should be viewed as static. The LGBTQ movement in Palestine can contribute to more sex-positive discourse if the topic is approached sensitively. This is a response to existing public discourse on sexuality in Palestinian communities and encompasses hegemonic gender and sexuality norms, including those that are homophobic. Queer Palestinians overwhelmingly do not want their queer struggle to be reduced to sex acts, just as the identities and experiences of heterosexuals should not be reduced to mere sex. What queer people do—or do not do—in their bedrooms is their business. They want to be able to make decisions about whether they should discuss their lives, pain, love, families, and relationships publicly without social ostracism or fear for their well-being. Straight Palestinians take for granted that they can do this in the public and private spheres because they can generally abide by conservative gender norms and heteronormativity. That is not even an option for many queer Palestinians. Homophobia is largely what accounts for this double standard.

The LGBTQ Movement in Palestine

Thanks to the queer Palestinian movement, there are activists on the ground who have paved the way for the emergence of a Palestinian discourse resisting homophobia. The year 2002 was foundational for the rise of the queer Palestinian movement in Israel/Palestine, with the establishment of Aswat (Palestinian Gay Women). They describe themselves as "a group of lesbian, bisexual, transgender, intersex, questioning and queer Palestinian women," and they promote "safe, supportive and empowering spaces to express and address our personal, social and political struggles as a national indigenous minority living inside Israel; as women in a patriarchal society; and as LBTQI women in a wider hetero-normative culture." Registered in Israel and based in Haifa, Aswat focuses on the queer experience for that population of queer Palestinians, and their emphasis on women's experiences bolsters their feminist approach to sexuality. They have reached hundreds of queer women in Israel/Palestine over the years. I have seen how their meeting spaces, with the support of the feminist organization Kayan, serve as refuges for many lesbian Palestinians. Aswat continues to function today with publications, workshops, and community engagement to support queer women, to shape the discourse on gender and sexuality in Palestinian society, and to contribute to the larger Palestinian struggle for rights and freedom.

In 2007, Al-Qaws (Sexual and Gender Diversity in Palestinian Society) was established and registered in Israel. Al-Qaws also has one office in Jerusalem. The organization works with queer Palestinian activists across Israel and the West Bank. Al-Qaws includes men and women and increasing numbers of trans as well as gender-nonconforming individuals. Both Al-Qaws and Aswat have boards, retain few paid staff members, and are largely dependent on foreign aid for their programming. Both also have women Palestinian citizens of Israel as their leadership's most visible global figures, namely, Ghadir Shafie for Aswat and Haneen Maikey for Al-Qaws.

Maikey had previously served as the staff member tasked with supporting queer Palestinians for the Jerusalem Open House, an Israeli LGBTQ organization. After disagreements with the Open House about how to best support queer Palestinians both within and outside of Jerusalem, Maikey worked with other queer Palestinians to establish their own institution, Al-Qaws. Al-Qaws shares Aswat's mission to create an alternative discourse on gender and sexuality within Palestinian society and to facilitate queer Palestinians becoming part of the larger Palestinian solidarity movement. Al-Qaws is known for its hotline, which is implemented in partnership with Aswat, that provides support for Palestinians with questions and concerns about their sexuality. Al-Qaws also organizes monthly queer Palestinian parties in Tel Aviv (these also serve as fundraisers for the organization). They engage in civil society outreach efforts with potential Palestinian partner institutions and facilitate ongoing queer Palestinian empowerment workshops that take place in the West Bank. Al-Qaws's work, which continues today, also includes creative projects such as the production of youth music that affirms and promotes gender and sexual pluralism in Arabic and in a manner that addresses fellow Palestinians.

During my fieldwork, I cofacilitated an LGBTQ workshop series and also spent significant time in the safe house that Al-Qaws set up for queer Palestinian activists in the West Bank. This is a place where they could gather, collaborate, and support one another. The precise location of the house was not known to others outside the queer Palestinian community. Strict proto-col around keeping the location of the house secret ensured that the space was protected. Al-Qaws has since shut it down. Although queer Palestinians do come together in spaces across the West Bank and Gaza Strip, the chal-lenges of securing queer-devoted activist space in the Occupied Territories are tremendous.

The members of Gaza's queer population are almost impossible to reach as a result of the Israeli- and Egyptian-imposed blockade on Gaza as well as Hamas control of the area, yet they often follow queer Palestinian activism online. Many queer Palestinians in Israel and the West Bank are also aware of Aswat and Al-Qaws. While most individuals in Gaza are not active with these organizations, they nonetheless follow their activities, press releases, social media accounts, and coverage in the global press with delight that such entities exist to represent queer Palestinians. We know this from queer Pal-estinians who had previously been completely in the closet and, after con-fiding in others, went on to share the boost in morale they experienced af-ter learning about queer Palestinian groups online. At the same time, other queer Palestinians feel that those activists cannot speak for them. Queer Pal-estinian activists do not purport to speak on behalf of all queer Palestinians, but local and international actors do sometimes take statements from leaders of these groups in an attempt to embody a supposedly authentic queer Pales-tinian voice. It is important to note that such a voice cannot exist.

In a context such as occupied Palestine, where there are so many layers of political and psychological violence, surveillance is necessarily multilayered also. The politics of hiding and revealing can be deeply painful. A gay Pal-estinian man unable to muster erections after being pressured to marry a woman suffers a particular form of anguish—with concerns about his erectile dysfunction being linked to his homosexuality—as well as the shame and hu-miliation of not meeting the masculinist community's overwhelming expec-tations of virility. Also, society, activists, and academics too often neglect to discuss the victimization of the women trapped in these situations. The sex-ual performance of Palestinian men and the fertility of their wives are often mechanisms not only for passing down the family's lineage but also for con-tributing to the national struggle in the face of ethnic cleansing.[50] LGBTQ Palestinians also experience anguish because they are unable to meet oth-ers for companionship, sex, love, and friendship in person and therefore de-pend on virtual spaces facilitated by queer websites. There is constant fear that one's family may find that browsing history or that an intelligence officer could be monitoring that behavior, therefore revealing poisonous knowledge and leading to any number of devastating outcomes.

Queer Palestinian activism aimed at ameliorating the negative effects of coming out to others in Palestine and at transforming the connotation of queerness from poison to love is to be lauded. Queer Palestinian solidarity activism around the world is then enhanced, and the extraordinary significance of ordinary queer Palestinian organizing and community-building in local contexts in Israel/Palestine is accounted for. Attention to the ordinary necessitates attention to the body—and the ontology of queer Palestinian bodies demonstrates how homophobia and imperialism cannot be divorced because they are simultaneously physically mapped onto subjects.

Activists must also confront the concern from other queer Palestinian activists, LGBTQ Palestinians in general, and Palestinians at large (and even internationals) that queer liberation is not a priority for Palestine at this time. This critique posits that Palestinians facing threats of displacement, dispossession, and detention from Israeli military occupation forces do not have the luxury of worrying about whether two men or two women should be allowed to be intimate in bed. Such simplistic logic reduces queer identities and experiences to specific and narrow sexual acts—disregarding varied LGBTQ understandings of self, struggle, and solidarity. The removal of homophobia from an intersectional articulation of liberation from all forms of oppression resuscitates homophobia. When a young lesbian Palestinian woman is forced by her family to marry a man, she must anticipate the high likelihood of a life of marital rape. Whether she seeks support before or after the marriage is consummated, or both, her priority may very well become the need to escape Palestine over resistance to Israeli occupation. The desire of a queer Palestinian activist to ensure that there are resources, options, and emotional support for such a person as she navigates pragmatic needs for survival cannot be dismissed as a luxury that must be subordinated to the struggle against Zionism.

LGBTQ Palestinians recognize that an end to Israeli oppression would likely make it easier to empower and liberate queer and trans Palestinians (assuming that the next system of governance for Palestinians would enable political freedom and individual liberties). Like their feminist counterparts and like many feminists among them, queer Palestinians cannot be required, even when some of them acquiesce, to halt the struggle against heteropatriarchy in Palestine. For most queer Palestinians, that struggle is no more and no less critical than the fight for Palestinian national self-determination. Although Palestinian feminists too have a long road ahead, the precedent they have established in Palestine is inspiring. For decades now, many Palestinian feminists have clearly articulated their rejection of the notion that discussions surrounding—and work toward—gender justice should wait until after Palestine is free.

The heart of Al-Qaws and Aswat's work is the determination to have queer Palestinians shape education about queer Palestinians, in both Israel and the Occupied Territories. This ability to define a queer Palestinian agenda happens when a professional advocacy group is created to train and support Palestinian therapists who are allies to the LGBTQ community, or when groups in the cities of Haifa, Tel Aviv, and Ramallah are nurtured to empower queer Palestinian youth in particular to have a space of their own with a trained facilitator. Al-Qaws established its local presence in Israel/Palestine when, in an effort to educate their society about LGBTQ issues, queer Palestinian activists produced a series of professional short videos circulated online about their experiences with homophobia. Defining a queer Palestinian agenda also happens when a volunteer spends an hour using newly gained conceptual tools to support the increasing number of Palestinians who identify as transgender and call the queer hotline for assistance. Al-Qaws realizes its mission while enabling community organizers to develop further programming for LGBTQ individuals from different parts of historic Palestine. Al-Qaws also simultaneously runs regular support groups for LGBTQ Palestinians and maintains Hawamesh, a monthly public discussion forum in Haifa to engage the public on gender and sexual diversity.

Queer Palestinian activists have published dozens of articles in Arabic and English in forums such as www.qadita.net (a widely read Arabic literature and politics website now on hiatus but with its entire archive available online) and *Jadal* (the journal of Mada al-Carmel Arab Center for Applied Social Research).[51] Al-Qaws contributes to developing further resources for queer Palestinians that speak to their particular experiences and local contexts. For example, www.qadita.net published an article in August 2011 by queer Palestinian activists in Arabic titled "The Palestinian Sexuality Movement: From Identity to Queer Politics,"[52] and *Jadal*'s twenty-fourth issue included five articles in English on gender and sexuality in Palestine. Some individuals on the right and left have attempted to undermine this activism by emphasizing the fact that much of it has been catalyzed by queer Palestinian citizens of Israel. These activists reject such attempts to sever them from the Palestinian social fabric in the Occupied Territories, particularly because the Israeli state is already invested in such severance. Other individuals critique queer Palestinian activists for their use of English (in addition to Arabic), even though these activists are, in fact, mainly using Arabic. At the same time, these activists are thoughtful about the need to reach wider audiences through English in an interconnected world in which they feel that solidarity from abroad is essential, including from queer Palestinians in the Diaspora.

Queer Palestinian activists, in joining mainstream Palestinian human rights activism that is not necessarily LGBTQ related, have helped Palestinians start to see LGBTQ individuals not as collaborating with Israel or as antithetical and foreign to Arab and Muslim values but instead as integral to the movement for national liberation. The queer Palestinian movement should not be defined merely by its resistance to Zionism—as is done by many heterosexual Palestinian activists. There must be increased space for queer Palestinians to resist oppressive internal social norms that are meant to dictate expressions of gender and sexuality. It is both in the public defiance of social taboos and in the ordinary defiance of everyday queer Palestinians (particularly those who are not activists with existing organizations) that the foundations for future gender and sexual pluralism in Palestine have been laid. It is in the linking of national and sexual struggles that a broader conception of emancipation is possible.

The ruptures to imposed patriarchy and heteronormativity, strict gender binaries, and marriage within Palestinian society do not often occur in the public sphere. These ruptures, however, are becoming more accepted in the private sphere and are nascent in the public sphere. The queer movement in Palestine needs not only to continue its work toward queer liberation but also to expand spaces in which sexual and national politics can come together. There are many examples of queer Palestinian activists asserting their existence and delineating their struggles within Palestinian society—and these voices need to be heard more vociferously in the global queer Palestinian solidarity movement.

When Al-Qaws activists sprayed graffiti in the West Bank of two men kissing in one spot and two women kissing in another spot, with the caption "Queers passed by here," they were addressing fellow queer Palestinians to let them know they are not alone. The activists were also addressing heterosexual Palestinians who expect queer Palestinians to remain completely invisible. In

May 2013, "hundreds of people attended the launch of an album featuring lo-cal Palestinian musicians"[53] in Haifa as part of an Al-Qaws event. The event was part of the project Singing Sexuality, in which artists produced "photo-graphs, videos, music and written testimonials and information"[54] in Arabic that challenged gender and sexual norms in Palestinian society.[55] Al-Qaws's Haneen Maikey contextualized Singing Sexuality "as part of the larger Pal-estinian struggle against Israeli occupation, colonialism and discrimination, both inside present-day Israel and the occupied West Bank and Gaza Strip."[56] She added, "Part of how I see and understand resistance is that when we de-colonize Palestine, I will have a society that I can rely on, a society that is ready to [respond to] different social and political processes, that can respect the Other, [and] have openness about different sexuality and behavior."[57]

Safa Tamish, director of Muntada, the Arab Forum for Sexuality, Educa-tion and Health in Palestine, reflected on this, explaining that "while sexu-ality in general and LGBT rights in particular are not openly talked about, Palestinian society has seen an increased willingness to discuss these issues in recent years."[58] Tamish also noted, "I think there has been a shift in peo-ple's perception. I'm not saying that Palestinian society is so pro-gay rights. I cannot say that, but I can say that it is more and more acceptable. The fact is that we know of many, many families that accepted their children."[59] She added, "Within Palestinian society, I see that there [has been] a real trans-formation in the last four or five years."[60] Tamish's insights reveal emerging trends that we see among some younger urban, more socioeconomically ad-vantaged Palestinians.

In December 2015, Aswat premiered its first queer Palestinian film festi-val. During the three-day event, "a handful of Haifa coffee shops and art ven-ues opened up a dialogue about the overlaps of occupation and sexuality; and of the borders of individual identity in the context of an uncertain interna-tional existence."[61] Hanan Wakeem, Aswat's educational director, stated that the festival was a response to the fact that "most films talking about gay Pales-tinians are made by Israeli or Western eyes, and they don't represent the real voice of Palestinians."[62] Aswat's work has been to reclaim queer Palestinian voices as they encounter criticism and appropriation from all directions.

Another example of resistance to gender and sexual norms in Palestin-ian society is the September 2016 article by Abdullah Hassan Erikat, who was a college student in the West Bank when his article was published in the widely-read Palestinian magazine *This Week in Palestine*. Erikat's piece, titled

"Coming Out as Grey," boldly and bravely pushed back at the "list of slurs" he has endured in Arabic from fellow Palestinians for not conforming to an "ideal masculinity."[63] These include *"Fafi, Tant* = sissy; *Luti* = faggot in the most insulting way, more professionally it means queer; *Nua'om, banoteh* = womanly."[64] Erikat writes, "My voice, body language, *nuomeh* (softness), and choice of clothes are inconsistent with the masculine pattern that each 'penis-born human' should adopt instinctively without claiming any difference that is not in line with this pattern."[65] Erikat also defends "women and LGBT people" and fights "the monster of the masculine paradigm" in Palestinian society.[66] Erikat's article, and the emotions and struggle that it captures, are yet another form of queer resistance in Palestine.

Several months later, Erikat published another article in which he narrated the experience of being told as a seventh grader: "This is how your future looks like." The friend who said that referred to a well-known man in their hometown who cross-dressed. Erikat was puzzled for years about why the fact that he did not reinforce Palestinian masculinity marked him so early and negatively in his society, a society that he describes as "worshipping" the gender binary.[67] He adds,

> Palestine needs to stop wearing the shadows of its historical struggle with Is-
> raeli occupation, which people are submerged in and which links it directly
> with masculinity, thus tightening the . . . rope. Our Palestinian-Israeli conflict
> and the continuing occupation is a tragic reality, yet people adopt it as an ex-
> cuse not to allow any other social issues to be tackled as they prefer not to be
> distracted.[68]

Erikat continues to write and speak openly and boldly about these queer issues and his personal experience. He has been an inspiration, especially to many other young queer Palestinians in the West Bank.

Queer Palestinian Epistemologies

As a native anthropologist, I minimize the use of the label "informant" to describe my interlocutors. This term is used by intelligence and security institutions as well as other sources under the empire of critique.[69] I am also cognizant of the political and ethical implications of designating queer Palestinians as "subjects" of my analysis, particularly as they already experience regimes of surveillance and scrutiny. Subsequently, I have protected the identities of all LGBTQ individuals in Palestine who are referenced in this text (whose references cannot already be found in the public domain). This book is not only a contribution to the production of knowledge but also a form of engaged scholarship so that my research can bring to light queer Palestinian epistemologies (emphasis on the plural). I envision this text serving as a resource and a source of empowerment for those queer Palestinians with whom these ideas resonate. Some of them have already been among my primary readers and interlocutors. Many queer Palestinians are invested in building a more inclusive, democratic, and efficacious movement, with intimate connections to other local, regional, and global queer movements. This book also delineates a road map for how we can potentially move toward realizing that goal.

My analysis was largely informed and inspired by the insights that queer individuals in Palestine shared with me. They are certainly capable of theorizing the reality of Queer Palestine (whether or not they choose to engage in public activism). If we pay close enough attention to them, it becomes clear that the activists sustaining the queer Palestinian movement along with other queer Palestinians attempting to lead their everyday lives have been engaged in compelling epistemological work to make sense of their experiences and to communicate those insights to one another and to the world. For instance, one queer Palestinian collective articulated a conception of queer politics that accounts for other systems of marginalization in robust ways. They write, "We must also question the logic of 'gay rights' as it is commonly understood and practiced—a single-axis politics based on one's sexual identity to the exclusion of other interconnected injustices based on race, ethnicity, class, gender, and other markers of difference."[70] Because queer Palestinians must confront Zionism in addition to homophobia, many of them see the world through an intersectional lens of resistance to both domains of ethnoheteronormativity.

In connecting queer Palestinian politics to discourses of visibility, Rauda Morcos, a former chair of Aswat, explained that "there are different kinds of visibilities" and that Western visibilities do "not work for everyone."[71] Morcos does not subscribe to "a refusal to leave the closet but a rejection of the language of the closet altogether, a reliance not on the projection of visible, intelligible subjects but on the subversion of the state's need to see in the first place."[72] The form of queer Palestinian activism that has resonated with Morcos is not "the collective movement out of the closet and into the space of the nation but the creation of a space, outside the state's regulatory gaze and beyond the reach of its checkpoints, where bodies, desires, and identifications—

queer or not—might proliferate, in all their perverse and incoherent glory."[73] Such a perspective and approach to challenging hegemonic queer Western notions of visibility and their relationship to the state demonstrates how the examination of queer Palestinian epistemologies enriches queer theory more generally.

Queer Palestinian epistemologies are also complex, with individuals conceptualizing visibility, sexuality, and the state differently, perhaps even adapting terms of Western origin—such as "the closet"—to the Palestinian context in a manner that is organic and resonates with other queer Palestinians. In my research and activism, I have seen how some queer Palestinians employ the Arabic term *khazaneh* ("closet") as a metaphor for the condition of living without disclosure of one's sexuality and the challenges of "coming out." Others prefer to think about disclosure in terms of "inviting in," in which LGBTQ Palestinians reveal aspects of themselves and their sexuality in a methodical, patient, and individual fashion and only with those with whom they have established trust and a sense of security. In this context, queer Palestinians have used the term "dance" to describe what it is like to navigate a world in which the boundaries between disclosure and nondisclosure and between legibility and nonrecognition require constant vigilance, recalibration, and flexibility. The spatial and temporal limits of the notion of the closet become evident; that is, many do not experience a teleological transition from one geographic positioning to another and from one period to another. The spaces overlap, the times are blurred, and the traumas are triggered when they must retreat or when they see another queer person they care about suffer. Queer Palestinians rarely feel that they are truly fully out of any closet, and life becomes a series of dances, alone or in a community, to survive, thrive, and find love and acceptance.

Ghadir Shafie has written about Aswat's commitment to educational programs on sexuality among queer Palestinians in Israel—and how this commitment has been hampered by the Israeli government:

> As part of this campaign, the [Israeli] Ministry of Education has been determinedly sabotaging all efforts made by Aswat—Palestinian Gay Women to provide professionals and service providers with training courses and study days on sexual rights and politics. In fact, over the past five years, the Ministry has been bent on excluding us from any project at all that aims to promote respect for diversity and tolerance within Palestinian societies. Instead, the Israeli government and many foreign embassies in Tel Aviv—including

the U.S. Embassy—allocate funds to Israeli organizations to work with our constituencies in Palestinian communities. On the one hand, Jewish and foreign funding brands sexual rights as a "Zionist" issue, thus hindering even further the advancement of sexual freedoms in Palestinian societies. On the other, Israelis wanting to "educate" Palestinians about gay rights ensures that sexuality education is only delivered condescendingly by non-Palestinians to Palestinians, ignoring cultural, language, and other particularities. The propaganda . . . deems Palestinians not "civilized" enough to understand, let alone respect, "gay" rights, while at the same time depriving them access to equal resources and opportunities. For "gay" Palestinians, "coming out" in this environment restricts their sexual identities to the Israeli Jewish understanding of LGBT, even if and when the parameters of such a narrow spectrum do not apply to their local contexts. . . . [There is investment in] maintaining backward, racist depictions of Palestinians in order to better justify oppression and unequal treatment of them, and its internal vicious cycle tokenizes "gay" Palestinians, who become not Palestinian enough in their own communities.[74]

Shafie rejects the bifurcation of the world between the West and others, in which the West and its epistemologies and political projects conceive of sexuality in a certain way, and societies such as Palestine are pathologized as homophobic and in need of outside intervention. Instead, she captures a consciousness among Aswat activists of the need of Palestinians for conceptual and practical resources and tools on gender and sexuality and also recognizes the challenges that global discourses pose for queer Palestinians. Shafie demonstrates that Palestinians have their own epistemological tools to engage in this work in their local contexts and at the level of the ordinary.

Meanwhile, the other major queer Palestinian organization, Al-Qaws, also connects the global to the local. They call

for a kind of queer solidarity based not on racist assumptions about "others" who look different, speak different languages, or live in different places but on a willingness to listen to each other and stand together against violence and repression, even when some among us try to justify it in our name. . . . It is a queer movement made up—not . . . of "oppressed" victims who identify with each other's suffering—but of courageous queer activists, thinkers, artists, writers, and everyday people who identify with the common dream of a better world for us all.[75]

This delineation of solidarity has also helped sustain queer Palestinian organizing. Al-Qaws's goal of "building an equal, diverse, and open Palestinian society . . . that internalizes the non-hierarchical diversity of sexual and gender identity" also demonstrates "that their politics is not a retreat from the public sphere."[76]

Ghaith Hilal, a queer Palestinian activist from the West Bank who has been part of Al-Qaws leadership since 2007, has connected queer Palestinian visibility with its relationship to language and political struggle.

> Language is a strategy, but it does not eclipse the totality of who we are and what we do. The words that have gained global currency—LGBTQ—are used with great caution in our grassroots movements. Simply because such words emerged from a particular context and political moment does not mean they carry that same political content when deployed in our context.
>
> The language that we use is always revisited and expanded through our work. Language catalyzes discussions and pushes us to think more critically, but no word whether in English or Arabic can do the work. Only a movement can.[77]

Hilal's eloquence is a testament to the rich epistemological work of queer Palestinians in Palestine.

Shifts toward Radical Purity

In more recent years, the queer Palestinian movement has shifted toward radical purism, and its growth has plateaued. Considering that Al-Qaws has emerged as the most recognized queer Palestinian institution in the global solidarity sphere, the public critiques leveled by Haneen Maikey, Al-Qaws's director, reverberate far and wide. Maikey's interventions have been part of a pattern of delineating which values, agendas, and political projects should fall under the domain of queer activism in Palestine and which should be under the domain of global queer Palestinian solidarity activism. These articulations have changed over time. For instance, Maikey has disavowed her prior commitment to the value of visibility for the queer Palestinian movement. She previously insisted that Al-Qaws's activism "comes down to visibility."[78] She took pride in what Al-Qaws had been able to accomplish and their visible work and presence in Palestinian communities. Yet this particular statement on visibility was published in 2012—shortly before the movement would begin experiencing the pull toward radical purity under the empire of critique. Maikey's positions on the importance of visibility in Al-Qaws's activism and on the LGBTQ axis of struggle are no longer salient in the context of her most recent priorities.

The axis of the struggle has therefore shifted under Maikey's leadership, because she does not integrate the LGBTQ identity and struggle as much in her epistemological approach. Her initial position on sexuality was articulated clearly in a 2009 article cowritten with anthropologist Jason Ritchie. Maikey and Ritchie drew on Al-Qaws's full name ("Al-Qaws for Sexual and Gender Diversity in Palestinian Society") to state:

> There are many openly gay and lesbian Palestinians, and they are not . . . an insignificant group of a "few lucky Palestinians" who are seeking asylum in Israel: they are actively engaged in changing the status quo in Palestinian society by promoting respect for sexual and gender diversity.[79]

This commitment to advocating for LGBTQ rights and pluralism then began to weaken.

In 2012, it was evident that Maikey's explication of queer politics was moving in a different direction, with Al-Qaws's official public discourse transitioning in lockstep:

> There is currently a sexual movement happening in Palestinian society and around the Arab world. Our discourse is shifting away from narrow LGBT "gay rights" and identity politics approaches, to more of a sexual rights approach. We are critical of the "rights" approach, but use it as a framework so people such as women, allies and bisexuals can be included and involved in challenging the different taboos in sexuality. We cannot discuss homosexuality and queer politics without challenging sexuality. This is why we think queer politics rather than queer identity could be the right framework.[80]

Maikey's incremental disavowal of sexuality has been accompanied by a turn in Al-Qaws's politics that she has mobilized. By 2013, her current priorities were coalescing. In a public lecture at Cornell University that year, Maikey described Al-Qaws as "a group for LGBTQ people and activists working to dismantle the sexual politics behind occupying Palestine." She elaborated, "We are not a gay organization. We are not working to achieve gay rights for the Palestinian gay movement. We don't think that kind of activism is sustainable, or relevant to the Palestinian conflicts." She also added that "Zionist colonialism . . . must be tackled *before* the group can have full conversations regarding sexuality" (emphasis added).[81]

In an article that Maikey wrote with Heike Schotten, the two extended such sentiments, stating that a "significant challenge" of queer Palestinian solidarity activism "has been to draw a line between queer involvement in the struggle for Palestinian liberation" and the integration of issues related to "queers and sexuality in Palestine/Israel."[82] They pushed back at the latter, asserting that the movement is "not about gay rights; it is not about gay Israelis (progressive or not); it is not about the status of homosexuals in Palestine; it is not about self-congratulatory gay Americans or Europeans."[83] Thus, Maikey's positions have embodied the vanguard of the queer Palestinian movement in its radical purist form. Many politically conscious queer Palestinians disagree with this approach, and their voices are found throughout this book as well. Those in this group question the decoupling of the struggle for political rights and the struggle for sexual rights in Palestine, particularly when that decoupling is promulgated by the organization receiving the most funds on behalf of the LGBTQ movement in Palestine.

This is not merely a semantic argument about whether the terms of "gay rights" as understood in the West are applicable or relevant to the Palestinian context; it's also about the very place of gender and sexuality in Al-Qaws's work. Al-Qaws gave itself that name to emphasize gender and sexual diversity. At times, the organization represents itself as one that's committed to both sexual and national liberation. At other times, it frames sexuality as a secondary or tertiary matter, subservient to the struggle for national liberation, or a sexuality-based agenda is rejected altogether. This reflects the lack of consensus among queer Palestinians about such priorities.

The voices of queer Palestinians for whom the struggle against patriarchy and homophobia is considered most pressing in the immediate context are largely missing from this analysis. They are also largely missing from the consciousness of global queer solidarity activists. The opposition to foregrounding gender and sexuality in the queer Palestinian movement does have an alienating effect on queer Palestinians—and queer individuals around the world in solidarity with them—who belong to other ideological camps. The first camp prioritizes resistance to Zionism over resistance to homophobia, and the second camp prioritizes the latter over the former. Individuals in the third camp do not agree with either approach; they believe that their national and sexual struggles cannot be disentangled. The first camp lists anti-imperialism as their paramount concern, given their belief that resistance to homophobia is linked to an imperialist agenda. Thus, radical purists in the first camp increasingly perceive the third camp's coupling of national and sexual liberation as a move toward *impurity*.

Al-Qaws and Aswat have had points of convergence and divergence. Certain Al-Qaws activists have criticized Aswat activists for being too slow to embrace forms of radical purity. There are some Aswat members who have had ideological reservations about strategies deployed by radical purists in the broader movement, while others have been concerned about potential political repression by the Israeli state if they moved in that direction as a registered NGO in Israel. One of Aswat's most vocal and visible activists (to local and international audiences), Ghadir Shafie, interweaves feminist, queer, and anti-Zionist struggles in her local and global advocacy work.

Both Al-Qaws and Aswat typically now reject funds from the US government, including the US Agency for International Development (USAID), in protest of US support for Israel. In fact, some queer Palestinian activists, in several interviews with me, criticized Al-Qaws for once accepting a grant from the Astraea Foundation, an institution that had received $4,000,000 in funds from USAID for global LGBTQ advocacy.

Al-Qaws activists have also criticized some Aswat activists for Aswat's previous dealings with the US government. This is one factor that has contributed to distance between these two organizations. When the US embassy in Tel Aviv organized a function for LGBTQ organizations in Israel, some Aswat activists expressed opposition to the embassy for not inviting Aswat and not including voices from LGBTQ Palestinian citizens of Israel. The position of these Aswat members at the time was that the US government should not exclude these citizens from initiatives including Jewish-Israeli queer organizations (these communities are already largely segregated). Segregation in Israel reflects the divide between these populations, for which the Israeli state is largely responsible. Some Al-Qaws activists then challenged Aswat for the expressed desire to engage the US government in this manner and accused them of reinforcing Western imperialism. These activists also felt that by contemplating an appearance alongside LGBTQ Jewish-Israeli organizations, Aswat was engaging in a form of legitimization of institutions aligned with the Israeli state. Aswat has since shifted their position officially, joining Al-Qaws in supporting the continued separation of queer Palestinians from the LGBTQ sector in Israel. By May 2016, Aswat had moved in the direction of Al-Qaws, rejecting all ties to the US embassy and calling for a boycott of Tel Aviv Pride as well as a boycott of the embassy's LGBTQ work. They even issuing a press release to condemn the US embassy.[84]

Queer Palestinian citizens of Israel who believe in resisting their forced segregation from Jewish Israeli society and who envision LGBTQ spaces that account for Jewish and Palestinian citizens of the state have been critiqued by fellow queer Palestinians as the movement moves toward purism. Therefore, these individuals who the purists perceive as politically compromised must organize outside of the institutional queer Palestinian spaces led by Al-Qaws and Aswat. I have seen how such internal critiques among activists have contributed to such queer Palestinians no longer identifying with the major LGBTQ Palestinian activist network, making these organizations more ideologically homogenous.

Queer Palestinians in the West Bank have also been feeling increasingly alienated from Al-Qaws, to the point that some activists have shared with me that they are thinking of establishing their own queer organization focused on the West Bank. A large part of the alienation is the natural result of Israel's forced separation of Palestinians from one another, with Palestinian citizens of Israel living under a physical regime of governance that is different from the military occupation rule endured by stateless Palestinians in the West Bank.[85] The overwhelming majority of queer Palestinians in the West Bank cannot access Al-Qaws's office in Jerusalem because of the Israeli permit regime and restrictions on movement. As a result, Al-Qaws's programming is largely available only to queer Palestinians in Israel, and while the organization does engage queer Palestinians in the West Bank, the challenge of securing spaces as well as the need to be discreet makes it much more difficult. It is no surprise then that so many queer Palestinians in the West Bank do not feel connected to Al-Qaws and its work. When they see images of hundreds of people at Al-Qaws's monthly queer Palestinian parties in Tel Aviv, they often feel agony. These West Bank Palestinians hope for Israeli permits so they can legally go to these parties, but sometimes they take the risk of traveling "illegally" in order to find such community and be in that joyful space.

Some queer Palestinians in the West Bank have critiqued Al-Qaws activists in Israel for their sources of income, not fully grasping the constrained economy for Palestinian citizens of Israel and the activists' need to survive and even thrive as racialized queer subjects in that ethnoheteronormative state. I remember one incident in which an academic who is also a queer Pal-

estinian citizen of Israel was critiqued by a fellow queer Palestinian for working at an Israeli university. Meanwhile, another queer Palestinian citizen of
Israel who was active in the queer Palestinian movement was critiqued for
working on Israeli LGBTQ films as a costume designer.

Some queer Palestinians in the West Bank and in Israel feel that Al-Qaws
has devoted too much time and too many resources to combat pinkwashing
abroad, including going on speaking tours in Europe, the United States, and
around the world. These individuals expressed their concern to me that this
global advocacy has come at the expense of serious investment in the creation
of a robust infrastructure of support on the ground across historic Palestine
for queer communities and individuals with a range of needs, some of which
can be urgent. I remember when one gay-identified Palestinian from the West
Bank, who was struggling with his sexuality, attempted to become part of
the Al-Qaws network. He was kept at bay without any explanation. Someone
then privately explained to him that some Al-Qaws activists were alarmed after discovering that he had a family member who worked with the Palestinian
Authority security services. This young man felt completely abandoned and
that Al-Qaws should adapt to be able to support as many queer people in Palestine as possible, regardless of background or politics.

Another individual, a trans woman (who was labeled as a gay man by
her community) was constantly physically threatened in public in the West
Bank for being overly feminine and was severely assaulted by a group of men.
She then applied for asylum to a European country and requested a letter of
support from Al-Qaws. She described to me how "degrading" it felt to "almost beg" for the letter, and although she received it in the end, she felt "shat-
tered" after an activist shamed her for wanting to leave Palestine, accusing
her of contributing to Israel's goal of expelling as many Palestinians as possible from the West Bank. She was ultimately able to leave and was granted
asylum in Europe. We have been in communication throughout her journey,
and she has described the relief she feels to be able to live as a woman—her
true self—but also how much she misses her family and Palestine. She said
that her heart aches for her community and her home. Her experience of being chastised without expressed concern for her physical safety—due to homophobia and transphobia—is consistent with an emerging critique leveled
by some queer Palestinian activists against other queer Palestinians: that they
are guilty of internalized pinkwashing and internalized colonialism. This is
part of a new discourse among queer Palestinian radical purists critiquing

those who name homophobia in their society as succumbing to and internalizing imperialist logic. The purists charge queer Palestinians seeking recourse from Israeli or international institutions with being pawns in the Israeli domination of Palestinians.

As for queer Palestinians in the Gaza Strip, the vast majority cannot leave the territory as a result of the Israeli blockade there—and even virtual connections to other queer Palestinians in Israel and the West Bank are limited as a result of surveillance. Surveillance by both Hamas and Israel certainly creates significant risks for queer Palestinians in Gaza.

Queer Palestinians in the Diaspora do sometimes attempt to engage Al-Qaws, but there are many instances of alienation. Hytham Rashid, a gay-identified man who grew up in Palestine, moved abroad, and returns to Palestine often, spoke with me during our interview about his painful experience with Al-Qaws. He volunteered for Al-Qaws on several projects. After expressing opinions on non-LGBTQ matters related to American politics with which an Al-Qaws leader disagreed, he received a message from a queer Palestinian activist informing him that he could no longer identify himself with the group. He described this experience as devastating but also ironic, because he had been bracing himself for exile from his family but did not envision being exiled from the organization that was meant to support queer Palestinians such as himself. Rashid also expressed his frustration with the queer Palestinian movement "labeling everything as pinkwashing" and his hope that queer organizing in Palestine will become more open to a wider range of LGBTQ Palestinians.

I have seen how it is possible for queer non-Palestinians who are in the global solidarity movement with Palestine and those who are interested in learning more or who are considering joining the movement to feel unwelcome. Although there is significant interest from journalists, tourists, NGO workers, diplomats, academics, and other visitors or foreign residents in Israel/Palestine who are LGBTQ to learn about Al-Qaws's work and to engage the community, there are times when Al-Qaws has had only one and a half paid staff members, a small volunteer board, and a network of volunteers across various cities. They, like their counterparts in Aswat, are troubled by academics, journalists, and others who employ Orientalist tropes or who exoticize them, and therefore, in many cases, the queer Palestinian activists do not engage with these groups at all. As one Aswat activist, Rauda Morcos, once stated, "Sometimes I feel humiliated. . . . They look at me as if I am in the zoo. . . . They have their ideas and stories, and they're not willing to ask whether that works for us."[86] As for Al-Qaws, I have seen how its members often treat foreigners with deep suspicion and ignore or even chastise them for their inquiries. This is not surprising considering the layers of surveillance under the empire of critique. Decisions about whom to engage are now being made according to a limited radical purist litmus test. This suspicion has also led to tension between queer Palestinians who want their epistemological work to be shaped by openness to transnational dialogue and the radical purists who want to fortify a queer Palestinian epistemology that is not tainted by any potential imperialist elements.

With such shifts of radical purism, resistance to Zionism has increasingly taken priority over resistance to homophobia. Queer Palestinian solidarity does not demand the inverse (that the struggle against homophobia be prioritized instead). Rather, the systems of Zionism and heteronormativity intersect and therefore need to be challenged simultaneously. As the queer Palestinian movement has become globalized, concerns have been raised about whether those from elsewhere who are in solidarity with Palestine are engaged in a colonial relationship. This worry is linked to the proliferation of internal critiques, which, combined with criticism from so many other sources, has led to a competition of sorts over who in the movement is the most radical and morally pure. The fear that working against homophobia could be imperialist is often accompanied by a lack of recognition that anti-imperialism's critique of empire can elide homophobia, leading to an empire of critique that, in fact, prolongs homophobia. Many queer Palestinians believe that what is needed instead are commitment to sexual and national liberation and recognition of how imperialism entrenches homophobia. It is yet to be seen whether activists in Palestine and around the world will be able to sustain a movement that can truly attend to the concomitant projects of national and sexual liberation. This is challenging in the face of ethnoheteronormativity, particularly with Zionist defense of the Israeli state, Palestinian homophobia, and internal radical purist critiques of queer liberatory aspirations as unwittingly neocolonial.

Queer Palestinian Subjectivities

During the biannual Al-Qaws retreats, several of which I have taken part in, the power of two-pronged resistance, to Zionism and homophobia simultaneously, is palpable. Because of the Israeli policy of physically isolating Palestinian populations from one another (in the Gaza Strip, the West Bank,

Israel, and the Diaspora), it is tremendously challenging for queer Palestinians to come together at one time at one place in historic Palestine. Nonetheless, at these Al-Qaws retreats, dozens of activists meet for several days at a site in the West Bank, where queer Palestinians from Gaza are sadly missing but those from Israel and the West Bank gather along with Diaspora individuals whenever that is possible. The number of cities represented in the group reflects what increased communication and organizing can accomplish across imposed geographic boundaries and fragmentation. During the retreats, these activists not only considered their relationships to each other, how to strengthen and improve Al-Qaws's work, and how queer Palestinians can serve the overall Palestinian national movement but also considered how they can support each other and others in navigating gender and sexual expectations within Palestinian society. I observed how all of this was done in Arabic, allowing queer Palestinians to further cultivate a lexicon and agenda that speaks in organic ways to their local, lived, and embodied experiences while also borrowing from inspiring examples set by queer activists across the Middle East/North Africa region and around the world. A number of queer Palestinian activists are connected to fellow activists in the broader region through networks such as the Regional Network Against Homophobia and the Arab Foundation for Freedoms and Equality.

At the Al-Qaws retreats, many participants are able to express their gender and discuss their sexuality in ways that are authentic and true to themselves. During one gathering, I experienced a drag performance in which cross-dressing was expected and makeup on cisgender men was welcome. Cisgender women could impersonate men, and scripts and body movements could be as outrageous as was possible in a Palestinian context. Two individuals sang Celine Dion's "My Heart Will Go On" from *Titanic* on a small handmade stage. In full costume, the woman impersonated Leonardo DiCaprio, and the man Kate Winslet. They acted out the iconic scene on the ship in which DiCaprio embraces Winslet from behind and both of her arms are extended forward. We clapped, cheered, and cried from laughter, and our hearts warmed. Yet the tears also came from a place of pain. Although no one mentioned it, we were cognizant of such performances as subversive acts of resistance. We knew that a free-spirited queer rendition enacted outside of that ordinary space, whether in public or at home, could very well place the lives of most queer Palestinians in jeopardy.

At the Palestinian Night at an Israeli gay bar, a Palestinian known as Madam Tayoush, who identifies as a transgender woman, drag queen, and performance and visual artist, created over several years the monthly radical queer drag ball parties called "Jerusalem Is Burning." In one drag performance, Madam Tayoush playfully orders her mixed Israeli and Palestinian audience to repeat after her. They repeat one Arabic letter after another, while the crowd goes wild. Once the word is spelled out, Madam Tayoush announces that they just spelled the Arabic word *ihtilal* ("occupation") backward. Many queer Palestinians and progressive Israelis cheer her on, while other Israelis respond with blank or even indignant looks. Madam Tayoush uses this platform simultaneously to resist the Israeli occupation; to refuse objectification by Zionists who believe in her subjugation as a Palestinian and are exoticizing her body in that space; to embrace solidarity from progressive queer Israelis and Palestinians; and to resist a Palestinian society that harshly condemns both transgender people and those who cross-dress.

Photojournalist Tanya Habjouqa captured a rare set of photos of Palestinian and Israeli drag queens in Jerusalem. Reflecting on the Israeli bar, Shushan, which has since closed, Habjouqa comments,

> In 2006, drag queens, LGBTQ communities and friends—both Palestinian and Israeli—defied political expectations and social convention with rambunctious displays of heels and makeup in a colorful denial of the darker elements of greater society. Shushan, a tiny West Jerusalem bar, was a magical place where performers would dress up as classic Arab divas such as Um Kalthoum. Whether for an Orthodox Jew or a West Bank Palestinian who had "snuck across," the place had an air of acceptance, if only an illusory one.[87]

Habjouqa's images capture one particular drag queen, Eman, backstage, onstage performing a belly dance, and in interactions with her Israeli friends, trans Palestinians, other drag queens, and enthusiastic bar patrons. Eman's blackness (she was from the Afro-Palestinian community) coupled with her open display of affection toward her Israeli counterparts added even more layers to her defiance and resistance to political and social limitations. This is precisely why ordinary acts in ordinary spaces take on such extraordinary meaning and valence for queer Palestinians. In my interview with Habjouqa, she shared her desire for the world to see these images so that they are more aware of the full range of queer Palestinian subjectivities, beyond representations of the dogmatic activist and the helpless victim.

During my fieldwork research in Palestine, I met a queer Palestinian male couple, "Hosni" and "Rayan,"[88] who had both recently come out to their parents as gay and were met with support from their families. They were understandably ecstatic and wanted to celebrate this monumental development in their lives in a special manner. Hosni had not been to Jerusalem or to the Mediterranean Sea for more years than he could remember, and he still had not attained an Israeli permit to travel there. A European friend of Rayan's, who worked for an international humanitarian organization, offered to take them in his car. The couple sat in the back, their European friend drove, and a blonde-haired, blue-eyed female American friend of theirs sat in the front passenger seat. As a Westerner, the European friend had a yellow Israeli license plate on his car and could access the Israeli settler roads. They drove onto one of those roads in the West Bank; then they approached a settler checkpoint leading into Jerusalem. The friend drove slowly past the soldiers and smiled at them, and the soldiers just waved them through, assuming it was yet another car full of Israeli settler passengers. All of their hearts had been pounding, and they screamed in joy and relief after passing the checkpoint. They had taken a risk that could have led to significant consequences from the Israeli military for all of them had they been stopped.

After driving through Jerusalem, they drove north to the Jaffa coast and then spent that night at a hotel in Tel Aviv. The European and American friends reserved the room in their own names because according to Israeli national policies these Palestinians from the West Bank could not do that. Rayan and Hosni were nervous going into the room with hotel security watching closely. They described dressing in beach attire, which helped allow them to pass as tourists alongside their friends. Rayan and Hosni described to me their feelings that night as they stood on the balcony of their hotel room. With the Mediterranean in front of them, they embraced and could not let go of each other. Rayan told me that he said to Hosni, "I wish we could do this openly in Ramallah. One day I hope we will. But Tel Aviv is also part of our homeland. No matter what anyone says, this will always be Palestine to us." It is a travesty that a queer Palestinian couple must go through such a struggle just for the ordinary act of seeing a part of their ancestral homeland, but their material pragmatism reflected the spirit of queer Palestinian resistance and resilience.

I have witnessed and experienced the latent networks and the vicissitudes of joy and sorrow among everyday queer Palestinians. The global queer Palestinian movement must account for submerged, informal context and for its ordinary struggles. At a party with fellow queer Palestinians during which we danced nonstop for hours to Arabic music, I saw a group of individuals enact a *zaffeh*, or the traditional entrance of a groom to his wedding. The *zaffeh* typically includes family and friends, mainly men, as they sing and dance and often put the groom on their shoulders. A cisgender man at the party dressed as the bride, and a cisgender woman enacted the groom's role, with her male friends placing her on their shoulders as they would for a groom at a wedding. As they sang some of the traditional songs, some of the men made the ululating sound, which Palestinian women normally do at weddings. The group was clearly enjoying this very much, but I could not help also thinking of the underlying pain.

It is difficult to capture in words the significance of marriage for Palestinian families. A queer Palestinian activist once shared with me her joke—that if you gave Palestinian parents a choice between their child getting married and a cure being discovered for cancer, the family would choose the former and hope that someone else finds the cure. Marriage is more than a rite of passage, an initiation into adulthood, or a way to honor one's family or serve the national struggle; it plays a role in the very definition of self. Being unmarried is highly stigmatized for women, and it creates other anxieties for men. An unmarried woman can quickly become thought of as a spinster of sorts, and the pressure intensifies with the passing of her prime years for reproduction.

Unmarried men have not yet completed "half of their religion." The Muslim population generally understands marriage as a fundamental religious requirement to fulfill one's faithfulness, and Palestinian Christians emphasize marriage to help ensure that their dwindling communities do not become extinct. Palestinian society also often perceives unmarried men as not fulfilling their sexual needs; thus there is the perception that these men may pose some risk to the people around them due to their improperly channeled sexual energy. Many queer Palestinians realize they are unable to marry and feel the agony every time their mother's eyes sparkle while discussing her dream of dancing at their wedding. An unmarried person must regularly encounter everyone around them saying, often daily, "May your day come next." This pressure is heightened every time another person in their social circle marries. That is why observing the group of friends enact a portion of this rite of passage in a queer space, subverting the gender norms as to whom the *zaffeh* belongs and reclaiming the Palestinian tradition of marriage in this queer way, moved me deeply. For many queer Palestinians, this is the closest they can get to authentically experiencing such a formative part of Palestinian social development.

The funeral of a queer Palestinian also illustrates the submerged nature of the LGBTQ Palestinian social movement and the politics of affect and the ordinary. The person who passed away was known as queer only to their closest friends. At the funeral, family, friends, and members of the congregation were devastated by the loss, and the level of grief made it an intensely mournful experience. The deceased had struggled with their sexuality, informing their closest confidantes that they were suffering from this turmoil and in perpetual fear that their family would discover their secret. Some good friends of the deceased expressed sadness that the person died without their loved ones knowing this about them and their relationships. As the queer Palestinians in that group of friends and acquaintances sat in the congregation and at the various funeral rituals, they were spread apart. Yet they looked at one another across the room, recognizing that they each were aware of their own queerness, one another's queerness, and the queerness of the deceased but that all of this was completely hidden, poisonous knowledge from the overwhelming majority of the people around them.

Although the hidden queerness added an additional level of grief, the friends' realization that they were not alone and that they were coalescing as a community to support one another—as those connected to the deceased but also as queer individuals—was a powerful revelation. There was a time when all of these individuals struggled with their sexuality completely on their own, and they know that for most queer Palestinians that remains the reality. And while they lost someone from the community who was dear to them, and that person could not live to experience unconditional love from their family, I experienced how we, the LGBTQ Palestinians in that space, were now legible to one another. We became resources to one another. This group organized on their own, outside of any queer Palestinian organization, and vowed to attend to each individual's pain, so that our friend's memory will have resulted in a strengthening of queer bonds of trust. Outside of the NGO and activist orbit, the potential for the democratic spirit of this queer movement was evident, free of political litmus tests and inclusive of all queer bodies with a shared purpose of support, love, and solidarity.

Democratic Visions

The emergence of the Queer Palestine movement is, in many ways, a miracle in the face of the forces of ethnoheteronormativity. Those who founded the movement have demonstrated remarkable leadership, and they have helped give a voice to queer Palestinians even as radical purism has taken hold of the leadership. The ethnography from within this Queer Palestine sphere that I have shared in this chapter is a contribution to social movement theory, specifically in the growing literature on submerged, latent, and informal social movements and networks. The chapter emphasized the importance of recognizing the heterogeneity of queer Palestinian voices, of not succumbing to the purist impulse to diminish the analysis of Palestinian homophobia, and of accounting for the range of subjectivities that animate queer Palestinian existence on the ground in Israel/Palestine. It is in our attention to the politics of the ordinary, and not just to the politics within the institutionalized sphere of queer Palestinian NGOs and activist groups, that the most democratic visions of queer Palestinian existence can be conceived and realized.

2 Global Solidarity and the Politics of Pinkwashing

MY PUBLIC TALKS to American audiences on pinkwashing and the intersection of LGBTQ and Palestinian rights often evoke varied responses, and I patiently try to engage everyone from across the political spectrum. In March 2014, I was participating in a panel at Boston University, and a fellow panelist, who identifies as Zionist, stated that my "gender choices" would not allow me to safely travel to the Islamist-ruled Gaza Strip, suggesting that this is simply a result of homophobic violence there. During the question-and-answer session, a student prefaced his question by identifying himself as gay and pro-Israeli and then shared his experience visiting the Palestinian town of Hebron in the West Bank. He stated that he logged onto Grindr, the gay dating application, and there were no profiles in the area. Then he looked at me and said, in an exasperated tone, "What's up with that?" During a talk I gave in October of that year at Harvard Law School alongside Darnell Moore, a queer Black American writer and activist who was one of the members of the first LGBTQ delegation to Palestine, a student—also in an accusatory tone—asked us why Hamas does not allow gay clubs in Gaza. In all of these interventions, the questioners contrasted Palestinian homophobia with the existence of queer spaces and expression in Israel.

These types of responses are painful to experience for any queer Palestinian, especially during a year such as 2014, in which the level of violence and the humanitarian crisis in Gaza were even more devastating than in previous years. I reiterated that I am outspoken in condemning patriarchy and homophobia in my society. I reminded my interlocutors that my inability to access Gaza is not just because of a Hamas policy—even though I am afraid of how they would treat me—but also because of Israel's closure policies and restriction of travel for Palestinians between the West Bank and Gaza Strip. I questioned how and why all Palestinians should be associated with Hamas. And how did Grindr become a marker of queer subjectivity? Is whether or not it is used among Palestinians a more important question than the conditions in Hebron that Palestinians endure as a result of the Israeli occupation there? How does use of Grindr become a marker of Palestinian civilizational value?

I also tried to remind my interlocutors that even if queer Palestinians in Gaza wanted to confront Hamas and establish a gay club, the Israeli blockade on Gaza would limit such a possibility. The United Nations predicts that by 2020, Gaza will be uninhabitable for human beings if the Israeli siege, which dramatically hinders people's access to clean water, electricity, and a proper sewage system, persists.[1] It perplexed me that the absence of gay clubs in Gaza is more outrageous to some people than is the reality of queer and straight Palestinians in Gaza struggling to survive amid unspeakable conditions imposed by Israel. It also highlighted to me the powerful grip of pinkwashing discourses in the United States and other parts of the Western world.

Queer Palestinian activists and their allies have defined pinkwashing as drawing attention to a purportedly advanced LGBTQ rights record in Israel in order to detract attention from Israel's violations of Palestinian human rights. As I see it, pinkwashing relies on a logic based on four pillars: (1) naming queer Israeli agency and eliding Israeli homophobia; (2) naming Palestinian homophobia and eliding queer Palestinian agency; (3) juxtaposing these contrasting queer experiences in Israeli and Palestinian societies as a civilizational discourse aimed at highlighting the superior humanity of the former and the subhumanity of the latter, who deserve to be dominated; and (4) representing Israel as a gay haven for Israelis, Palestinians, and internationals in order to attract tourism and other forms of solidarity and support.

This chapter applies conceptions of victims and saviors to the debates on pinkwashing and pinkwatching. It explicates four examples of pinkwashing: that of the late Palestinian leader Yasser Arafat, that of the emergence of Queer Birthright trips for Jewish North American youth to Israel, that of propaganda surrounding the Gaza flotilla's humanitarian mission and its interception by the Israeli navy, and that of the response to the murder of Palestinian teenager Mohammed Abu Khdeir at the hands of Israeli extremists. I then provide an overview of homophobia and LGBTQ rights in contemporary Israel, recognizing the elision of Israeli homophobia and elevation of Israeli queer empowerment in pinkwashing discourse. The final section of this chapter offers an analysis of hegemonic critiques of use of the terms *pinkwashing* and *pinkwatching* in the contexts of (a) the charge of singling out Israel for criticism, (b) the invocation of the presence of queer Palestinians in Israel, and (c) debates surrounding the salience of the Israeli occupation. It is in the interplay between pinkwashing and pinkwatching that the queer Palestinian movement has catalyzed global solidarity.

Victims and Saviors

Pinkwashing logic is deployed by individuals and organizations using the tropes of victim and savior. My delineation of how victimhood informs dynamics of conflict is inspired by Sarah Schulman's explication of this in her book *Conflict Is Not Abuse: Overstating Harm, Community Responsibility, and the Duty of Repair*. Schulman cautions against maintaining "a unilateral position of unmovable superiority by asserting one's status as Abused and the implied consequential right to punish without terms."[2] She elaborates,

> This concept, of having to earn the right to have pain acknowledged, is predicated on a need to enforce that one party is entirely righteous and without mistake, while the other is the Specter, the residual holder of all evil. If conflicted people were expected and encouraged to produce complex understandings of their relationships, then people could be expected to negotiate, instead of having to justify their pain through inflicted charges of victimization. And it is in the best interest of us all to try to consciously move to that place.[3]

One of the primary case studies that Schulman examines in her book as an application of her framework on victimization is the Israeli state's 2014 war in Gaza. She demonstrates how the pain of Israelis contributes to their perpetual self-understanding as the ultimate victims, which enables them to righteously inflict harm on Palestinians without being held accountable. This chapter connects Schulman's framework to debates over Israeli harm to LGBTQ communities. I recognize Israeli suffering at the hands of Palestinians but problematize Israel's claim to a privileged victimhood status. I also acknowledge Israel's disproportionate victimization of Palestinians as well as the infliction of harm by Palestinians on queer bodies and subjects.

Israeli state actors, their satellite institutions around the world, and their allies often represent their relationship with Palestine as dichotomies of victims and saviors. According to pinkwashing logic, the queer political landscape can be seen as including only victim and/or benevolent Israelis and victim and/or malevolent Palestinians. In this worldview, Israelis, both straight and queer, are victims of Palestinians, while queers, both Israeli and Palestinian, are saved by Zionism. When Palestinians and their non-Palestinian allies identify such instances and patterns of pinkwashing discourses in efforts to resist them, Palestinian solidarity organizers have termed their activism to be *pinkwatching*. These pinkwatchers invert the pinkwashing discourse on victims and saviors. Pinkwatchers assert that it is actually Palestinians, both straight and queer, who are victims, and they are such at the hands of Zionism. They contend that pinkwashing further victimizes queer Palestinians. Pinkwatchers are concerned about pinkwashers drawing attention to queerness in order to obfuscate Israeli state victimization of Palestinians. The pinkwashers subsequently engage in *discursive disenfranchisement*, attempting to prohibit queer Palestinians from speaking for themselves and instead speaking for them. Pinkwashers cast the Israeli victimizer of the queer Palestinian as the savior. Queer Palestinians often feel that pinkwashing also victimizes them because such a discourse severs the queer Palestinian subject from the larger Palestinian body politic, much as the forces of Palestinian homophobia disavow the queer Palestinian subject.

By resisting pinkwashing, queer Palestinians engage in "discursive enfranchisement." They claim their place within the Palestinian body politic and social fabric, rejecting Zionist and homophobic attempts to negate their existence and struggle. In naming themselves as victims of Zionism alongside those in the broader Palestinian society, queer Palestinians are thus able to be met with increased inclusion from heterosexual Palestinians by articulating a queer vision that is deeply Palestinian in nature. Using this method, queer Palestinians can powerfully reclaim their agency and have that agency recognized in Palestine and abroad in the global Palestinian solidarity movement.

There are two other forms of discursive disenfranchisement that queer Palestinians and their allies encounter. One is the undermining by Israeli state supporters of the ability of queer Palestinians to identify as victims of Zionism. Another is the contestation by Israeli state supporters of queer Palestinian recognition of pinkwashing as a discourse, ideology, and practice. These Israeli state supporters charge queer Palestinian activists with denying Palestinian homophobia and singling out Israel for criticism. Queer Palestinians point to such accusations as further evidence of attempts to silence their voices. Nonetheless, they and their allies have been successful at raising consciousness among LGBTQ populations around the world about Israeli pinkwashing.

There is currently a split among queer Palestinian solidarity communities between those who name both Zionism and homophobia as systems of oppression that queer Palestinians face and those who prioritize Zionism and see recognition of homophobia as reinforcing a central feature of pinkwashing rhetoric. Those who engage in the elision of Palestinian homophobia tend to be the most purist. Moving so far in this direction puts discussions of this issue to the right of the political spectrum and misses opportunities for the left and for queer Palestinians to historicize, contextualize, and shape their own narratives surrounding homophobia in Palestinian society.

The Israeli state's attempts to improve its global image through a pinkwashing agenda has catalyzed the transnational reach of the queer Palestinian solidarity movement. It is now the case that often where pinkwashing is found, pinkwatching is also found. Pinkwatching has not only empowered queer Palestinians as a form of resistance to ethnoheteronormativity but also activated non-Palestinian allies in solidarity with queer Palestinians. Additionally, queer Palestinians in the Diaspora have found an entry point for expressing their identity and contributing to a global social movement that has made opposition to pinkwashing and imperialism its primary focus outside of Palestine. In this way, queer Palestinians have resisted being relegated to the permanent condition of victimhood and have rejected the notion that there must be a Zionist savior in service of this condition.

Examples of Pinkwashing

Any time that queer discourse is invoked by advocates of the Israeli state, it is likely to raise concerns about pinkwashing by a queer Palestinian solidarity activist. I will delineate four examples of pinkwashing in practice.

The first example pertains to Yasser Arafat, the chairman of the Palestine Liberation Organization. After Arafat died in 2004, some supporters of Israel and some Israeli media outlets circulated rumors that Arafat was gay. A subsequent article, written by pro-Israel journalist James Kirchick for the popular gay American magazine *Out*, also reinforced this notion. Kirchick wrote that "the Palestinians ought to have the honesty to accept that the father of their nationalist movement might have been gay."[4] He referenced three sources to put forward this theory. The first was a statement by Ahmad Jabril, a Palestinian politician, that a French medical report had supposedly indicated that Arafat had died of AIDS. The second source was the memoir of Mihai Pacpea, a former head of Romanian intelligence, in which he claims to have knowledge that Arafat slept with one of his male bodyguards. And the third was the claim that "Arafat had an immune system suppressing blood disease, lost 1/3 of his weight, and was suffering from mental dysfunction, all tell-tale signs of AIDS."[5] Kirchick, a critic of the queer Palestinian solidarity movement, cited this to undermine the widely believed notion among Palestinians that Israel poisoned Arafat.

In the article, Kirchick also included an image of Arafat walking with a limp wrist, which reifies a stereotypical image of effeminate gay men. He did not problematize the homophobia that was among Israel supporters who promoted the rumor about Arafat being gay and that undergirded the linking of homosexuality and terrorism. Instead Kirchick drew attention to Palestinian obliviousness and denial about Arafat's alleged homosexuality and failed to mention that Palestinians may have been skeptical because these assertions were unsubstantiated. Palestinians point to the fact that Arafat had been married to a woman (Suha Arafat) with whom he'd had a daughter.[6] Kirchick used his article as an opportunity to contrast Palestinian homophobia with Israeli acceptance of homosexuality, even though he explicitly relied on homophobia to further his argument. He wrote, "Palestinian society like Muslim society in general is violently homophobic. The harassment and torture of homosexuals is a tried-and-true practice of the Palestinian Authority, and a burgeoning gay underground of refugee Palestinian homosexuals thrives in Tel Aviv, the gay capital of the Middle East."[7] In having to grapple with the dynamics and consequences that such a narrative about Arafat's sexuality presented, queer Palestinian solidarity activists understood Kirchick's intervention as a form of pinkwashing meant to negate Israel's responsibility in the alleged murder of the Palestinian leader.

The LGBTQ Birthright Israel trips are the second example of pinkwashing (and pinkwatching). Each year, the program Birthright Israel takes thousands of Jewish North American youth on all-expenses-paid trips to Israel, with the aim of deepening the relationship between Israel and the participants. Birthright has included some meetings with Arabs in their programs in the past, but they have discontinued such meetings, and the Palestinian question is not addressed in a robust way. Zizo Abul Hawa, a queer Palestinian activist who has met with some of these delegations, publicly criticized Birthright's decision to altogether exclude Arab voices such as his.[8] Abul Hawa has been met with critiques from radical purist queer Palestinian activists who do not agree with his willingness to speak to Zionist audiences on these queer delegations to Israel.

The first specifically LGBTQ Birthright Israel trip took place in 2008. Whereas regular Birthright Israel trips include Israeli soldiers as tour guides, the LGBTQ trips include gay soldiers. Jayson Littman, a supporter of LGBTQ Birthright Israel trips, articulated their purpose: "Having an LGBTQ Birthright trip allows participants to have a space where they can explore their Jewish identity and connection to Israel through an LGBTQ lens."[9] In a subsequent article, Littman mocked the charge of pinkwashing leveled against participants in these trips, stating that this discourse emanates from "a small, influential group of LGBT activists" who criticize Israel for "promoting its gay-friendliness to distract from other policies."[10] He goes on to write, "Does Israel also have policies that I don't agree with? Yes, but that doesn't take away from the fact that Israel does gay rights pretty well."[11] In his piece, Littman described his admiration for Israel and the importance of such LGBTQ engagement with the country. He described the LGBTQ trips as a response to queer and trans Jewish North Americans who request such experiences, and he said that individuals could meet with Palestinians once the trip was over. In his description of his own one day in the West Bank, Littman stated that a Palestinian with whom he spoke "went on a rant on how disgusting homosexuality was and informed me of the rightful honor killings of homosexuals in Palestinian society."[12] Littman then used that alleged statement to take issue with pinkwatching activism: "I immediately wondered about the anti-pinkwashing activists who never discuss the mistreatment of gays in the [Palestinian] territories, but are quick to criticize Israel for the gay rights it affords to its people."[13]

Israeli commentator Ofer Matan offers a different perspective on the LGBTQ Birthright Israel trips, writing of the contradictions at hand. For instance, he noted the "anachronism" between "the flexible, pluralistic (even 'cool,' some would say) forms of non-Orthodox Judaism dominant in North America, and the state-sanctioned Israeli form of Orthodoxy."[14] Matan added contextual dimensions: the state that supports LGBTQ initiatives simultaneously "refuses to recognize marriages among gays" and "discriminates against same-sex couples in the allocation of social benefits, and . . . some MKs are openly homophobic."[15] While the Israeli state provides the queer Jewish North American trip participants with "first-class treatment," it transmits "mixed messages" to its gay citizens.[16] Matan characterized the ruling party of the Israeli government as "largely homophobic."[17] He asked whether the goal of the program is for the participants to "return home and tell others that Israel is gay-friendly." After all, program organizers openly acknowledge that a major objective of the trips is to have the participants return to American and Canadian universities to "shatter the simplistic discourse about Israel often heard on campuses."[18] Matan also added that while visiting dunes in Israel on the trip, key information was left out, such as "the fact that the Palestinian villages that existed on those dunes are ignored—including the [destroyed Palestinian] neighborhood of Manshiya, whose mosque remains very visible from Jaffa today."[19] He concluded by raising a concern about whether the participants, upon returning to their campuses, will be able to respond to the accusation "that Zionism is a colonialist movement."[20] This example highlights how pinkwashing is damaging to both Palestine and Israel—queer Palestinians are erased from consideration as having agency, and Israeli homophobia is obfuscated.

Queer Palestinian solidarity activists, inhabiting many global queer spaces, view their pinkwatching work as part of the larger anti-Zionist movement. Their repudiation of the LGBTQ Birthright Israel trips has usually been private, although public criticisms of regular Birthright Israel trips are common within the larger global Palestinian solidarity world. Common concerns include the Israeli government's partial financial support of the program, its strict exclusion of young diasporic Palestinian Christians and Muslims,[21] the absence of Israeli dissident and Palestinian voices on the trip, and the itinerary's militaristic nature, evident in its support of the Israeli army and that army's occupation of Palestine. Liza Behrendt, a queer Jewish American who previously participated in Birthright Israel and who has become anti-Zionist and a Palestinian solidarity activist with Jewish Voice for Peace (JVP), has supported efforts to dissuade others from joining the program. She has stated, "Birthright makes participants feel as if questioning Israel's policies is to question their own Jewishness. . . . In the experience it creates, it renders Palestinians and the Palestinian area invisible on the trip."[22] Examination of these trips also elucidates how Zionism requires the interpellation of transnational ties and loyalties (cultivating Jewish subjects from other countries as part of Israeli policies) to justify continued occupation. At the same time, the trips try to limit international Palestinian solidarity.

In reflecting on her participation in a gay Birthright delegation, Zoë Schlanger, in an interview published in *Newsweek*, contextualized the experience not only "to talk about how our queerness connected to our Jewishness"[23] but also to talk about pinkwashing. Schlanger delineated pinkwashing as "the practice of using progressivism on gay rights to justify military interventions or to violate the civil liberties of another group of people—or in Israel's case, to obfuscate its human rights violations in Palestine. While one 'other' (LGBT people) is embraced, a second 'other' (Palestinians) [is] obliterated."[24] Schlanger also cited journalist Raillan Brooks's writing that one function of pinkwashing is attempting to justify the "blithe military alliance with Israel (one of whose expansion stratagems is to pitch Tel Aviv as a gay mecca reclaimed from the gay-murdering Palestinians)."[25] As a result, pinkwashing "gets liberals to consent to intervention after intervention in the names of queer people."[26]

Cases of pinkwashing are much clearer when there are direct connections to Israeli state institutions, as we will see in the third example. Queer Palestinian solidarity activists have been vigorous in these contexts in helping to shape global public discourse on how LGBTQ domains intersect with the Israeli-Palestinian conflict. This issue was evident in a 2011 incident, as described by Tom Jones in his article on Israeli pinkwashing.

> As organizers prepared to launch the second Gaza Freedom Flotilla in 2011, the Israeli Government Press Office tweeted a link to a YouTube video. The activist in the video claimed that organizers had refused to allow him to participate after discovering he was gay. "Look, this is what I want to say to all the people fighting for human rights all over the world," the man concluded. "Be careful who you get in bed with. If you hook up with the wrong group, you might wake up next to Hamas."[27]

Palestinian solidarity activists revealed the video to be a hoax, ultimately designed to smear the flotilla campaign.

This form of pinkwashing is aimed at improving Israel's international image while disavowing global solidarity with Palestine. The Gaza Freedom Flotilla to which Jones referred was part of an effort by Palestinian rights activists from around the world to break the Israeli and Egyptian siege on the Gaza Strip by delivering humanitarian supplies to the Palestinian population there via boats across the Mediterranean Sea. That year, the Israeli navy intercepted those boats in international waters, killing nine civilian activists and detaining and then deporting the others. In response to this incident, Israeli prime minister Benjamin Netanyahu made a statement to peace activists in light of the global concern for Gaza: "Go to the places where they oppress women. Go to the places where they hang homosexuals in town squares and deny the rights of minorities. . . . Go to Tehran. Go to Gaza. . . . Anyone for whom human rights are truly important needs to support liberal democratic Israel."[28] Ironically, the international flotilla activists that were blocked by Israel *were* trying to reach Gaza.

The video[29] to which Tom Jones referred featured a young man who identified as Marc; he was an LGBTQ activist on an American college campus who claimed he had wanted to join the flotilla but was turned away by homophobic flotilla organizers. After subsequent research, Marc came to the conclusion that these pro-Palestinian activists and their flotilla efforts were supporting terrorism. This video circulated online and was a powerful tool in the undermining of these Palestinian solidarity and humanitarian efforts.

One of the first individuals to tweet the video was Guy Seemann, a staffer in the prime minister's office. Queer Palestinian solidarity activists exposed the man in the video as an Israeli actor named Omer Gershon. In an investigative report on the video, journalist Justin Elliott described Gershon as a "public-relations guru who has worked for several Israeli government agencies."[30] One of the individuals who expressed the "embarrassing" nature of this hoax video was Hagai El-Ad, "executive director of the Association for Civil Rights in Israel and former head of [an] LGBT community center in Jerusalem, where he also organized the first annual pride parade in 2002."[31] Referring to the video as an example of pinkwashing, El-Ad contextualized it as a strategy

> that has been branded as quote-unquote Israel Beyond the Conflict. This means trying not to have a conversation about the occupation, about the rights of Arab Israelis, but to have a different conversation about other issues in Israel. In no other arena has that been used in a more cynical way than in the context of LGBT rights.[32]

Queer Palestinian activists were in disbelief at the false narrative that Gershon put forward in the video, when in reality, openly queer individuals had actually participated in these flotillas. The video exemplified pinkwashing in that it was a deliberately propagandistic method of drawing attention to a false instance of Palestinian homophobia in order to obfuscate Israel's violations of Palestinian human rights. Queer Palestinian solidarity activism helped to expose the video as fabricated and used the incident to keep moving pinkwatching activism forward.

In a May 2012 investigation by the *Guardian*, members of the Palestinian solidarity team for the Gaza flotilla in London confirmed that they had not received the type of inquiry that Gershon (or "Marc") had described in his video and that they would not have discriminated against an LGBTQ individual. The journalist then interviewed Omer Gershon, who admitted that what he had stated had not been true. He said that he was acting in the video "as a favor" for a friend he could not name. Gershon stated, "My friend sent it to another friend of his who works at the prime minister's office [in Israel] and he put it on their website."[33] Nonetheless, the damage had been done, and many of the individuals who watched the video around the world believed that that the humanitarian flotilla to Gaza reflected Palestinian homophobia and should be a warning call to LGBTQ people not to align themselves with the Palestinian struggle. The pinkwashing video was an effort to position Israel as a savior of queer people too easily manipulated by homophobic Palestinian extremists and to deflect attention from the reality of queer internationals and Palestinians being victimized by Israeli state violence.

In the fourth example of pinkwashing, Queer Palestinian solidarity activists found it especially challenging to respond to the murder of sixteen-year-old Palestinian Mohammed Abu Khdeir in Jerusalem in 2014. This killing caused widespread pain across Palestinian society, but it was particularly traumatic for many queer Palestinians because of the pinkwashing dimensions that added salt to their wounds. The murder of Abu Khdeir came after three teenage Israeli yeshiva students—Naftali Fraenkel, Gilad Shaar, and Eyal Yifrach—were kidnapped and killed by Palestinian militants in the West Bank. Israeli settlers then kidnapped Abu Khdeir in what appeared to be a revenge attack. Joseph Ben-David, a twenty-nine-year-old resident of a West Bank settlement, then confessed to Israeli investigators that he had murdered Abu Khdeir and that he and his accomplices had stated, "They took three of ours—let's take one of theirs."[34] They beat Abu Khdeir and set him on fire while he was alive. A testimony revealed that Abu Khdeir's final words were "Allahu Akbar" (God is great).[35] It went on to add, "An autopsy showed he had soot in his lungs, indicating he had been burned alive after being beaten and forced to swallow petrol by his attackers."[36]

Israeli police placed a gag order on their investigation before they knew who was responsible for Abu Khdeir's murder, informing the *Times of Israel* that they were investigating whether Abu Khdeir "was murdered in a family honor killing."[37] The invocation of "honor killing" here promoted anti-Muslim and anti-Arab sentiment in order to obfuscate the identity of the perpetrators as Israelis.

The Israeli press referenced Israeli reports that "indicate that the abduction likely was carried out by Arabs and that the murder was an 'honor killing' or another kind of criminal murder."[38] The Israeli journalist Mairav Zonszein later reported on the rumors that many believe were initiated "by the Israel Police itself . . . that this was an inter-family honor killing, possibly because the victim was gay."[39] The narrative about Abu Khdeir being gay and killed by his family was salient among many supporters of Israel despite the belief that the rumors were started by the Israeli police. Another Israeli journalist, Lisa Goldman, wrote, "It's obvious that if the police knew for certain that the culprit were a Jew, they would not have dared to suggest the theory that the murder might have been committed by Palestinians in the name of 'family honor,' because the boy was suspected of being a homosexual, etc."[40] The suspicion of Abu Khdeir's homosexuality was based on "a single photo of a boy who does not fit the stereotype of a Palestinian man with a thick beard, a keffiyeh and a weapon" and who is "physically gentle."[41] But it was made to fit the form of the queer body—skinny, gentle, and subsequently targetable by the very stereotype he was not: a barbarous Palestinian with a thick beard, *kufiyyeh*, and a weapon.

In his article translated from Hebrew, queer Israeli writer Shaked Spier stated that the narrative of the Palestinian gay honor killing among Israelis on social media reflected what Spier considered the "intersection of racism and homophobia in order to discriminate against a person or a collective."[42] Spier argued that Israelis were going even further by "instrumentalizing the individual in order to project homophobia that originated in *our* patterns of thought onto *them*. Moreover, this instrumentalization is already based on a generalized picture of the Palestinian—a picture that originates in *our* patterns of thought."[43]

Writer Lara Friedman considered the Abu Khdeir gay honor-killing narrative to be a "blood libel against all Palestinians." Friedman inverted the discourse of blood libels that has generally been used to describe European and Christian anti-Semitic tropes against Jewish individuals. She elaborated:

Where is the outrage and shame for the blaming of the victim and defamation of Mohammed Abu Khdeir, his family, and his society? Where are the voices denouncing the blood libel manufactured by cynical officials; spread unchallenged by lazy or credulous media; and seized on—whether naïvely or cynically—by people inside and outside Israel to deflect responsibility from Israel and Jews?

Because while it is now known that Mohammed Abu Khdeir's killers were Israeli Jews, not Palestinians, his death has been framed for the entire world in a dehumanizing, defamatory narrative suggesting that while Palestinians may be innocent of this particular crime, in the more general sense they are always guilty.[44]

In writing about the Israeli media's "floating" of the honor killing theory even after the Israeli police "abandoned" it, journalist Sigal Samuel asserted in her article, "The Pinkwashing of Mohammed Abu Khdeir," that "they attempted to make Israel look good by making Palestinians look bad, and they attempted to do that by using a dead teenager's possible sexual orientation (note that we still don't actually know whether Mohammed was gay or not) as a tool against his own people and his own family."[45]

The queer Israeli scholar Aeyal Gross argued that the case of Abu Khdeir was "evidence of the success of pinkwashing—the use of LGBT rights as propaganda to portray Israel as an enlightened democracy and Palestinian society as homophobic."[46] In his article, Gross referenced Israeli posts on social media with Abu Khdeir's picture and the caption "The Arabs killed him for being gay." He also discussed how the executive director of the Jerusalem Open House for Pride and Tolerance had to clarify that, contrary to what was being circulated, Abu Khdeir was not known at that LGBTQ center, and they had not issued a statement about his death. Gross wrote, "The willingness to believe those rumors uncritically has another significance: The marking of Palestinians as barbaric and homophobic, as people who would murder their own children for being gay."[47]

The Israeli police and their right-wing supporters readily advanced the pinkwashing propaganda that Abu Khdeir was a queer victim of his homophobic family and society and that the Israeli security state is the savior of queers. This Israeli pinkwashing in turn reinforced homophobia. During my interview with one of Abu Khdeir's cousins from Jerusalem, she told me how this rhetoric revictimized Abu Khdeir and his family. For many queer Palestinians in Palestine, and for Palestinians more broadly, watching the debates surrounding this brutal murder was a source of trauma. Queer Palestinians had to navigate the emotions brought on by these debates amid the real forces of ethnoheteronormativity shaping their lives. Within the global queer Palestinian solidarity movement, the pinkwashing of Abu Khdeir's death created a collective wound for activists that still has not healed. This case and the three pinkwashing examples presented before it in this section reveal examples of the wide reach of different domains of pinkwashing.

Homophobia in Israeli Society

Many Zionist critics of pinkwatching activism often express frustration with what they perceive to be an almost obsessive focus among queer Palestinian solidarity activists on Israel. Such critics are concerned that these activists around the world eagerly await any instance of homophobic violence or marginalization internal to Israeli society in order to undermine Israel's claim to gay tolerance. The pro-Israel critics also believe that little genuine empathy is felt or expressed by the pinkwatching movement toward the Israeli LGBTQ community when Israelis are victimized and that the queer Palestinian movement does not express any form of solidarity when queer Israelis attempt to address the discrimination that queer Israelis experience from the Israeli state and society. Although solidarity with queer Israelis is missing from the global queer Palestinian solidarity movement, acknowledgments of Israeli homophobia are largely missing from the queer Israeli solidarity movement outside of Israel. Pinkwashing relies on the framing of Israel as a savior of gays to deny Israeli homophobia and Israel's victimization of Palestinians.

Examples of homophobia in Israeli society include the fraught history of Jerusalem Pride parades. For instance, at the 2005 parade, Yishai Schlissel, an Israeli religious extremist, stabbed and injured three people. After being released from prison in 2015, he targeted that year's pride parade, injuring five and killing sixteen-year-old Shira Banki. Israeli government officials and religious leaders have spoken against the parade in homophobic terms. For example, Prime Minister Ehud Olmert made a statement in 2007 that he "does not think that Jerusalem is the appropriate location for holding gay-pride parades due to the special sensitive nature of the city."[48] In 2008, during a debate in the Israeli parliament on whether to ban Jerusalem Pride, Nissim Ze'ev, an Israeli parliamentarian, stated that homosexuals were "as toxic as bird flu" and are "carrying out the self-destruction of Israeli society and the Jewish people."[49]

In 2012, Israeli parliamentarian Anastasia Michaeli stated her view that most gay people experienced "sexual harassment at a very young age and it just gets worse. . . . They are miserable, those homosexuals. In the end they commit suicide when they reach the age of 40 and it's those same guys that want to be women."[50] Another Israeli parliament member, Bezalel Smotrich, called the gay pride parade the "March of the Beasts."[51] After expressing regrets for that statement, he referred to LGBTQ people as "abnormal." "Every person has the right to be abnormal at home," he said, "but he can't ask of me as a state to see the idea as normal."[52] He later called the pride parade the "abomination march" and articulated his promise "to object no less vehemently to the recognition of same-sex couples in the Jewish state. . . . I will fight any attempt to besmirch traditional Jewish family values."[53] Parliamentarian and agricultural minister Uri Ariel called on the Israeli military to stop recruiting gay people. He said, "If I were the decision maker, I wouldn't enlist homosexuals into the [Israel Defense Forces] IDF, because some things interfere with the military's ability to fight. . . . We must conduct ourselves in accordance with Jewish law. The Torah forbids homosexuality and demands that those who behave in such a manner be punished."[54] Figures such as Shlomo Benirzi, who in 2008 was a member of the ultra-Orthodox Mizrahi Shas party and was also a member of the Israeli parliament, have blamed earthquakes in Israel on homosexuals. Benirzi once urged his fellow parliamentarians to stop "passing legislation on how to encourage homosexual activity in the state of Israel, which anyway brings about earthquakes."[55] Another member of the Israeli parliament, who was an education minister, stated that gays "are not people like everyone else," and that "their lifestyle harms the Jewish people."[56]

In 2015, Israel's former chief rabbi and member of the High Rabbinical Council stated, "I believe that this phenomenon will wane and disappear, because most of the public is disgusted by it and detest it."[57] That same year, the Israeli interior ministry denied asylum to a Ghanaian citizen by arguing that she "chose to be a lesbian." Aviv Himi, the committee's chairman, wrote,

> Her statements show that she consciously and rationally adopted a lesbian lifestyle. This wasn't a preference she had had all her life, forming an integral part of her identity, so her claims of a clear sexual preference are unacceptable. Since arriving in Israel she didn't meet women or act on her alleged preference, even though free to do so. This is contrary to what might be expected of someone fleeing persecution for a sexual preference.[58]

Even more overt state-sanctioned homophobia was evident the following year, in 2016, when the Israeli lawmaker Bezalel Smotrich described himself as a "proud homophobe." He later clarified that "being a homophobe would mean I am afraid of homos. . . . I am not afraid of homos . . . or of Arabs. . . . I am not afraid of anything."[59]

A 2011 survey exposed Israeli homophobia with the revelation that Israeli "LGBT soldiers are often victims of verbal and physical violence" within the military, with rates of abuse against gay soldiers reaching 40 percent.[60] Additionally, "almost half of the out gays and lesbians serving in the Israeli military have been sexually harassed by other servicemembers."[61] Another report revealed that in 2012, rates of HIV among Israeli men increased by 55 percent, and yet "many of the basic rights of HIV carriers are still being violated."[62] These violations include significant stigmatization from others in Israeli society, lack of access to proper insurance or nursing care, an inability to secure a mortgage for a home, and even discrimination from dentists.[63] Also in 2012, many in the LGBTQ Israeli community lamented the closing of Minerva, what was then Tel Aviv's last lesbian bar, due to the "owner's wishes to turn the building into a luxury high-rise."[64] This closing illustrated to progressives within Israel's queer community that the increased neoliberalization of the Israeli economy would have adverse effects on the availability of accessible spaces for LGBTQ individuals of different classes and backgrounds. Such neoliberalization helps facilitate homophobic efforts to constrict queer spaces in Israel, even as other gay spaces emerge in gentrifying parts of Tel Aviv.

Violence against the LGBTQ community in Israel reached an alarming state in 2009, when a "black-clad, masked"[65] Israeli gunman stormed the Israel Gay and Lesbian Association building in Tel Aviv and opened fire on LGBTQ teenagers at a weekly support group, killing two and wounding fifteen. The police indicted Hagai Felician for the crime but then released him seven months later without charge. They also ruled out homophobia as the cause and attributed it instead to "personal revenge" as a result of a statement by Felician in which he claimed that he wanted to avenge the sodomization of his young male relative by someone at the center. The police then also ruled out that cause as well, because there was no evidence for the sodomization rumor. Many queer Israeli activists have argued that the rumor itself was a result of homophobia. Aeyal Gross stated that pinkwashing was "propaganda" and an "ideology" and was evident in this case, as the Israeli authorities wanted to "deny familial and societal homophobia."[66] In 2013, Felician was arrested, four years after the crime, and confessed to an "undercover police officer planted in his jail cell" that his shooting was a "clean job" as a result of his belief that the Bible forbids same-sex acts.[67] The Israeli state prosecution then reversed the decision that had failed to recognize the attack as motivated by antigay bias and instead considered it a hate crime. Felician was subsequently indicted for the murder of twenty-six-year-old Nir Katz, the LGBT youth center instructor, and sixteen-year-old lesbian teenager Liz Turbishi.

Tel Aviv saw another act of violence against the LGBTQ community in 2014, when a "group of gay men" were "assaulted by young attackers."[68] It later emerged that the attackers were eleven Israeli soldiers on leave. One of the victims then described the daily assaults that transgender women she knows experience as well as the harassment they face from the Israeli police who treat them "contemptuously."[69] That same year, eleven individuals assaulted a transgender woman in Tel Aviv with "pepper spray and an electric shocker."[70] The Israeli police reported that the youth responsible for the latter incident were motivated by "boredom" and not homophobia, while Israeli LGBTQ activists urged the police to consider the possibility that this was a hate crime since "these assaults take place across the country."[71] Such physical violence has led to "half of Israel's transgender population"[72] experiencing attacks, as documented in a 2015 Israeli study. That same year, a European Social Survey of seventeen countries found that "Israel tops the list of European countries in which people experience discrimination based on sexual orientation."[73] Although Israel is located in the Middle East (on the Asian continent), its relative tolerance of homosexuality is meant to serve as an additional colonial marker of its civilizational proximity to Europe. Such pinkwashing elides the very real forms of homophobia that endure in Israeli society and the racism that persists against Palestinians and Israel's Arab neighbors. It also masks the systematic intolerance and violence, including discrimination in employment and health, that LGBTQ people in Israel face.

In 2014, the Israeli LGBTQ community was shocked to learn that the deputy education minister, Avi Wortzman, in response to concerns about homophobic discrimination, stated that, "A family is a father, mother and child," thereby denying that same-sex couples can be considered families.[74] A 2014 report indicated that "only 13 percent of gay teens felt comfortable talking about the subject of sexual identity with their teachers. Also, 65 percent said they suffered homophobic comments in the hallways, with 17 percent saying their teachers did nothing about it."[75] At the university level, LGBTQ students in Israel have had to deal with such incidents as Bar-Ilan University initially refusing to "allow an event marking Gay Pride Week on the campus, with the institution's spokesman likening the planned event to a gathering of pedophiles." Bar-Ilan backtracked after public pressure.[76] Queer Israelis have also experienced discrimination in the domain of housing, with LGBTQ individuals in cities such as Tel Aviv often experiencing homophobia from landlords due to a lack of legal protection preventing it. As one reporter wrote, "And just as they can discriminate against individuals of a particular sexual orientation, they can also discriminate against individuals of a certain religion or ethnic group."[77]

In 2016, an Israeli rabbi, Shlomo Amar, stated that gay people are an "abomination" and that homosexuality is a "cult."[78] The Israeli television authority then banned an advertisement for backing "gay marriage and Arabic language."[79] That same year, the combination of Israeli militarism and transphobia sent Aiden Katri, a young transgender woman, to prison for refusing to serve in the Israeli military. She spoke of her motivations as a conscientious objector and feminist. An article about the incident stated that "before being sentenced, Katri explained that her actions [were] driven by a sense of solidarity with Palestinian women living under Israeli military occupation, and the feminist struggle against the discriminatory treatment between men and women in the army itself."[80] Katri has also spoken about her Mizrahi identity and the racism her community experienced as Middle Eastern (non-European) Jews in Israel. She said, "I struggle against my oppression—my gender oppression as a trans woman and my ethnic oppression as a Mizrahi Jew, and if I turn a blind eye to an oppression of another people, this would be hypocrisy."[81] Despite her identification as a woman, the Israeli military sentenced her to a men's prison.

Marriage remains elusive for many LGBTQ Israelis. In Israel, "marriage is in the control of the Orthodox rabbinate," which is "firmly opposed to gay marriage."[82] Within the state, each religious group (Judaism, Christianity, Islam, and Druze) has its own authorities that perform marriages in that tradition. Two Jewish Israelis seeking to marry in Israel must do so through the Orthodox rabbinate, and they must be a heterosexual couple. A gay couple, or a Palestinian Christian or Muslim citizen of Israel or Jewish Israeli, for example, must marry outside of the country and then apply for state recognition once they return. Right-wing political parties, which are gaining increased representation in the Israeli parliament, have expressed their opposition to civil unions for gay couples as well. For instance, in 2013, a senior party official from Habayit Hayehudi stated, "There's not a chance we'll allow civil unions for gay couples, and it doesn't matter whether it's a government-sponsored bill or a private member's bill."[83]

The combination of homophobia and the right-wing agenda in Israel led to a frightening incident in January 2016. Shai Glick, a right-wing Israeli activist, discovered that Yuli Novak, the Israeli executive director of Breaking the Silence, an organization exposing the Israeli military's human rights violations against Palestinians, was planning to marry her girlfriend. Glick stated that "he hope[d] Novak [was] jailed but if she [wasn't], that he [would] 'protest at the wedding of an enemy of the Jews.'"[84] Right-wing activists circulated at the address and time of the wedding. The specter of right-wing protestors appearing to intimidate a lesbian Israeli couple with whom they disagreed politically while the couple was celebrating their love and commitment to one another demonstrated the limits of queer life in Israel. As a result, there has been increased talk about what some are referring to as Israel's "gay exodus."[85] Queer Israeli academic Hila Amit (who herself now lives in Berlin) explained that Israelis "whose appearance is not 'normative'—such as transgendered people or lesbians with a masculine appearance—experience discrimination, violence and humiliating treatment."[86] In another piece, Amit elaborated that queer Israelis who have chosen to emigrate do so "whether because of growing homophobia or their criticism of the occupation," and they "say they're not coming back."[87]

In September 2016, Ivri Lider, a popular gay Israeli singer, experienced both support and condemnation from the settler community in the run-up to his performance in an illegal Israeli West Bank settlement. Those who opposed him declared his presence a form of "desecration" and said that he is a "declared pervert."[88] Two months before that, the Israeli press had addressed other incidents of Israeli homophobia. In July 2016, *Haaretz* revealed that the Israeli military was appointing Col. Eyal Karim as its chief rabbi. The *Times of Israel* reported that he previously "seemed to permit wartime rape" by writing the following: "Although intercourse with a female gentile is very grave, it was permitted during wartime (under the conditions it stipulated) out of consideration for the soldiers' difficulties. . . . And since our concern is the success of the collective in the war, the Torah permitted [soldiers] to satisfy the evil urge under the conditions it stipulated for the sake of the collective's success."[89] He later retracted these comments. *Haaretz* reported that Karim's belief is that homosexuality is to be treated as a sickness and that it is the "opposite of nature" and destroys nature.[90] That same month, 250 Israeli rabbis signed a letter in support of Rabbi Yigal Levinstein, head of an Israeli military academy, after he was criticized in Israel for calling homosexuals "perverts."[91] Such homophobic discourse, and the reality of deepening homophobia in Israel, undermines the Israeli government's marketing of the Israeli military as willing to embrace LGBTQ Israelis.

The LGBTQ Israeli community dealt with an additional blow that summer after the cancellation of the gay pride parade in the Israeli city of Be'er Sheva. The local police "forbade participants from marching through the city's main road" by citing security concerns and responding to pressures from local Jewish religious institutions.[92] The police noted "that the parade's original route was to pass close by several synagogues and religious institutions."[93] The LGBTQ community refused to be diverted from the main road and therefore filed a petition with the Israeli High Court of Justice. The High Court denied the petition and sided with the police. The parade organizers thus canceled the march and instead decided to protest outside of the Be'er Sheva municipality building. Be'er Sheva witnessed its first pride parade the following year, in June 2017, with 3,500 participants and marchers carrying signs with messages such as "It's okay to be gay in Be'er Sheva, too."[94] Israeli police arrested two ultra-Orthodox men near the parade, "one of whom was carrying a knife. . . . The other tried to break into the closed off section with force."[95] Fortunately, no one was hurt. Such cases do not feature in pinkwashing discourses, in an effort to elide the power of homophobic religious institutions in Israeli public life.

In 2017, Israeli homophobia remained part of public discourse and policy. Yair Netanyahu, son of Israeli Prime Minister Benjamin Netanyahu, posted an accusation on Facebook that the son of Ehud Olmert, a previous prime minister, was in a relationship with a Palestinian man. The younger Netanyahu asserted that Israeli reporters were not investigating this connection with the Palestinian man and its repercussions for "Israeli security" due to an alleged bias against his father, Benjamin Netanyahu.[96] Ariel Olmert, the son of Ehud Olmert, responded by clarifying that this was false and that he is straight and not in a relationship with a Palestinian man. Ariel Olmert also condemned Yair Netanyahu's homophobia. Yair Netanyahu, in defending his father amid a corruption scandal and investigation in Israel, drew on homophobic tropes to argue that previous prime ministers and their families were not treated the same way as Netanyahu and his family and that the Israeli media was conspiring against them. Shaul Olmert, Ariel Olmert's older brother, wrote, "I read what my brother wrote and I'm happy to see he's [Ariel Olmert] not a racist, a homophobe, a bully, a fascist."[97] Shaul Olmert was, of course, lambasting Yair Netanyahu for being all of those things. Accusing a male political rival of having sex with another man, who is also Palestinian, is a doubly harmful blow given the hold that ethnoheteronormativity has over contemporary Israel.

The summer of 2017 yielded several devastating decisions regarding LGBTQ rights in Israel. The Supreme Court ruled that "same-sex marriage is not a right," with the judges unanimously affirming that Israeli civil law would not permit gay marriages and that this would remain "under the jurisdiction of the rabbinical courts."[98] Also, the Israeli Social Affairs and Justice Ministries informed the High Court of Justice that it was opposed to same-sex adoptions. The policy of allowing homosexual adoption only for children "for whom no heterosexual married couple can be found" would remain in place, despite its discriminatory nature and the difficulty that same-sex couples have in adopting, with exceptions for children from the most "at-risk families."[99] Responding to this decision, several Israeli lawmakers stated, "This is a foolish and discriminatory decision that is accompanied by unprecedented homophobia." They also said that "the Israeli government is again abandoning the gay community and this highlights government's cynical use of the community: In English they boast about [being a gay-friendly country], but in Hebrew they deny basic rights."[100] Aeyal Gross points out that the Israeli government nonetheless states that Israel is considered to be "one of the most accepting [states] of the LGBT community, recognizing the rights of its gay citizens—including, it claims, same-sex couples' full and equal rights to adopt."[101] According to Gross, this is yet another example of pinkwashing. In September 2017, Yigal Guetta, an Israeli lawmaker from the Orthodox Shas party, had to resign from the Israeli Knesset for attending his gay nephew's wedding and wanting him "to be happy." This was despite Guetta's statement that the Torah forbids gay weddings and considers them an "abomination."[102]

Queer Palestinian solidarity activists around the world often feel that queer supporters of Israel downplay the realities of Israeli homophobia as part of pinkwashing campaigns. Queer pro-Israel solidarity activists often take issue with such charges, asserting that they do acknowledge such homophobia. Israel's queer advocates do not argue that Israel is perfect, but they want the progress of the LGBTQ movement in Israel to be recognized as well, and they expect the global queer Palestinian solidarity movement to appreciate this. Because these two movements are in conflict and are so interconnected, I would argue that one cannot discuss queer Palestinians without also discussing queer Israelis and vice versa. Because queer Israelis and queer Palestinians are often victims of the same Israeli state—and the homophobic logic that undergirds its policies—there needs to be more robust understanding among queer Israelis and Palestinians of how their lives, experiences, and future struggles are intertwined.

LGBTQ Rights in Israel

Queer Israel solidarity activists who are critical of the term *pinkwashing* often argue that queer Palestinian solidarity activists ignore or downplay significant advancements of LGBTQ rights in Israel. The former see the Jerusalem and Tel Aviv Pride parades as monumental achievements. They recognize allies among Israeli governmental figures, school officials, civil society leaders, health care providers, judges, and even police. For instance, these activists celebrated when the Jerusalem police first authorized the 2007 Jerusalem Pride parade and provided seven thousand police officers to help protect them amid right-wing protesters.[103] In James Kirchick's account of marching in the parade, he relayed a statement by ultra-Orthodox rabbis in advance of the march: "To all those involved, sinners in spirit, and whoever helps and protects them, may they feel a curse on their souls, may it plague them and may evil pursue them."[104] Kirchick also described the "hundreds of anti-gay activists [who] lined the route shouting imprecations and holding hateful signs," but he wrote that he felt protected by the "over 7,000 police and army officers" and the "snipers [who] were placed on the rooftops of nearby buildings."[105] A decade later, at the 2017 Jerusalem Pride parade, Israeli police permitted one hundred members of Lehava, an antigay and antimiscegenation group, to protest "several hundred meters away from the marchers and under heavy guard from police officers."[106] Twenty-two thousand people marched peacefully, and police arrested twenty-two individuals, one of whom was carrying a knife.[107]

Since 2006, the Israeli government has registered same-sex marriages performed abroad, although this does not constitute full legal recognition. Critics of pinkwatching activists also point to developments in Israel such as the permissibility of openly gay service in the Israeli military starting in 1993 and "survivor benefits" for partners of Israeli military veterans.[108] They also acknowledge employment protection for LGBTQ workers, with Israel being "the only country in the Middle East that outlaws discrimination based on sexuality."[109] British journalist Brian Whitaker wrote of a case pertaining to El Al, the Israeli airline; an Israeli court forced El Al "to provide a free ticket for the partner of a gay flight attendant, as the airline already did for the partners of its straight employees."[110] Israel went on to lower the "minimum age requirement for gender reassignment surgery"[111] from twenty-one to eighteen, which was significant for the trans community. Such advancements do not feature in the global queer Palestinian solidarity movement's discourse on LGBTQ rights in Israel. In fact, many in the movement consider the mere mention of these cases to be a form of pinkwashing. I disagree with such positions, as recognition of these realities does not necessarily result in the erasure of the Israeli occupation of Palestinians from anyone's analysis. The challenge is in engaging queer Israelis to connect their struggle against Israeli homophobia to the queer Palestinian struggle against ethnoheteronormativity.

Israeli LGBTQ activists point to 1988 as a historic moment in the struggle for queer rights, considering the repeal that year of the ban on homosexual sodomy in Israel. Other critical junctures for them include the 1992 LGBTQ employment-discrimination ban,[112] a series of rulings between 1994 and 1996 extending common law and other benefits to same-sex couples, a 2000 decision enabling pensions for same-sex couples, and a 2008 decision by the Israeli attorney general that "gay couples will be allowed to jointly adopt children that are not biologically linked to either partner."[113] These decisions have held, even with opposition from individuals such as the Israeli Deputy Welfare Minister Avraham Ravitz, who is firmly against gay adoption.

Political scientist Lihi Ben Shitrit summarizes LGBTQ rights in Israel:

> Legally, LGBT citizens in Israel do enjoy rights that are unavailable in neighboring countries. For example, homosexual acts were decriminalized in 1988, discrimination based on sexual orientation in employment was banned in 1992, since 1994 same-sex couples are entitled to equal spousal benefits as heterosexual couples in the public and private sectors. . . . In addition, the visibility and acceptance of a spectrum of sexual identities in mainstream culture has improved, particularly in big urban areas and especially in Tel Aviv, whose extravagant annual parade is touted as evidence of Israel's progressiveness and is used by the Israeli government to attract LGBT tourists.[114]

The Association for Civil Rights in Israel (ACRI) has affirmed Ben Shitrit's evaluation of Israeli LGBTQ rights. ACRI has worked within Israel to further these causes, and they have celebrated their achievements.

> ACRI has achieved many significant victories in the struggle for LGBT rights, in particular concerning the rights of same-sex couples, including with regards to marriage registration for marriages conducted outside of Israel, spousal and medical benefits for same-sex partners, protecting inheritance rights, recognition of same-sex partners by the Israeli Military, recognition of adoption by same-sex couples, prohibiting discrimination based on sexual orientation, and ensuring equal access to medical treatment, housing and mortgage assistance, pensions, and life insurance.[115]

Many critics of pinkwatching activism take pride in the work of ACRI and other Israeli LGBTQ rights activists and institutions.

Such critics of the global queer Palestinian solidarity movement draw attention to additional reasons why LGBTQ rights in Israel cannot be reduced to mere propaganda to be deployed by pinkwashers. These include the reality of "LGBT celebrities whose careers haven't been hurt by their coming out" and the sight in Tel Aviv of "more than 100,000 people attend[ing] its most recent Pride parade."[116] And even when there is homophobic violence, they are grateful for the ability to protest, such as at Take Back the Night in 2014. This event was organized by Gila, Israel's transgender advocacy group, and over one thousand protestors were present. Some of the protestors spoke passionately that night, with one saying, "We won't remain silent over injustice, violence and discrimination based on gender identity or sexuality. These are human rights, we're not prepared to be second class citizens, and everyone should understand this."[117] Another protestor stated, "We've got to speak out! Israel has a hate crimes law but it's rarely applied or enforced, instead attacks on LGBT people are often classified under much more lenient offences, that's totally unacceptable."[118]

Israeli LGBTQ activists continue to celebrate victories, such as the August 2016 decision of the Tel Aviv–Jaffa municipality to allow an NGO called Hoshen to extend LGBTQ programs that were previously only in middle and secondary schools to preschools and elementary schools in Tel Aviv. *Haaretz* reported that "Shirli Rimon-Bracha, director of the city's education administration, told Hoshen staff that the city has decided to expand its subsidies for the organization's activities to include teachers at preschools and elementary schools."[119] The Hoshen staff emphasized the importance of broadening Israeli children's consciousness of gender starting in preschool, which is when the "socialization process begins."[120]

With each of these victories for LGBTQ populations in Israel, the reality of entrenched homophobia in Israeli society is also ever present. A queer Jewish Israeli who is cisgender, white, Ashkenazi, male, wealthy, and living in Tel Aviv is likely to fare very well in Israeli society, yet a queer Black Jewish Israeli woman of Ethiopian background living in poor economic conditions in that same city or elsewhere in Israel is likely to struggle from homophobia and other forms of marginalization in the context of ethnoheteronormativity. Pinkwashing discourse highlights visibility for narratives of the former while eliding the realities of the latter.

"Singling Out Israel"

Queer Zionists, Palestinians, and others continue to animate the debates regarding the term *pinkwashing*. There are arguments that *pinkwashing* and *pinkwatching* should not be used at all, arguments that they should be used extensively, and arguments about everything in between. Many terms have a contested nature, but no concept at the intersection of Israel/Palestine and queerness is more deeply and publicly contested than pinkwashing. The ways in which pinkwashing is contested hinge on a rubric of the centrality of the state and state exceptionalism. Critics of pinkwatching activists claim that such activists are just searching for anything to muddy the name of Israel, making Israel into an exceptional victim of unwarranted critique that is beyond the critique other nations receive. Pinkwatching activists argue that such criticism of their work is merely another example of pinkwashing, meant to obfuscate Israel's violations of Palestinian human rights and portray Palestinians as in a state of exceptional victimhood and Israel as in an exceptional state of impunity from critique and accountability. These activists also say that this pinkwashing falsely represents Israel as a savior. In many cases, the critiques that pinkwatching activists receive from those who engage in pinkwashing are deployed as forms of discursive disenfranchisement aimed at decentering and even silencing queer Palestinian voices. Furthermore, these pinkwatching activists often reiterate that they are not singling out Israel for criticism but merely responding to the Israeli government's preexisting attempts to single out Israel. They point out that the Israeli state represents the country as exceptional in the Middle East and as a role model for the positive treatment of queer people globally (including queer Israelis, Palestinians, and international visitors to Israel).

In working to resist oppression they face and in building networks of solidarity, queer Palestinian activists, particularly those in Palestine, have no choice but to name the Israeli source of that oppression. Although many queer Palestinian solidarity activists aspire to build a truly intersectional movement that is committed to social justice and human rights for people across the world, limited resources and capacity have meant that they must prioritize what is to be delineated as part of their struggle. As Palestinians and as queer people, they name Zionism and homophobia, respectively, as the two primary reasons for their marginalization. Yet pro-Israel queer advocates such as Jayson Littman relegate Zionism to an "other issue" from LGBTQ rights. For queer Palestinians, Zionism and homophobia are fundamentally connected through ethnoheteronormativity. Queer Palestinian activists also experience the Zionist demand not to "single out Israel" as a lack of ability to even articulate the source of their oppression. They take this demand as an additional hostile external expectation that they must name every oppressive state when attempting to speak of their particular conditions as queer Palestinians. Their discursive disenfranchisement is evident when the naming of Israeli oppression is accepted only if all other oppression is also named. The impossibility of the latter is therefore meant to also make the former impossible. Such discursive disenfranchisement has become a quintessential form of whataboutism: it is common for supporters of the Israeli state to attempt to shift the discourse to other contexts when confronted with the realities of Israeli human rights violations.

Many queer Palestinian solidarity activists in the United States and elsewhere are involved in local social justice struggles, and it is that activism closer to home that propelled them to recognize injustices in Israel/Palestine. For instance, Katherine Franke, a legal scholar and prominent member of the global queer Palestinian solidarity movement, wrote this on pinkwashing:

> Of equal importance, the pinkwashing critique applies to *all* states, not just Israel. In the United States there are many of us who have expressed concern that the Obama administration is using its good gay rights record (repealing "don't ask/don't tell," backing away from defending the Defense of Marriage Act, and endorsing marriage equality rights for same-sex couples, for example) to deflect attention from its otherwise objectionable policies (aggressive

deportation of undocumented people, use of drones to execute civilians, and failure to prosecute anyone or any entity in connection with the 2008 financial crisis for example). As some states expand their laws protecting the rights of LGBT people, pinkwashing has become an effective tool to portray a progressive reputation when their other policies relating to national security, immigration, income inequality, and militarism are anything but progressive.[121]

There is ample evidence of this broader understanding of pinkwashing among global queer Palestinian solidarity activists. For instance, at the Homonationalism and Pinkwashing Conference at the City University of New York, these concepts were applied to cases and domains from around the world. This included Darnell Moore's piece, which reflected on his experience as a queer Black American solidarity activist with Palestine. Moore drew connections between pinkwashing in Israel/Palestine and pinkwashing logics and dynamics in the United States. Moore lamented what he described as United States pinkwashing, with the Supreme Court's 2015 ruling that legalized same-sex marriage in all states and a simultaneous ruling that undermined the Voting Rights Act. Thus, Moore analyzed how attention to the advancement of gay rights pinkwashed the political disenfranchisement of African Americans through suppression of their ability to vote.

Even critics of the queer Palestinian solidarity movement such as Jay Michaelson, a queer Jewish American writer, recognize that queer Palestinian solidarity activists do often adopt a more universal approach to their movement building. For instance, Michaelson has written that activists such as trans Jewish American legal scholar Dean Spade are "quick to point out" that the latter's critiques of pinkwashing are "critiques of America even more than of Israel."[122] Michaelson also recognized that pinkwashing does occur in some contexts, and he takes issue with some of his fellow critics of pinkwatching activism when he writes, "Pinkwashing is real, notwithstanding the hysterical denials of some."[123] At the same time, queer Palestinian solidarity activists have shared with me how alienated they have felt by Michaelson's work. Michaelson had previously assumed that Dean Spade is not Jewish, explicitly asserting that in one of his articles. This prompted the editors of *The Forward*, a Jewish newspaper, to issue a correction to the assertion to the article on their website.[124] Although Michaelson responded that this was merely a mistake on his end, for Spade and Spade's fellow LGBTQ anti-Zionist Jewish allies, the false assertion fit with a pattern of behavior among many Zionists. This pattern is one of questioning the Jewish identity of anti-Zionist Jews merely because their views on Israel/Palestine do not align with supporters of the Israeli state.

Michaelson has argued that Israel's promotion of gay tourism to Israel is "about money, not politics."[125] He elaborated, "[Michael] Lucas [the Zionist gay porn star and anti-Palestinian activist] is right when he says that critics of Israel can't accept that it does anything for the right reasons. . . . One can talk about LGBT people in Israel, as A Wider Bridge [an American pro-Israel LGBTQ advocacy organization] does, without using it for hasbara [propaganda] purposes, as the Israeli Consulate sometimes does."[126] In another piece, Michaelson writes that pinkwatching activists are not "all as thoughtful as Spade is about situating their critique in a coherent radical context. Spade isn't just anti-Israel; he's anti-nationalism and anti-capitalism. That context is exactly what is missing from many less reflective critics of Israel—which enables conservatives like Lucas to allege bias."[127] Queer Palestinian solidarity activists often disagree that this larger context is missing from their movement, instead finding that their fellow activists in the movement overwhelmingly share a commitment to social justice along these numerous axes.

The expectation for queer Palestinian solidarity activism to necessarily be linked to other axes places a burden on queer Palestinian solidarity activists issuing their calls for solidarity. When these activists identify the struggles against Zionism and homophobia as their points of departure and simultaneously call for accountability from the United States and other nations that are complicit in these systems of subjugation, the question of what additional struggles to bring into this fold is far from a point of consensus among queer Palestinians. There is a danger that activists within the movement and critics of the movement will fuel the empire of critique by authorizing themselves as arbiters of when the movement is at an acceptable threshold of intersectional solidarity and alliance building. For example, criticism of the movement for not disavowing nationalism (and for the movement's commitment to nationalism) persists from the right and the left. While there are many antinationalists among global queer Palestinian solidarity activists, not all queer Palestinians subscribe to an antinationalist framework. The latter identify Palestinian nationalism as a manifestation of the subaltern and anti-colonial impulse of a people struggling for self-determination.

The question of nationalism makes the movement perpetually vulnerable to the charge of singling out Israel *because* of its self-definition as a Jewish state. As the queer Jewish antipinkwashing activist Wendy Somerson has written,

Pro-occupation commentators purposefully confuse the issue by using tele-scopic vision to zoom in on one piece of the controversy in order to obscure the larger power dynamics. By accusing the [pro-Palestinian] protesters of anti-Semitism, these [pro-Israel] critics can position the organization and people who are aligned with a powerful state, Israel, as the protesters' victims. Focusing excessively on tactics is part of their [pro-Israel activists'] effort to distract attention from the real issue that the protest highlights: the increas-ing insistence on including Palestine in all of our struggles for social justice.[128]

Debates about whether queer Palestinians—in their call for solidarity—have sufficiently disavowed Palestinian violence, anti-Semitism, US militarism, capitalism, or any other measure stem from demands from actors across the political spectrum. Such debates on whether this disavowal has then been ef-fectively realized globally in the solidarity movement further shifts the fo-cus away from queer Palestinians and their struggle in Palestine. I believe that a robust integration of intersectional organizing, including the resistance against anti-Semitism, is essential for the future of the global queer Palestin-ian solidarity movement. Yet there are instances in which calls for the move-ment to incorporate additional dimensions come not from a place of critique in the spirit of solidarity but from critique as a disciplining mechanism aimed at silencing or disempowering queer Palestinians through discursive disen-franchisement. Critiques from radical purists also often contribute to the splintering and weakening of the queer Palestinian solidarity movement.

Queer Palestinians in Israel

Pro-Israel critics of pinkwatching activism have argued that the lack of an-tihomosexual legislation on the part of the Palestinian Authority does not translate to Palestinian tolerance of homosexuality and in fact does not curb Palestinian homophobia under the Islamist Hamas in Gaza or the secular Fa-tah in the West Bank. As evidence, these critics point to the search by some queer Palestinians from the Occupied Territories for safety and livelihoods in Israel. Meanwhile, pinkwatching activists charge the pro-Israel critics with overstating the scale (and sometimes even existence) of that phenome-non. The queer Palestinian solidarity activists point to the tremendous inse-curity that queer Palestinians from the West Bank and Gaza Strip experience in Israel, when they are in the rare position of having gotten there. In 2014, Aguda, the Israeli LGBTQ organization, estimated "that around 2,000 Palestinian queers live in Tel-Aviv at any one time, most of them illegally."[129] This figure increased from 2003, when the BBC estimated that there were "300 gay Palestinian men secretly living and working in Israel."[130] The BBC also reported that year that "many Palestinian gays say they would still rather live under house arrest in Israel, where homosexuality is not considered a crime, than at home."[131] This is because of their fear of homophobic violence from fellow Palestinians.

Queer Jewish academic and Palestinian solidarity activist Ashley Bohrer added further context to what the BBC reported. She wrote, "The dismantling of economic stability and opportunity inside Palestine forces LGBT Palestinians to leave their homes and to live as undocumented, precarious workers in Israel, where they have no protections against harassment, rape, intimidation, or job discrimination, and in which . . . safe housing and steady employment are scarce."[132] Global queer Palestinian solidarity activists insist that Israel's illegal and brutal military occupation and the economic burdens it places on Palestinians must be taken into account in this context.

Queer Israel solidarity advocates such as David Harris argue that it is a "shame" that Palestinian solidarity activists do not share "how many gay Israelis have fled to Palestinian-controlled territories to avoid harassment, and how many gay Palestinians have fled to Israel."[133] Harris's commitment to juxtaposing the figure of zero for the former with the higher figure for the latter was an attempt to highlight the superiority of Israeli society. Others, such as Milo Yiannopoulos, have overstated this phenomenon. In a 2014 post on the far-right site Breitbart, Yiannopoulos asserted that "for over ten years, gay Palestinians have been fleeing their own country and settling in Tel Aviv, one of the most gay-friendly cities on the planet."[134] Jay Michaelson stated that he has "met Palestinians who sneak across the green line to hide from vengeful relatives, to find queer community, and even to dance at gay bars."[135] James Kirchick argued that there are "countless gay Palestinians who have fled to Israel after being tortured or receiving death threats by Hamas or Fatah agents."[136]

It is important to note that such pro-Israel commentators typically do not count queer Palestinian citizens of Israel in their analysis. They use the term "Israeli Arabs" to refer to those indigenous Palestinians who come from families that were able to remain inside the borders of Israel after Israel was established in 1948 (most other Palestinians experienced forced displacement from what was Palestine and became Israel), thereby denying their connections to

Palestinians from the Occupied Territories.[137] The experience of the limited numbers of queer Palestinians who make it to Israel from the Occupied Territories is significantly different, on average, from that of the queer Palestinians who are Israeli citizens and have only ever lived on their native land in Israel. Pro-Israel advocates often shape the narrative using the scale and experiences of queer Palestinians in Israel from the Occupied Territories. In fact, these Palestinians lead precarious lives in hiding and in most cases cannot speak openly to the public about themselves. When their voices are appropriated or instrumentalized by queer advocates for the Israeli state, the relative powerlessness of these queer Palestinians prevents them from being able to resist such narratives.[138]

The limits of Israel's acceptance of queer Palestinians seeking refuge there and the lack of asylum for them becomes evident when such individuals do receive asylum in a third location. When a queer Palestinian from the Occupied Territories makes it to Israel, that person's experience, regardless of how uncommon it is, reinforces a central pillar of pinkwashing logic. That pillar is predicated on the existence of Palestinian homophobia, which critics of pinkwatching activism argue is conveniently elided within the global queer Palestinian solidarity community. At the same time, that queer Palestinians in Israel so often need to seek refuge and asylum because they feel hunted by the Israeli state reflects that they are still oppressed, even if being hunted in Israel is preferable to what might happen to them in the Occupied Territories. Yet global queer Palestinian solidarity activists in most cases do not want to wrestle with the reality that Palestinian homophobia contributes to some queer Palestinians preferring to live as a hunted subject in Israel.

In a report by law professors at Tel Aviv University, Michael Kagan and Anat Ben-Dor have written that "Israel's continued refusal to consider asylum claims from gay Palestinians violates the general rule of international law—recognized by Israel's High Court—against returning a foreigner to a territory where his or her life or freedom may be in danger."[139] Another writer, Tom Jones, has argued that "Israel's reputation as a 'safe haven for gay people' is also dubious."[140] Jones cited a case in which a gay Palestinian citizen of Israel was "granted asylum in the United States."[141] He convinced American authorities that "he would face violence from his own family and tribe if forced to return to Israel. Lack of adequate action by Israeli police played a role in the approval of the request, his attorney said."[142] Palestinian homophobia coupled with Israel's lack of protection for queer Palestinians made life in Israel precarious for this gay Palestinian citizen of Israel, dispelling a central logic of pinkwashing.

Nonetheless, Israel advocates persist in expressing frustration that queer Palestinian activists do not acknowledge Israel's role in creating a supposed gay haven for both Israelis and Palestinians in Tel Aviv. Such acknowledgment is expected despite evidence that the Israeli government has articulated its explicit rejection of asylum cases from gay Palestinians. The state (through a 2014 committee with representatives of the Israeli justice, foreign, and interior ministries as well as the prime minister's office) has provided the explanation that "there is no systematic persecution based on sexual orientation in the Palestinian Authority" and that "life-threatening cases are rare."[143] Queer Palestinian activists assert that Israel's stance is actually motivated by racism, homophobia, and Israel's desire not to establish a legal precedent for the right of return of Palestinian refugees to their ancestral lands in Israel. Palestinian refugees across the Middle East would then attempt to utilize this precedent to secure the ability to return to their ancestral lands in Israel. Queer Palestinian activists also point to a hypocrisy here: that the Israeli government invokes Palestinian homophobia to further pinkwashing propaganda but denies Palestinian homophobia to disallow Palestinian rights in Israel. Israel recognizes Palestinians as victims only when the perpetrators are also Palestinian and when doing so is convenient for Israeli state narratives.

Critics of the global queer Palestinian solidarity movement also express concern that the movement disregards Palestinian homophobia, overstates the power of queer Palestinian organizations, and fails to recognize that those few organizations are based and registered in Israel. Jay Michaelson described them as "three miniscule advocacy organizations" that are "courageous, but totally marginal."[144] Queer Palestinians in the movement and on the ground in Israel/Palestine often find such diminishing characterizations of their presence and work to be deeply insulting. These discussions take place in popular American queer forums and contribute to the dehumanization of queer Palestinians and their allies in the mainstream press. For instance, James Kirchick writes, in general terms, that when pinkwatching activists around the world put forward the accusation of pinkwashing and support Palestinians, they are "making excuses for people who kill homosexuals."[145] He went on to write, "And whatever law might be on the Palestinian Authority books has yet to persuade the leaders of Aswat, a Palestinian lesbian organization, to relocate their headquarters to Ramallah from Haifa."[146] Pro-Israel writer Roberta Seid, in her critique of queer Palestinian solidarity activist Sarah Schulman, argued that Schulman is "sliding over the fact" that "two Palestinian lesbian groups . . . have had to make their base in Israel, not the West Bank where they could not function."[147] The reality is that Schulman had referred to one Palestinian lesbian organization. The other organization is open to all LGBTQ Palestinians, including men and those in the West Bank. The latter has functioned and continues to function in the West Bank.

It is true that both organizations have needed to be registered with the authorities in order to function, that they are registered with the Israeli government, and that neither one is registered with the Palestinian Authority. Registering with the Palestinian Authority would not be possible, largely as a result of Palestinian homophobia. Zionist commentators such as Kirchick and Seid use this reality to undermine pinkwatching activism. Queer Palestinian solidarity activists argue that such points do not compromise the overall thrust of their argument against Israel's attempts to draw attention to LGBTQ rights in order to detract from its gross violations of Palestinian human rights. Queer Palestinians groups also face critiques internally and from radical purists for being registered in Israel, since there are members of the global queer Palestinian solidarity movement who do not want to see the movement embrace NGO models, let alone register those NGOs with the bureaucratic apparatus of the Israeli state.

Pro-Israel critics of pinkwatching activism also point to the denial of Palestinian homophobia as a contributor to the eliding of queer Israeli-Palestinian solidarity in Israel, particularly when progressive queer Israelis attempt to support queer Palestinians. Arthur Slepian, founder and executive director of A Wider Bridge, has stated,

> The truth is that Israel is a good place to be LGBT. . . . It is so because there are countless people within Israel doing amazing, courageous work every day, especially with LGBT teens and families, saving lives, including the lives of young LGBT Palestinians who often have nowhere else to turn. Their work deserves to be supported, and their stories deserve to be told. It is not pinkwashing to tell the truth.[148]

Individuals such as Slepian are concerned that organizations like the Tel Aviv University Public Interest Law Program and the LGBT organizations in Israel, including Aguda, that work to provide legal and other services to queer and trans Palestinians in Israel have been erased from the analysis of pinkwatching activists. When faced with pressure to acknowledge these groups, some queer Palestinian activists, especially those who are radical purists, will assert that these queer Israeli institutions reinforce pinkwashing—whether intentionally or in effect—to project an enlightened image of queer Israel and an inferior Palestinian society.

Israeli writer Yossi Klein Halevi described the work of Shaul Ganon of the Tel Aviv–based Agudah-Association of Gay Men, Lesbians, Bisexuals and Transgender in Israel, who "heads the Association's outreach to Palestinian gays."[149] Ganon "spends his nights on the Tel Aviv streets where Palestinian gay prostitutes gather, providing food and clothes and trying to keep them off drugs and out of jail."[150] In 2002, Klein Halevi wrote, "Over the last four years Ganon has waged essentially a one-man campaign to try to interest human rights groups in Israel and elsewhere in their plight."[151] He elaborated,

> According to Ganon, during the last year police have generally stopped arresting and deporting Palestinian gays because of his efforts. He has even worked out a quiet arrangement with Tel Aviv police, providing them a list of Palestinian gays under his sponsorship and providing those gays with Association membership cards to show their affiliation. The goal is to reassure local police, who are primarily on the lookout for Palestinian terrorists, that these Palestinians pose no threat. (The exceptions to this arrangement are Palestinian gays with security records and those from Gaza, whom the Israelis see as *inherent security risks* because of Hamas's popularity there.) Some Palestinian gays, though, say they see no recent change in police policy and still feel hunted (emphasis added).[152]

Ganon referred to a group of "teenage prostitutes, [Palestinian] refugees from the West Bank," who "live in an abandoned building" in Tel Aviv as "my children."[153] Klein Halevi reported that Ganon asks them, "Does anyone need condoms? How about clothes? Who hasn't eaten today, sweethearts?"[154] They tell the journalist "that sometimes a client will offer them a meal and a shower instead of payment; sometimes a client will simply refuse to pay in any form, taunting them to complain to police. And sometimes police will beat them before releasing them back to the streets."[155] Gay and trans Palestinian prostitutes continue to try to make a living in Israel—although their presence is limited—because the sex market for these Palestinians in Israel remains. And just as critics of pinkwatching activists dismiss the impact of queer Palestinian solidarity activism, the work of queer Israelis in solidarity with queer Palestinians, such as Ganon, is dismissed as "miniscule" and "totally marginal" by many pinkwatching activists.[156]

Although there are cases in which pinkwatching activists completely ignore Palestinian homophobia in their public discourse, other pinkwatching activists do integrate a recognition of Palestinian homophobia. For instance, Sarah Schulman has written,

> How Homophobic is Palestine? The Occupied Palestinian Territories are homophobic, sexist arenas. The goal of Pinkwashing is to justify Israel's policies of Occupation and Separation by promoting the image of a lone oasis of progress surrounded by violent, homophobic Arabs—thereby denying the existence of a Queer Palestinian movement, or of secular, feminist, intellectual and queer Palestinians. By ignoring the multi-dimensionality of Palestinian society, the Israeli government is trying to claim racial supremacy that in their minds justifies the Occupation. Yet, nothing justifies the occupation.[157]

It is essential to name and contextualize Palestinian homophobia and to acknowledge when queer Palestinians choose to live vulnerably in Israel as a result. At the same time, the politicization of Palestinian homophobia to absolve Israel from its oppression of Palestinians or to justify that oppression against Palestinians revictimizes queer Palestinians while purporting to be concerned with their well-being and to save them. Juxtaposing the status of queer Israelis and Palestinians by representing each in monolithic terms and not recognizing critical differences in contexts between them—such as that one of these groups lives under military occupation—is often a disingenuous attempt to champion queer rights while serving as a smokescreen for another system of oppression. Hence, the concerns of pinkwatching activists about pinkwashing are often valid. Although pinkwatching activists should be subject to legitimate and fair criticism, the critiques leveled against them are often not well founded or ethically deployed. It is particularly disconcerting when supporters of Israel instead cast Israeli state sources of victimization as saviors of queer Palestinians.

The Occupation

The sharpest divide between the queer Palestinian solidarity movement and their critics in the queer Israeli solidarity movement is over where Israel's military occupation of Palestinians must fit in the analysis of queer rights in

Israel/Palestine. Pinkwatching activists argue that the struggles against homophobia and the occupation are intertwined and thus that any conversation on queer Israel/Palestine that does not foreground a condemnation of the occupation is pinkwashing par excellence. But queer Israel advocates often see the occupation as a separate question from LGBTQ rights, and they arrive at different positions on its ethics and legality despite a near consensus among the international community on the occupation's immorality and illegal features. Many queer pro-Israel activists do object to the ills of the Israeli occupation and its harmful effects on Palestinian civilians. These queer Zionist activists often also feel that every utterance on gay rights in Israel should not have to mention the occupation and should not be dismissed as pinkwashing. While queer anti-Zionist activists often identify the occupation as a profound moral evil in the world today, queer Zionist activists often diminish the brutality of the occupation, referring to it instead as merely a "conflict," "issue," or "question" that can be bracketed from discussions of queer rights in Israel.

One example that blurs the lines between constructive critique and counterproductive criticism is Jay Michaelson's admonishment of pinkwatching activists for viewing "all of Israel through the single lens of the Israel/Palestine conflict."[158] Jayson Littman shares a similar critique, saying, "I don't necessarily have to agree with all the policies of the Israeli government. I would encourage our community not to create a queer value of condemning a nation that has progressive LGBT rights to its citizens just because there are other unresolved conflicts."[159] Tyler Lopez takes this critique further when he says, "Linking the gay rights movement to Israel's geopolitical conflict merely refreshes age-old Zionist conspiracy theories by using one of today's most prominent social issues."[160] Like Michaelson, Littman, and Lopez, Arthur Slepian also invokes the discourse of "conflict."[161] He states,

> Discourse about Israel must be all about the occupation all the time, or face charges of bad faith. If every visiting Israeli LGBT leaders' event can be cast as a bid to divert the attention of Americans away from the conflict, if anything touched by the Israeli government automatically becomes *treif*, there is always a simple choice between good and evil. Simple, all too simple.[162]

Furthermore, Slepian writes that pinkwatching activism is "for those who want to demonize Israel, or turn every conversation about LGBT progress in Israel into an argument about the Israeli-Palestinian conflict."[163] He adds, "There are those for whom the *only* frame through which to see Israel is the conflict, with a one-dimensional country cast as a colonial, racist oppressor worthy of the pariah status of South Africa in the days of apartheid."[164] Slepian also writes, "I reject that frame, along with the portrayal of Israel as a nation that can do no wrong. Israel is a complicated, challenging, messy, inspiring, and exhilarating country. It is a land full of seeming contradictions that cannot be reduced to simplistic slogans."[165]

Most queer Palestinian solidarity activists would argue that the need to unequivocally condemn the occupation and to reiterate this condemnation for as long as the occupation persists is indeed right, simple, and irrefutable. They add that no amount of complexity should obfuscate the harm of the occupation. They posit that it is impossible—without reifying pinkwashing—to ethically discuss LGBTQ rights in the context of Israel/Palestine without discussing the plight of Palestinians, queer and straight. And they claim that the erasure of Palestinians from this discourse, as Slepian's statements exemplify, is an extension of the erasure of Palestinian bodies from the political imagination. For instance, Tom Jones writes that "scrutiny" should be directed not to Israel's "noble gay rights record" but to "Israel's human rights record toward the Palestinians."[166]

Katherine Franke adds,

In Israel/Palestine, gay rights and human rights more broadly are necessarily connected to one another, and treating one domestic minority well does not excuse or diminish the immorality of the state's other rights-abridging policies. Had South Africa enacted good gay rights laws during the Apartheid era no one would have seen that as excusing their treatment of black and colored people.[167]

Queer Israel advocates often respond with the clarification that their silence on the "conflict" with Palestinians should be interpreted not as an excuse for the occupation but as not wanting to spend time discussing a contentious issue, on which they hold different positions, at the expense of LGBTQ rights. Jay Michaelson elaborates that "some queer Jews emphasize their solidarity with all victims of oppression, while others feel more solidarity with the Jewish state. Some of us feel pulls in both directions. . . . To suggest that queers should all have a certain view . . . is the kind of essentialism one usually finds among homophobes."[168] Pinkwatching activists then argue that to be silent on Israel's domination of Palestinians is to support the status quo, thereby enabling the occupation. These activists also claim that a proper vision for queer liberation in Israel/Palestine must encompass Palestinians. Ashley Bohrer asserts that "to refuse to do so retrenches the all-too-common neoliberal strategy of divide and conquer. The idea that Israel must be defended regardless of its human rights abuses or racist violence, separates LGBTQ liberation from larger social and structural phenomena."[169]

In his critique of pinkwatching activism, Tyler Lopez reiterates the concern that, even while attempting to link homophobia and occupation, queer Palestinian solidarity activists are elevating occupation over homophobia while critiquing others for the reverse. He writes, "Of course, LGBTQ rights aren't the only marker of social change or human rights. But suggesting that they're separate from any other universal human right is dangerous. An accusation of pinkwashing presumes that gay human rights causes are less salient than Palestinian human rights causes, when in fact they're all equal."[170] James Kirchick states, "The first fallacy of the pinkwashing meme is that it is a non sequitur. No one is saying that Israel ought to be immune from criticism because it treats gay people humanely.[171] Jay Michaelson argues that it is a fallacy for pinkwatching activists to assume that discussions of LGBTQ rights in Israel necessitate the muting of condemnations of the Israeli state. Pinkwatching activists critique Michaelson for such statements, which, for example, deny the realities of Israel's targeting of gay Palestinians.

One of the most criticized representatives of the Israeli state by the global queer Palestinian solidarity movement has been Ron Huldai, the mayor of Tel Aviv, who created shockwaves in the international press in June 2016 when he linked the escalation of violence perpetrated by Palestinians against Israelis explicitly to the Israeli occupation. He stated, in the same month as Tel Aviv Pride, that "we, as a state, are the only ones in the world with another people living among us under our occupation, denying them any civil rights."[172] He added, "The problem is that when there is no terrorism, no one talks about [the occupation]," and he said that "nobody has the guts to take a step towards trying to make some kind of [final status] arrangement. We are 49 years into an occupation that I was a participant in, and I recognize the reality and know that leaders with courage just say things."[173] This is the same Huldai that had simultaneously championed the Tel Aviv gay pride parades and gay tourism. Some queer Palestinian solidarity activists saw this as a victory for years of pinkwatching activism, in which Huldai had finally been compelled to speak openly about the occupation, using his significant political platform for that end, and likely a result of years of critiques leveled against him for pinkwashing the occupation. At the same time, some queer Israel solidarity activists interpreted this as a vindication of all their critiques of pinkwatching: that Huldai's comments meant that celebrating gay rights in Israel is not necessarily a smokescreen for the occupation. Thus, Huldai's statements were critiqued from both the right and the left. Numerous Israel supporters expressed concern that Huldai could be seen as an apologist for Palestinian violence. Numerous Palestinian solidarity activists understood his recognition of the occupation as far from ideal for acknowledging the suffering only of Palestinians in the Occupied Territories and not acknowledging the Israeli oppression faced by Palestinians who are citizens of Israel or Palestinian refugees in exile.

Saving Brown Homosexuals

This chapter established both the contested nature of delineating what constitutes pinkwashing and the debates between queer Israeli and Palestinian solidarity activists on the nature of pinkwatching. The global reach of pinkwashing and pinkwatching has propelled the queer Palestinian movement to its transnational frontiers. The chapter makes clear how deeply political the juxtaposition of Palestinian homophobia and Israeli queer agency is within pinkwashing discourse. The shifting parameters of pinkwashing revolve around contrasting Israel's alleged gay friendliness with Palestinian rejection of queer and trans individuals among them. This should be interrogated, because homophobia is not an ontological phenomenon but a social one, and, as such, there are different homophobias (that is, homophobia can be racialized). Discourses surrounding sexuality cannot be divorced from ideologies surrounding race. Race-based and gender- or sexuality-based hierarchies co-constitute and shape the human experience of being dominant and/or dominated. Furthermore, how we understand social status is intimately linked to our own racial position and how we perceive and treat racial others.

I call for an analysis that does not use civilizational logics that cast particular communities as having superior claims to rights and humanity and that therefore enable systems of domination over others. It is possible, and in fact imperative, to speak of homophobia in Israeli and Palestinian societies as well as of the advancement of LGBTQ rights in Israel (no matter how limited) without reproducing pinkwashing. A central feature of pinkwashing is the cynical appropriation of queer bodies to elide the possibilities of Palestinian gay agency and the realities of Israeli homophobia. This discourse is used to justify Israel's military occupation of Palestine. Thoughtful juxtapositions accompanied by proper contextualization can be used to distinguish between cynical pinkwashing, which must be opposed, and a multidimensional consideration of the fact that Israeli and Palestinian societies harbor homophobes and also contain queer activists.

Even as queer Palestinians have been successful in entering the global sphere and raising consciousness among LGBTQ populations worldwide on the politics of pinkwashing, there are radical purists within the solidarity movement today who continue to prioritize the struggle against Zionism. The focus on resisting pinkwashing among these purists can inadvertently contribute to reinforcing homophobia. This happens when queer issues are raised only in the context of exposing a nefarious Israeli state-sanctioned project that deploys a queer discourse in the service of gross violations of Palestinian human rights. When the only messages about LGBTQ people that Palestinians are exposed to in their broader society are homophobic ones (such as that homosexuals are alien, immoral, corrupt, and mentally and physically ill), the queer Palestinian movement has a responsibility to introduce alternative representations of queer subjects in the local public discourse. When queer Palestinians and their allies focus on critiquing global pinkwashing, they risk entrenching even more negative representations of queer subjects in Palestine, namely, highlighting queer Zionist pinkwashers who are instrumental to advancing Israeli oppression. This just reinforces existing local homophobic tropes about queerness in Palestine. Pinkwashing is bolstered when pinkwashers are granted a monopoly by the right and the left on claiming and defining queerness. Breaking down hegemonic homophobic Palestinian understandings of queerness can help facilitate resistance to homophobia *and* Zionism in the face of ethnoheteronormativity.

To help minimize the entrenchment of homophobia in Palestinian society, activists can simultaneously engage in naming homophobia, correcting stereotypes about LGBTQ people, challenging pinkwashing, openly identifying themselves as queer and their movement as a queer struggle, and introducing more positive representations of queer subjectivities into the public sphere. During my interview with scientist and musician Huda Asfour, she reflected on her concerns about the movement's "overemphasis on resisting pinkwashing." Asfour also felt that there was a subsequent entrenchment of homophobia at the expense of representing queer Palestinian agency, creativity, and resilience. She stated passionately, "Our [queer Palestinian] experiences cannot be reduced to pinkwashing."

There are queer Palestinians who maintain a commitment to tackling both of the domains of ethnoheteronormativity, thereby reclaiming their voices in the face of multiple sources of discursive disenfranchisement from across the political spectrum. Whereas the previous chapter delineated the internal Palestinian contributors to the empire of critique under which queer Palestinians must survive, this one has revealed the role of queer activists who defend the Israeli state in the empire of critique.

Throughout this chapter, I have disentangled pinkwashing allegations. I pointed out the specific institutions that individuals allege are participating in pinkwashing and also identified the positions of those who critique the use of the term *pinkwashing* in the first place. In order to not reproduce the logic of pinkwashing, we must identify what specific regimes of power these institutions and individuals are in, so that we can think about Israeli homophobia and Palestinian homophobia in their own contextual manifestations rather than reducing them both to a transhistorical homophobia that enables us to gauge which community is "better to its gays." Within the pinkwashing debate, there are fundamentally different paradigms with which queer activists in solidarity with the Israeli state—versus those in solidarity with Palestinians—approach this domain. Analysis of these paradigms shows that the former camp often attempts to diminish the place of the occupation in their discourse, while the latter attempts to center their discourse on Israel's system of oppression.

The pinkwashing examples illustrated here exemplify the larger pattern that is on display in many pinkwashing campaigns. The hegemonic reach of pinkwashing discourses has the potential to produce both effects and affects and has implications for how we read history. Although pinkwashers do not always intend to have these effects, the operation of power lies in effects, not intentions. Just as Gayatri Spivak problematized the "white men saving brown women from brown men"[174] discourse that became part of colonial dynamics, I identify the same fallacy with regard to much of pinkwashing—which is that "white men are saving brown homosexuals from brown heterosexuals." This is precisely why queer Palestinian activism is so important, as is where this book fits into that activism, because this text constitutes a historical archive that clears the pinkwashing record and renders more nuanced narratives related to Queer Palestine.

3   Transnational Activism
and the Politics of Boycotts

IN JULY 2012, a video went viral across queer Palestinian solidarity
networks showing pinkwatching activists protesting that year's World Pride
Parade in London. The subject of protest was the parade's inclusion of a marketing campaign aimed at promoting gay tourism to Israel. "At London's big-
gest outdoor party for the gay community," Tel Aviv was promoted as "fun,
free, [and] fabulous."[1] Two gay Israeli acts appeared on stage, including an
Israeli singer and four drag queens from Tel Aviv. At the same time, however, "a sea of Palestinian flags sprang up in the audience and were waved
high above the crowds." Sarah Colborne, director of the Palestine Solidarity Campaign, recalled that "World Pride host and television presenter, Gok
Wan, tweeted [a photo] from the stage to his 990,000 followers show[ing] Palestinian flags and the Palestine Solidarity Campaign banner waving prominently in the crowd."[2] The video that went viral was produced by queer Palestinian solidarity activists in London and featured a link to their website,
www.nopinkwashing.org.uk/. Set to the song "We Found Love" by Rihanna,
the video depicted their pageantry, signs, and slogans at London Pride, where
they chanted refrains such as "Stop Pinkwashing!" and "No Pride in Israeli
Apartheid!"[3]

According to queer studies scholar Natalie Kouri-Towe, the year 2012 was
critical for the momentum of the global queer Palestinian solidarity movement because of the World Social Forum (WSF) in Porto Alegre, Brazil. The
World Social Forum is an annual conference bringing together tens of thousands of representatives from global civil society to collectively envision a

counterhegemonic future for globalization. That year, the theme of the conference was "Free Palestine," and it featured Palestinian solidarity activists and organizations from around the world. Queer solidarity activists planned a Queer Visions component focusing on transnational initiatives to combat Israeli pinkwashing.[4] At the WSF General Assembly, activists pushed for the adoption of pinkwatching activism as a priority to broaden international engagement on Palestine.[5]

The activism that year in Britain and Brazil are examples that reveal the global reach of queer Palestinian solidarity. Once queer Palestinians began organizing in Palestine, diaspora Palestinians and their allies around the world joined them in giving international voice to queer Palestinian demands. As I demonstrated in the previous chapter, the transnational reach of the movement was catalyzed by local responses to Israeli pinkwashing efforts on multiple continents and the rise of a shared pinkwatching discourse. In this chapter, I explore the discourse and practice of boycotts in this transnational activism.

Underlying the development of pinkwatching was the emergence of boycotts as a primary strategy of the queer Palestinian movement. In addition to the Pinkwatching Israel initiative, LGBTQ Palestinians launched the Palestinian Queers for Boycott, Divestment, and Sanctions (PQBDS) collective in 2011. PQBDS became the queer branch of the global BDS movement, which was a response to the 2005 Palestinian civil society call to boycott and divest from institutions and initiatives complicit with the Israeli occupation. The three demands of the BDS movement are an end to the Israeli occupation of the West Bank and Gaza Strip, equal rights for Palestinian citizens of Israel, and the right of return for Palestinian refugees. Boycotts have become the major tool and mode for engaging with Palestine solidarity globally, including in many LGBTQ communities. The formal endorsement of BDS by the queer Palestinian movement has provided LGBTQ Palestinians with a seat at the Palestinian civil society table, thereby challenging Palestinian homophobia and altering perceptions of queer Palestinians within Palestinian society. It has helped transform the image of queer Palestinians from suspect subjects into nationalist subjects deeply embedded in the Palestinian struggle for freedom.

But many queer Israeli solidarity activists are also passionate about supporting Israel. The two opposed camps intersect globally in the context of campaigns that engage international audiences on the relationship between queerness and Israel/Palestine. While queer Zionist organizers object to the term *pinkwashing* as a description of their work, queer Palestinian solidarity activists insist on the label and call on allies to boycott pinkwashing initiatives. Pride parades are critical sites of contestation, with activists having confronted one another at parades in Tel Aviv, Jerusalem, Toronto, Madrid, Berlin, New York, and other cities around the world. Tel Aviv Pride has emerged as the central tourism pillar that undergirds pinkwashing campaigns. In addition, the conflict plays out at global meetings, conferences, and forums. The link between queerness and Israel/Palestine has been intensely debated at sites such as the US Social Forum in Detroit, the GALEI queer Latinx organization in Philadelphia, the Brown University and Ohio State University Hillels, the University of Pennsylvania, the Creating Change conference in Chicago, and a range of other activist, queer, and Jewish venues. Efforts to boycott pinkwashing events as well as counterefforts to boycott the boycotters have become part and parcel of the queer activist landscape.

The first section of this chapter traces how the conflict over boycotts maps onto successive Tel Aviv Pride parades. It examines queer Palestinian calls to boycott Tel Aviv Pride, decisions to participate in the parade by queer antioccupation activists, and the emergence of resistance to the Israeli state by mainstream LGBTQ organizations in Israel. The chapter then focuses on two cities that emerged as early epicenters of the pinkwatching and boycott debates—Seattle and New York—highlighting the victories as well as the challenges encountered by queer Palestinian activists and queer non-Palestinian solidarity activists in these cities. The next section examines the politics of boundary policing as they played out on multiple fronts. I further delineate the phenomenon of radical purism and its public critiques of integral movement participants. This chapter then turns to a critical moment in the summer of 2017, when conflict between pinkwashers and pinkwatchers came to a head and surged into the national media spotlight. In particular, it addresses the events that unfolded at the Celebrate Israel Parade in New York, the Chicago Dyke March, and SlutWalk Chicago. Finally, this chapter demonstrates that we have been equipped by social theory and peace and conflict studies with conceptual tools to transcend the present impasse of queer Palestinian transnational activism.

On Heteroglossia and Conflict Transformation

My analysis is informed by the work of political theorist and activist Andrew Robinson, who in turn draws on the work of the philosopher Mikhail

Bakhtin. The ongoing conflict between queer Palestinian solidarity activists and queer pro-Israel advocates reflects elements of what Bakhtin has termed *monoglossia*. In calling for resistance to this tendency, I turn to Robinson's formulations of *heteroglossia* and *dialogism* as tools for imagining alternative trajectories for queer activism regarding Israel/Palestine. In addition, I draw on John Paul Lederach's notion of conflict transformation to consider how the impasse between pinkwashing and pinkwatching might be transcended.

Bakhtin argues that *monoglossia* is present whenever we observe the "dominance of a single ethical world-view over a much more complex reality, to the exclusion of living historical forces."[6] Bakhtin developed this concept in the context of literature and language, but it is no less applicable to the study of social phenomena. Adapting Bakhtin, Andrew Robinson identifies *monologism* and its opposite, *dialogism*, as they play out in activism and everyday life. He writes, "From the often arbitrary moderation of web forums to informal hierarchies in activism, there seems to be a plague of monologisms in the modern world, often reinforced by mutually exclusive categories and roles, conventional expectations of authority, and an emphasis on efficiency and 'getting things done.'"[7] On Robinson's reading, Bakhtin calls for the "rupture" of "monoglossical dominance" in favor of *heteroglossia*—interruption "by other voices." It is imperative that we see the world from other perspectives and that we remain open to contesting, discussing, and even changing our views and incorporating those of the other. Heteroglossia introduces nuance to our "social values, world-views and intentionalities" and enables us to communicate effectively beyond our particular "speech-genre" and "across different groups of activists, or between activists and non-activists."[8]

Lest we draw the wrong conclusions, Robinson clarifies that

> Bakhtin's vision is not one of an empty juxtaposition of opinions, or a flattening-out of discourse so that all perspectives are equivalent. Different perspectives are not partial, complementary truths. Rather, the dynamic interplay and interruption of perspectives is taken to produce new realities and new ways of seeing. It is incommensurability which gives dialogue its power.[9]

To interrupt the monologues of actors who would foreclose on the possibilities of dialogism, writes Robinson, is an "insurrectionary act." The encounter with the other can and should have "self-altering, or even self-destroying, effects."[10] Modifying the self-understanding of those who refuse to acknowledge Palestinian humanity is a major objective of the queer Palestinian solidarity movement. I contend that we must resist the monologism that radical purism seeks to impose against engagement with the other.

Peacebuilding scholar John Paul Lederach also argues that "a capacity to understand and sustain dialogue" is "a fundamental means of constructive change" when it comes to transforming conflict.[11] Transformation, in Lederach's view, extends well beyond mere resolution, beyond simply removing "something not desired." Rather, it means building something desired and moving from a "content-centered" approach to a "relationship-centered" one, from addressing the current problem in its immediacy to promoting "constructive change processes" and "engaging the systems with[in] which relationships are embedded." Real transformation requires thinking beyond the short term and adopting a "mid-to-long range" horizon, one in which conflict is conceptualized "as a dynamic of ebb (conflict de-escalation to pursue constructive change) and flow (conflict escalation to pursue constructive change)."[12] At each turn, Lederach urges us to transcend the conflict resolution formulas so often bandied about and instead to imagine how human connections, cultures, and social structures can be radically and durably transformed.

Tel Aviv Pride

Two trans women (or drag queens) in flowing dresses walk alongside a camel, steering it as they go. They arrive at the Mediterranean coast, in Tel Aviv, where they find gay men in Speedos. Standing on either side of a muscular gay Israeli wearing an unbuttoned shirt and sunglasses, the two begin to dance as a troupe of male backup dancers, including the men in Speedos, suddenly materializes. The Israeli hunk looks on approvingly. The two individuals in beautiful dresses return to him, flirting with him ostentatiously, and just when it appears that they are going to kiss him, they kiss each other instead, ignoring the befuddled muscle man and skipping away to join two white, apparently European women doing yoga along the Mediterranean.

Set to Mizrahi music, these scenes feature in an online video promoting the Arisa gay dance party, a cultural celebration of Jewish Israelis from the Middle East/North Africa region. The video concludes with the logo of the official Israeli government website (www.tel-aviv.gov.il) advertising 2013's Tel Aviv's Pride. The muscle man in the video is gay Israeli model Eliad Cohen, the country's most visible spokesperson for queer tourism. Cohen is known for appearing shirtless, displaying his chest hair, and wearing a necklace with the Hebrew word *chai* ("life"), a symbol that the pro-Israel LGBTQ group A Wider Bridge describes as "a sign of [Cohen's] pride in Israel."[13] As one of the most prominent gay Israeli entrepreneurs, he leverages his international fame to promote parties such as Arisa and other events associated with Tel Aviv Pride. On its website, A Wider Bridge underscores Cohen's three years of service "in an elite combat unit"[14] in the Israeli military.[15]

The message of the Arisa advertisement video and others like it is clear. The images therein—the Mizrahi music in Hebrew with some Arabic words and beats; the European women; the dark-skinned and light-skinned Israeli men—portray Israel as a unique gay tourism spot in which East meets West. The camel alongside the yoga, the effeminate alongside the hypermasculine, the Mediterranean, the tall buildings, the blue sky—they all signal that Tel Aviv has everything to offer the gay tourist. Such messages and the reinforcement they receive in the international Western press have succeeded in branding Tel Aviv a gay hub and boosting the city's gay tourism industry.[16] The Municipality of Tel Aviv reports that two hundred thousand people attended the 2016 gay pride festivities in the city.[17]

Local governments and Israeli state institutions regularly collaborate with private sector advocates of gay tourism. For instance, in 2010, the Tel Aviv tourism board launched a $90 million campaign to brand the city as "an international gay vacation destination."[18] The following year, the Israeli Ministry of Foreign Affairs participated in Berlin's International Tourism Fair with an exhibit called "Tel Aviv Gay Vibe" geared toward promoting gay tourism. (Palestinian solidarity activists protested the display.) Supporters of gay tourism in Israel employ other playful marketing techniques, such as distributing novelty condoms at international gay events with the Israeli flag and the words "Israel, It's Still Safe to Come" emblazoned on the wrappers. Other strategies include pushing stories about Tel Aviv as a gay city in the global press and producing promotional videos for gay events that target an international gay clientele.

Needless to say, the queer Palestinian solidarity movement views such activities as pinkwashing. This view rests on the well-founded assumption that the Israeli government invests resources to promote Israel as a gay haven not only because of the economic benefits of tourism but also to project a positive image of Israel intended to elide the state's violations of Palestinian human rights. When gay tourists arrive in Tel Aviv, they often remain within gay bubbles, interface with Israelis in privileged spaces, and remain oblivious to the realities only miles away in the Gaza Strip, in the West Bank, and even in Palestinian enclaves within Israel. Enthusiasts of Israel's gay scene then return to their respective Western countries to further propagate the erasure of the Palestinian voices, bodies, and experiences. As Tel Aviv city councilman Yaniv Weizman remarked, "Every foreign tourist turns into an ambassador, and gay tourists to Tel Aviv often come back."[19]

The debates over pinkwashing were made visible to tourists and supporters of Israel at the June 2012 Tel Aviv Pride parade. On June 11, the Israel Defense Forces' (IDF) Facebook page published an image of two soldiers holding hands with the caption, "It's Pride Month. Did you know that the IDF treats all of its soldiers equally? Let's see how many shares you can get for this photo."[20] The image went viral, with popular websites such as Gawker reposting it (unironically) and touting the IDF's gay rights record.[21] The *Times of Israel* later reported that the photo of the "gay soldiers" was "staged" and is "misleading" since the soldiers in the image "are not a couple," "only one is gay," and both served in the IDF spokesperson's office.[22] Activists in the queer Palestinian solidarity movement highlighted this as an example of pinkwashing, arguing that queerness was being cynically exploited to promote sympathy for Israel and to divert attention from the fact that the IDF imposes a military occupation on millions of Palestinians. The merging of militarism and queerness has become an aspect of the marketing of Tel Aviv Pride.

Alongside campaigns aimed at pressuring internationals to boycott Tel Aviv Pride and related events, Palestine solidarity activists have launched a number of reactive mobilizations against the initiatives and partnerships of queer pro-Israel organizing. In 2009, StandWithUs, an American pro-Israel advocacy organization, created iPride, an initiative to bring prominent LGBTQ Americans and Europeans to Israel for a five-day seminar on sexuality in conjunction with Tel Aviv Pride. The trip included meetings with Israeli politicians, military officials, filmmakers, and others, ostensibly to learn about the LGBTQ community in Israel. Noa Meir, the coordinator of iPride, bluntly stated, "We decided to improve Israel's image through the gay community in Israel; we found that the issue is not familiar around the world."[23] In response, queer Palestinian solidarity activists circulated an image by artist Michael Levin of a mock iPride flyer that read, "Don't ask, Don't tell about the Nakba?"[24] The image drew attention to what activists felt iPride was designed to conceal:

Even the expansive expenditures of Israeli public relations campaigns—like those organized by "Stand With Us"—cannot obscure the fact that the cost of establishing the state of Israel was the dispossession of another people from their land. This Nakba [catastrophe] continues, as the state of Israel even now engages in ethnic cleansing and population transfer, violates international law, inflicts disastrous collective punishment on the civilian population of Gaza, and continues to deny to Palestinians their human rights and national aspirations.

Still, this creative response failed to completely undermine the iPride initiative.

That year saw other high-profile pinkwashing initiatives, such as the Israeli government's decision to sponsor a gay Olympics delegation in order "to help show to the world Israel's liberal and diverse face."[25] In October, the International Gay and Lesbian Travel Association (IGLTA) held a conference in Tel Aviv "with the goal of promoting Israel as a 'world gay destination.'"[26] Queer Palestinian solidarity groups protested both events. Helem, an LGBTQ organization in Lebanon, called for a boycott, noting that Israel "has built walls, blockades, and systems of racist segregations to hide from the Palestinians it oppresses. . . . Leisure tourism to apartheid Israel supports this regime. It is not neutral, and it certainly is not a step toward real peace, which can only be based on justice."[27] Four other groups issued a joint letter in support of Helem's boycott: Queers Against Israeli Apartheid (QAIA) Toronto, Queers Undermining Israeli Terrorism (QUIT), the International Jewish Anti-Zionist Network, and a group of queer Israeli BDS activists from within Israel. Their statement called on "LGBTQI people and friends around the world to join us in our protest against IGLTA's promotion of leisure tourism to apartheid Israel. We demand that IGLTA cancel its planned conference in Israel and cease any promotion of tourism to this country."[28] As with iPride, the protests did not put a halt to the IGLTA's gay tourism event in Israel.

The queer Palestinian solidarity movement was finally able to claim a victory in 2009 when it convinced Sarah Schulman to refuse an invitation to speak at Tel Aviv University. Schulman chose to honor the Palestinian boycott call and heeded the advice of queer Israeli activist Dalit Baum, who suggested she instead undertake a solidarity trip to Israel/Palestine to meet with queer Palestinians and their Israeli allies. Inspired by her visit, Schulman then organized Al-Tour, a six-city speaking tour of the United States, for three of the queer Palestinian activists she met: Ghadir Shafie, Haneen Maikey, and "Sami."[29] In February 2011, the activists spoke at LGBTQ community centers, conferences, and universities across the country, attracting over a thousand attendees. Schulman's strategy was to partner with high-profile queer American figures who could help promote the Palestinian speakers. For instance, Judith Butler, the renowned queer theorist, did just that as a Jewish anti-Zionist and outspoken BDS proponent. She has been among the most recognizable supporters of the global queer Palestinian solidarity movement. Al-Tour amplified the voices of queer Palestinians in a profound way,[30] and Schulman is now well-known for her joke encouraging fellow queer solidarity activists to spell out the BDS acronym, "boycott/divestment/sanctions," so that it will not be confused with BDSM, or "bondage/domination/submission."[31] By catalyzing transnational linkages between Palestine and the United States, Schulman's activism has helped expand the global queer Palestinian solidarity network.

In 2011, Palestinian Queers for Boycott, Divestment, and Sanctions (PQBDS) emerged on the global scene, partly as a result of its IGLYO Out of Israel campaign. The International Gay and Lesbian Youth Organization (IGLYO) had decided to hold its general assembly in Tel Aviv that year. In June, PQBDS began lobbying the organizers to reject Israeli governmental support for this event and to choose an alternative location. The campaign had mixed results. On one hand, in July, IGLYO decided to cancel the general assembly, a move that PQBDS applauded. The transnational reach of the queer Palestinian solidarity movement became clear when groups such as the International Gay and Lesbian Cultural Network and specific IGLYO member organizations (including those in the United Kingdom, Ireland, Lebanon, and Turkey) expressed support for the boycott. On the other hand, IGLYO's official statement announcing its decision to cancel made no reference to Palestine, mentioning only "recent legal decisions in Israel." The group also encouraged its member organizations to participate in the International LGBTQ Youth Leadership Summit slated for later that year in Tel Aviv, an event organized by Israel Gay Youth, one of IGLYO's organizational partners. Al-Qaws and PQBDS condemned the decision,[32] but Israel Gay Youth proceeded with its Tel Aviv summit, whose stated purpose was to train "the next generation of leaders of the international LGBTQ community for social activism."[33] Solidarity activists lamented this as a form of pinkwashing but were heartened by the cancellation of the original IGLYO event, the outpouring of solidarity from IGLYO member organizations, and their overall success in raising consciousness around BDS and queer Palestinian activism.

Tel Aviv continues to loom large in the global LGBTQ imaginary. In June 2017, tourists arrived in Tel Aviv for that year's pride parade. At the same time, some fifteen thousand internationals were attending the International Defense and HLS Expo (ISDEF) at the Tel Aviv convention center. ISDEF describes itself as "the largest defense and security exhibition ever held in Israel."[34] According to journalist Tanya Rubenstein, "Throughout the exhibition, Israel [sells] its technological developments to foreign countries, including those under arms embargoes for violating human rights."[35] She adds,

> It's no accident that Israel is one of the world's biggest military exporters. The territories and people under Israeli occupation enable the military to develop, test out and perfect new technologies on the battlefield. As a result, Israel can compete with world powers in the global arms trade, and is prepared to sell its wares to the highest bidder—no matter the human rights situation in the purchasing country.[36]

For queer Palestinian solidarity activists, the intersection of Israeli militarism, LGBTQ pride celebrations, international tourism, and the erasure of Palestinian suffering is the hallmark of pinkwashing.

In response to the previous year's Tel Aviv Pride advertisements, activists from Pinkwatching Israel called for a boycott of the parade and released a number of videos highlighting the pinkwashing dynamics at play. One was a spoof of the official Israeli advertisement from 2016,[37] which had set images of Tel Aviv, belly dancers, tattoos, and lesbian sensuality to Aerosmith's "Pink." Pinkwatching Israel's subsequent version featured the same music and aesthetic but replaced Tel Aviv and gay revelry with images of checkpoints, soldiers, settlers, and the IDF's bombardment of Palestinian homes. Under the signature of "Israeli queers against occupation," a title at the end of the video reads "You can't wash away the OCCUPATION" in both Hebrew and English.[38] In the leftist Israeli online magazine +972, Fady Khoury, a queer lawyer and Palestinian citizen of Israel, lamented that "there is no room for Palestinians at [the 2016] Tel Aviv Pride Parade"[39] due to the refusal of mainstream Israeli LGBTQ organizations to integrate Palestinian rights into their platforms as well as their willingness to be co-opted by state-sponsored pinkwashing efforts. Khoury had likewise boycotted the 2015 parade, citing Israel's "attempt to divert the discussion away from the violation of Palestinian human rights, and toward the relative freedom enjoyed by (Jewish) sexual minorities in Israel."[40]

Queer Israeli Pinkwatching Activism

From the very beginning of the LGBTQ movement in Palestine, a small group of queer Israelis, based primarily in Tel Aviv, have continuously protested the occupation and exhibited solidarity with Palestinians. Their mother organization is Black Laundry, a queer antioccupation group cofounded by queer Israeli activist Dalit Baum. Since at least 2002, their supporters, sometimes 250 demonstrators strong, have been showing up to protest Tel Aviv Pride.[41] In recent years, queer Israelis in the Palestinian solidarity movement have unfurled banners and painted graffiti around Tel Aviv bearing antioccupation slogans in both Hebrew and English, hoping to reach queer Israelis, gay tourists, and (via photography and social media) other international audiences. Yael Marom, a supporter of these efforts, writes that her Israeli LBGTQ community "must not remain silent. It must not be used as fig leaf to maintain Israel's image of normalcy, while in our name people are being blackmailed over their sexual orientation, while we live in a situation that is anything but 'normal.'"[42]

At Tel Aviv Pride in 2013, activists from the queer Israeli group Mashpritzot painted themselves pink[43] and staged a die-in amid the paradegoers, later releasing a video of the action in which they articulate their opposition to pinkwashing and call for an end to the occupation.[44] In 2015, Israeli journalist Shai Zamir argued in the Hebrew-language *Yedioth Ahronoth* that the annual pride spectacles in Tel Aviv were more for domestic than foreign consumption.

> In English, they call it pinkwashing—the methodical concealment of violations of human rights through the exploitation of pink "fuck me" underwear, which the hunks on floats wear. But the well-funded campaign by the Tel Aviv municipality and the foreign ministry to present a tolerant, gay-friendly Israel isn't meant for outsiders as is generally believed. First and foremost it's directed internally toward Israelis who like to think of themselves as a sort of burbling brook of democracy in the midst of the primitive dark eastern savannah. . . . The relative tolerance the gay community enjoys lives on borrowed time, because it isn't founded on a genuine belief in equality, but on a superficial claim of acceptance of the Other. Gays and lesbians must know that Israeli society exploits them in order to maintain the semblance of a free society in a nation for which millions of Palestinians have no importance. A nation which charges anyone who dares to speak of human rights in the Ter-

ritories as an anti-Semite. The real truth is that anyone who doesn't love Arabs can't love gays. And those who don't really love gays should stop pretending.[45]

Zamir's indictment of pinkwashing reflects the small but increasing number of LGBTQ Israelis who are challenging their own relationship to the state and recognizing the interest in equality they share with Palestinians. Such progressive queer Israelis experience agony as they confront militarization, homophobia, and the appropriation of their struggle and their bodies by the same state that renders their lives precarious.

Queer Palestinian solidarity activists, for their part, attempt to center the conversation around the complicity of mainstream LGBTQ Israelis with the state and its occupation. Pinkwatching activists emphasize the precarious lives of all Palestinians, both queer and straight, who on average face far greater tribulations than do queer Israelis. Although acts of resistance by leftist Israeli radicals are uplifting, queer Palestinians often wonder how mainstream queer Israelis can envision freedom for themselves without freedom for their queer Palestinian counterparts. A true queer agenda—more expansive than an LGBT one—must account for all queer bodies in Israel/Palestine, whether Jewish Israeli or Palestinian Christian or Muslim. The absence of such an agenda renders LGBTQ Israeli actors vulnerable to the charge of pinkwashing, which is simultaneously propaganda, ideology, and practice. The queer Palestinian movement is still grappling with how to integrate queer Israelis into the struggle against ethnoheteronormativity.

The seeds of pinkwatching resistance have been growing among Jewish Israelis, although less out of concern for Palestinians than for Israel's queer community itself. In 2016, a political earthquake ensued when gay Israeli activists called for the cancellation of that year's Tel Aviv Pride parade. They cited the Ministry of Tourism's decision to invest $2.9 million to market the parade to gay tourists and fly them to Israel in a rainbow-colored jet (literally). The $2.9 million figure was ten times the combined annual budgets for all LGBTQ organizations in Israel, underscoring the state's inadequate financial support for these groups.[46] Israel's National LGBT Task Force expressed opposition to what had been an implicit arrangement up until that point, which was that "the government supports the LGBTQ community as long as it stays in Tel Aviv and makes itself colorful and pretty in marches on an international stage and allows itself to be used."[47] But LGBTQ Israelis had recently grown frustrated at the repeated failure of legislation aimed at ensuring their equal treatment. For instance, in June 2015, the Israeli newspaper *Haaretz* reported that Israel's cabinet rejected a sexual orientation nondiscrimination bill, despite the fact that "many of the ministers who voted against the bill are on record as supporting the LGBT community and some [had] even attended the Gay Pride parade in Tel Aviv" a week earlier.[48] Aeyal Gross observed that Netanyahu's government had "done close to nothing to end legal discrimination against the LGBT community. Behind the pinkwashing, and alongside the many LGBT-rights achievements made by members of the community and court rulings, it turns out that homophobia in its worst forms exists within the Israeli government."[49]

In February of the following year, outrage erupted as protestors from the LGBTQ Israeli community confronted the Israeli Parliament (Knesset). Just one day after the Knesset's first LGBT Rights Day, lawmakers voted down legislation aimed at codifying LGBTQ rights in Israel. Named in memory of Shira Banki, the sixteen-year-old girl who was stabbed to death by an Israeli extremist at the Jerusalem Pride parade earlier that year, the "Banki Bills" included "government recognition of civil unions, a ban on so-called ex-gay or conversion therapy of minors, and a [requirement that] medical students study sexual orientation."[50] One openly gay Knesset member from the right-wing Likud party spoke passionately in defense of the LGBTQ population, saying, "They cannot get married in their country, bring children into the world in their country, be their partners' heir if he or she dies, and not because they are hostile to the state, do not serve in the army or pay taxes, rather, because they are gay or lesbian."[51] He even compared the struggles of LGBTQ citizens to the historic persecution of European Jews.[52] A day earlier, Benjamin Netanyahu had appeared in the Knesset to express his own support, affirming that "every man was created in the image of God."[53] Nonetheless, the government rejected all five bills promising equal rights for LGBTQ Israelis.

The rejection spawned protests, with Israel's largest queer organizations threatening to boycott the upcoming pride parade and hold demonstrations instead. Journalist Yael Marom interpreted the outrage as "a sign that we, the LGBTQ community, are finally realizing our strength. . . . We're starting to understand that we deserve more than being used as enlightened fig leafs [sic]. It is time to stop dancing to the tune of hasbara [pro-Israel propaganda]."[54] Recent reports had documented a surge of homophobic incidents in Israel, and Marom condemned the hypocrisy of the government's pinkwashing efforts.

It is about time that the state stop using us as a public relations tool to cover up what is really happening here: racism, hate crimes, violence, occupation, segregation and separation, intolerable economic gaps, the discrimination and marginalization of various groups in our society. It's time the state stops using us as a liberal, pink cloak to sell Israel to the world as something diametrically different than what it is. As much as we might want to think we're on our way there, we are not a tolerant, open or liberal society.[55]

In the run-up to the 2016 Tel Aviv Pride event, the Israel National LGBT Task Force successfully negotiated with the Israeli government to direct more funds into local LGBTQ organizations. Many queer Israeli activists considered this a significant victory, particularly because the Task Force, the largest LGBTQ association in Israel, had long been criticized for being apolitical and assimilationist. Israel's mainstream LGBTQ community then proceeded with Pride as usual, marching alongside queer tourists from around the world.

It does not detract from the major thrust of pinkwatching activism to acknowledge that the Israeli state reifies homophobia in certain domains and simultaneously creates conditions that enable gay Israelis to challenge homophobia in other domains. It is exactly because the state is so invested in pinkwashing that it agreed to provide the Israeli LGBTQ community with increased resources for its pressing advocacy work. The Knesset's rejection of LGBTQ civil rights reflects the conservative, religious base of Israel's governing parties. At the same time, the state's pinkwashing-based concessions to LGBTQ organizations helps raise consciousness in the fight against homophobia and for queer rights. The state both buttresses and undermines homophobia simultaneously, and the more Israel fashions itself as a gay haven and invests in that self-image, the more opportunities queer Israeli activists will have to point out the discrepancies between image and reality and to call for action toward bridging those gaps.

Palestinian solidarity activists often perceive little or no benefit in queer Israeli organizing. Many queer Palestinians view pinkwashing as only further entrenching the oppressive structures under which they live. But it is possible to imagine the eventual merging of the struggles for queer and Palestinian human rights in a way that could catalyze decolonization in Israel/Palestine—and perhaps it is precisely such a vision that Israelis and Palestinians need to help move them beyond the current impasse. Efforts like the June 2017 "Declaration: LGBTQs against the Occupation" represent an inspiring step within Israel in this direction. The document, signed by fifty LGBTQ activists and NGO workers in solidarity with Palestinian human rights and in opposition to pinkwashing, ends with a call to fellow LGBTQ Israelis: "Our safety and security cannot depend on the trampling of others' security. We are here to stay, and we will continue to tell our community: End the occupation, end the repression and end the discrimination. We all deserve a better future."[56]

In asserting their demands for Tel Aviv Pride in 2016, Israeli queer activists managed to resist one major tool of pinkwashing: their appropriation by the Israeli state for global propaganda purposes. But another dimension of pinkwashing—namely, the erasure of Palestinians—persisted. I hope to see a future in which the mainstream LGBTQ movement in Israel integrates resistance to all pillars of pinkwashing into its activism, including reversing complicity in the erasure of Palestinians. In the meantime, I also aspire to a future in which the LGBTQ Palestinian movement could combine struggles with LGBTQ Israelis. Even as we recognize the tremendous asymmetry in power between these movements—movements whose separateness reflects the broader segregation imposed by Israel on Israelis and Palestinians—we can also affirm that queer liberation in Israel/Palestine will be fully realized when anticolonial solidarity between queer Israelis and Palestinians is achieved. The fact that Israelis and Palestinians are not there yet is not an argument for the inevitably or the intractability of the present. The voices of progressive queer Israelis work in concert with those of pinkwashing's victims to puncture the durability of the pinkwashing enterprise. It is essential that we, academics and activists alike, distinguish between the state and nonstate actors involved with pinkwashing as well as between its perpetrators and victims. Such an analysis might be challenging, but it is essential.

Even though this section has focused on Tel Aviv Pride, I must emphasize that my conception of queerness is considerably broader. In some contexts, queerness is reduced to specific symbols or slogans or categories, and those can be significant for the self-realization of many queer people. But other LGBTQ individuals may be indifferent or even alienated by those same slogans, and neither experience is more authentically queer than the other. Queerness encompasses the right to fetishize symbols as emancipatory or to celebrate, disavow, interrogate, or criticize those symbols. A queer political project, as I understand it, is one that creates spaces of possibility in which anyone who chooses to identify as LGBTQ is free to articulate their sexualities and shape their lives and relationships as they see fit as long as they do not cause harm to others. I recognize that individuals with a higher socioeconomic status are able to benefit from increased mobility, choice, and possibilities for queer self-expression and self-actualization. For many individuals, coming out is dangerous, and pride parades are the least of their concerns. For those who have the luxury to empower themselves and others, visibility is often critical, even though social movements also depend on politics beyond the public gaze. Enacting queerness when hegemonic symbols circulate transnationally can be an exercise fraught with political implications. This is particularly true in our imperialist world, but that does not diminish the profound importance of anti-imperialist queer solidarities across borders, a phenomenon exemplified by the global queer Palestinian solidarity movement.

Epicenters of Conflict

The American city of Seattle, Washington, has emerged as a major site of conflict between queer Palestinian solidarity activists and queer pro-Israel advocates. In 2012, Seattle pinkwatching activists waged a campaign in response to a regional speaking tour by a delegation from the Alliance of Israeli LGBT Education Organizations (AILO). Sponsored by StandWithUs in partnership with A Wider Bridge, the delegation included four LGBTQ Israeli leaders and activists: Irit Zviel-Efrat, Avner Dafni, Iris Sass-Kochavi, and Adir Steiner. These delegates represented three Israeli LGBTQ organizations—Hoshen (education and outreach), Israel Gay Youth, and Tehila (Israel's version of PFLAG)—and the Tel Aviv Municipality. In response to the initial call for the tour's cancellation on the grounds of pinkwashing, one of the delegation's meetings was moved to a synagogue in Olympia, and the Tacoma and Seattle meetings were cancelled. The Seattle LGBT Commission had planned to meet the delegation along with members of the Seattle City Council. According to StandWithUs, the purpose of the aborted meeting was for delegates "to share the innovative work they are doing in Israel, to learn from their counterparts in the US, and to build relationships for future collaboration."[57]

Dean Spade, a member of the first LGBTQ delegation to Palestine, worked with the Seattle chapter of Jewish Voice for Peace (JVP) and with queer Palestinian activists in the Seattle area to successfully lobby the Seattle LGBT Commission to cancel the event. In a letter to the commission, Spade wrote, "I would strongly urge you to reconsider hosting this event, recognizing its broader significance. It is part of a large, government-funded public-relations campaign to conceal apartheid and violence, which I trust the Commission does not mean to support."[58] In response, the commission wrote that it "values the comments of Dean Spade, who recently brought to our attention the concerns of the Israeli and Palestinian conflict and agenda of pinkwashing to cover up said crimes and corruption of the Israeli government."[59] Spade was invited to express his concerns at the commission's public comments section the following day, just twenty-four hours before the Israeli delegation meeting was scheduled to occur. He attended, along with queer Jewish and Palestinian activists who provided several hours of testimony.

According to one journalist, the JVP activists "cleared away the debris of anti-Semitism accusations," while the queer Palestinians "detailed the racist and violent effects of Israeli policy in their own lives, and the way that Pinkwashing has furthered that violence by invisibilizing their lives, identities, and communities."[60] Following a vote, the commission decided to cancel the event because it felt ill-equipped "to facilitate an event surrounding such complex topics."[61] Queer Palestinian solidarity activists considered the decision a significant victory. That very night at Seattle's Capitol Club, they organized a "party to celebrate the cancellation of the pinkwashing event."[62]

Unsurprisingly, the commission soon experienced tremendous pressure and criticism from pro-Israel institutions and sympathizers. Journalist Dan Avery noted that the Israeli speakers represented nongovernmental organizations and that they might have criticized Israel's policies in their remarks. He posed the question, "Are anti-pinkwashers like Spade now saying that all gays from Israel should be silenced in the public arena, lest they accidentally encourage someone to visit their homeland?"[63] He continued by saying, "If the Seattle event *hadn't* been canceled, someone could have legitimately asked these groups if their message wasn't compromised because they received funding from pro-Israel sources to travel here."[64] Responding to the charge of pinkwashing, A Wider Bridge doubled down. StandWithUs accused the commission of discriminating against the delegates "simply because they are Israeli."[65]

Queer Palestinian activists responded by drawing attention to the fact that one of the delegation's speakers, Iris Sass-Kochavi, was "living in the illegal settlement of Mitzpe Shalem. In fact, she serves in the Megilot Dead Sea Regional Council, which pursues the interests of the bloc of illegal settlements situated near the Dead Sea."[66] Sass-Kochavi was also identified as the former board director of Ahava Dead Sea Laboratories, a cosmetics company that relies on the illegal extraction of Palestinian natural resources from the West Bank. And Jewish Voice for Peace responded to the charge that they were discriminating against Israelis based solely on their country of origin. In a press release, the JVP Seattle chapter wrote,

> We are not against dialogue, and would be happy to hear stories from Israeli LGBT activists, were they not funded by the Israeli government and Stand With Us. . . . Any true dialogue on queer issues in the Middle East has to address the Occupation and include queer Palestinian voices.[67]

Stefanie Fox, JVP's director of grassroots organizing, wrote in the *Seattle Times* that the Seattle LGBT Commission "was right to cancel the reception for visiting Israeli gay leaders." Identifying herself as "a Seattle citizen who is queer and Jewish," Fox pointed out StandWithUs's "ongoing alliance with the virulently homophobic pastor John Hagee and his group Christians United for Israel (CUFI)." Hagee, she noted, "infamously argued that 'Hurricane Katrina was, in fact, the judgment of God against the city of New Orleans,' because 'there was to be a homosexual parade there on the Monday that Katrina came.' He also claimed the anti-Christ was 'a homosexual.'"[68]

Nonetheless, criticism of the Seattle LGBT Commission continued pouring in. The Jewish Federation of Seattle issued its own press release, expressing disappointment and writing, "By choosing to cancel their planned event with LGBTQ activists from Israel, the LGBTQ Commission gave into pressure from a small, but loud community of activists."[69] Future Seattle mayor Ed Murray, then a state senator, accused the commission of undermining Jewish-LGBTQ relations. "I personally met with the Alliance of Israeli LGBTQ Educational Organizations during their visit to Olympia," Murray noted. "These are people who are moving rights for gays and lesbians forward, people like Adir Steiner, whose work led the Israeli military to recognize committed same-sex relationships as equal to the marriages of straight couples." Murray was not the only official to circumvent the boycott. The *Seattle Times* reported that "Councilmembers Sally Bagshaw and Jean Godden and City Attorney Pete Holmes arranged a hurried, lunchtime meeting with the delegates and apologized for the snub."[70]

In the end, the LGBT Commission officially apologized to all parties, writing,

> Our intent to vote to cancel the meeting was not to make a stand for either side, but to recognize that we could not facilitate a neutral space for dialog

and learning and keep the conversation focused on LGBTQ issues versus the larger issues of the Israeli-Palestinian relationship. . . . We also have heard from many who celebrate the cancellation of this event. We flatly reject the suggestion that there could be any joy or celebration in this outcome.[71]

Although events did not unfold as the queer Palestinian solidarity activists in Seattle had hoped, they produced a film to chronicle and document this experience. Titled *Pinkwashing Exposed: Seattle Fights Back*, the film has become a major resource for queer Palestinian solidarity activists in the United States.[72]

Three years after the initial controversy, Ed Murray, who had since become mayor of Seattle, traveled to Israel "to march in Tel Aviv's Gay Pride parade, meet Israeli political and military officials, and give a keynote at a conference celebrating Israel's LGBTQ rights record."[73] His trip received logistical and financial support from the Israeli Ministry of Foreign Affairs and A Wider Bridge, but Murray came under fire when it was revealed that his pinkwashing junket cost Seattle taxpayers $36,000.[74] Queer Palestinian solidarity activists highlighted the double standard inherent in Murray's support for a boycott of the US state of Indiana after it passed anti-LGBTQ legislation while openly flouting the Palestinian call for BDS. QAIA Seattle described Murray's trip as an attempt "to gain sympathy for Israel, covering up human rights abuses in the Palestinian territories."[75] Murray held fast, "respectfully" disagreeing with the protestors and declaring it "an honor to speak"[76] in Israel. When pro-Israel advocates pointed to Murray's planned meeting with two Palestinians in Ramallah, journalist Alex Shams excoriated the idea that "participation in a multi-day trip coordinated by the Israeli government with the support of pro-Israeli advocacy groups and including meetings with Israeli military officials can be 'balanced out' by a few hours in the West Bank."[77]

The spotlight was again on Seattle in April 2017 when the Seattle LGBT Commission decided to host Lt. Shachar Erez, the first trans officer in the Israeli military, who was on yet another speaking tour sponsored by StandWithUs (in the time since the 2012 tour, press reports revealed that StandWithUs received more than $1 million from the Israeli prime minister's office).[78] Dean Spade reprised his earlier letter to the commission, and queer solidarity activists once again mobilized. Two commissioners resigned in protest of the event, calling it "an act of pinkwashing."[79] One of them, Luzviminda Uzuri Carpenter, wrote, "We all have issues that we stand for and for me I stand for the boycott, divest and sanctions movement. For me, it is an is-sue similar to South Africa apartheid." She added, "I personally stand against the genocide of Palestinian people and cannot support militarized efforts or military personnel regardless of gender identity, gender expression, or sexual-ity or other identity markers."[80] The *Forward* wrote that "Erez rejects the no-tion that the IDF, which features his story on its website, is using him in order to deflect criticism about the military's treatment of Palestinians."[81] Erez also denied the charge of pinkwashing, saying, "Israel is progressive about LGBT rights and it has nothing to do with the Israeli-Palestinian situation."[82]

The recurring conflicts in Seattle reveal the fundamentally divergent frames of reference that many queer Zionists and anti-Zionists bring to the ta-ble. Pro-Israel advocates routinely interpret advocacy for Palestinian human rights as anti-Semitism, accusing queer solidarity activists of singling out Is-rael, justifying Palestinian violence, and tolerating various forms of authori-tarianism and oppression. Queer Palestinian activists, conversely, identify in the rhetoric of pro-Israel advocates a form of anti-Semitism directed against Jews who exhibit solidarity with Palestinians. Many queer Jewish anti-Zionist activists in the queer Palestinian solidarity movement have shared with me that they have experienced anti-Semitism from Zionist-leaning Jewish indi-viduals. This is because these Jewish pro-Palestine activists face attacks from the right and the center as Jews merely because their leftist views do not con-form to a set of preconceived notions about Jewish people being monolithic in their politics.

The Palestinian solidarity activists accuse the Israeli solidarity activ-ists of support for Israel's occupation, complicity in pinkwashing, and per-vasive anti-Arab racism and Islamophobia. The activists who speak out for each of these two political camps are frequently the loudest, most passion-ate, and most polarizing voices representing their respective causes. Nonethe-less, we must resist false equivalences. What is at stake in the conflict between pro- and antipinkwashing activists is the very integrity of the international queer rights movement. If we are to uphold the intersectional character of the struggle for sexual liberation, we must protect the movement from being hi-jacked by pinkwashing initiatives that seek to secure one group's freedom at the expense of another's.

The conflicts that unfolded in Seattle are similar to forms of contestation in other American cities, particularly in New York. In 2011, the struggle be-tween queer Zionists and anti-Zionists played out at the Lesbian, Gay, Bisexual & Transgender Community Center (LGBT center) in New York City. Siege Busters Working Group, a New York–based queer organization whose membership was half Jewish, was preparing to join an international flotilla to Gaza in hope of breaking Israel's multiyear siege of the impoverished seaside enclave. To that end, they had been renting space at the LGBT center, where they held regular organizing meetings. One member of Siege Busters, a Jewish American art student named Emily Henochowicz, later lost an eye when she was shot in the face by an Israeli soldier in Israel/Palestine as she peacefully protested the siege on Gaza. When Siege Busters planned to host a Party Against Apartheid fundraiser at the LGBT center, the center's leadership banned the party and announced that Siege Busters would no longer be permitted to use the space. Queer Palestinian solidarity groups protested outside the center and circulated a petition signed by queer activists.

It turned out that one of the instigators of the ban was pro-Israel gay porn star Michael Lucas, who had threateningly declared that he was "preparing to organize a boycott that would certainly involve some of the [LGBT] Center's most generous donors."[83] Lucas characterized Siege Busters and the broader Palestine solidarity movement as "anti-Semitic," alleging that they use "the pretext of support for Palestinians to stoke old anti-Semitic hatreds and perpetuate Jewish stereotypes."[84] Displaying his characteristic Islamophobia, he added, "They're also growing increasingly and aggressively pro-Islam."[85] Speaking at Stanford University a few years earlier, Lucas had declared, "I have a problem with people separating terrorists from the world that breeds them, from the world that originates them, which is the world of Islam."[86]

The petition circulated by pro-Palestine activists, which garnered the signatures of high-profile queer Jewish leftists such as Judith Butler and Sarah Schulman, protested the "attempt to manipulate hatred of anti-Semitism to draw attention away from the ongoing Israeli crimes of dispossession, systematic racism, collective punishment and wholesale warfare on a population guilty of nothing other than their own existence."[87] Citing Lucas's Islamophobia, many queer Palestinians, Arabs, and Muslims felt that the LGBT center was no longer a space in which they could engage their intersectional identities and experiences. When the center announced its cancelation of the Siege Busters event, Lucas sent out a celebratory email saying, "We prevailed! Congratulations to everyone who stood with me in support of Israel. With your help it only took eight hours to accomplish our mission."[88] Despite Lucas's explicit threat to organize a donor boycott of the LGBT center, he claimed in an interview that he "[had] no financial influence on the center. . . . If I [did], I would use it immediately. They use that stereotype a lot—the rich Zionist pornographer-mogul is shaking his checkbook."[89] At the same time, according to the interviewer, Lucas "failed to mention that his husband, the businessman Richard Winger, is the former president of the centre."[90]

Following the Siege Busters controversy, QAIA New York successfully rented space for three meetings at the LGBT center but was banned shortly after the first meeting. The center then introduced an "indefinite moratorium" on renting space to groups that organize around Israel/Palestine, complaining that it had been "forced to divert significant resources from its primary purpose of providing programming and services to instead navigating between opposing positions involving the Middle East conflict."[91] For the next two years, QAIA campaigned to reverse the center's ban, a campaign that intensified in 2013 when the center denied the group's request to host a reading of Sarah Schulman's book *Israel/Palestine and the Queer International*. Schulman described the center's rationale for the moratorium as a "weird kind of anti-semitism combined with a profound lack of intelligence and integrity." The center's leadership, she observed, "seems [to] hold cliched and stereotyped beliefs about punitive rich Jews who will pull out their Jew-money if anyone criticizes Israel, and it was this misguided prejudice that lead them to defensively ban any criticism of Israel."[92] In February 2013, QAIA celebrated the lifting of the moratorium on Israel/Palestine–related events, and the center finally hosted Schulman's book reading the following month. In introducing the event, QAIA member Leslie Cagan rejoiced, saying, "After two years, we are proud to be meeting here in this room, in this building, as Queers Against Israeli Apartheid."[93]

Policing Boundaries

In April 2013, I visited my colleague Katherine Franke in New York and participated in a discussion at her home about pinkwashing and Israel/Palestine. I first met Franke, the Isidor and Seville Sulzbacher Professor of Law at Columbia University, when she participated in the LGBTQ delegation to Palestine I had co-led in 2012. As director of Columbia's Center for Gender and Sexuality Law and a faculty affiliate at the Center for Palestine Studies, she has long been one of the most vocal figures in the Palestinian solidarity movement and outspoken proponents of BDS.

The previous year, from her position in New York, Franke had helped spearhead resistance to the Equality Forum conference in Philadelphia. Equality Forum hosts the largest annual LGBTQ conference in the United States, and organizers of the 2012 event decided to spotlight Israel as the summit's "featured nation."[94] This included six days of LGBTQ-oriented panels and activities related to Israel, including some that promoted the country's gay tourism industry, and a keynote address by Michael Oren, Israel's (straight) ambassador to the United States. Oren's speech was classic pinkwashing. As Aeyal Gross wrote, "Oren claimed in his speech that Israel provides asylum for LGBT Palestinian organizations that cannot freely operate in the territories. In reality, Israel has refused to take in LGBT Palestinians."[95] Queer Palestinian solidarity activists, including Franke, protested Equality Forum's decision to partner with the Israeli embassy in Washington, DC. They also pointed to the irony of Michael Oren being scheduled to speak alongside homophobic pastor John Hagee not long after Oren's Equality Forum speech. In addition to condemning homosexuality, Hagee "has a record of making racist, sexist, anti-Catholic, Islamophobic and anti-Semitic remarks."[96] Activists emphasized the opportunistic and unprincipled character of the Israeli government's approach to homosexuals and homophobes alike, one that instrumentalizes both groups in order to sustain US support for Israel.

PQBDS and Pinkwatching Israel also issued a joint statement condemning the Equality Forum's decision, labeling Oren a "propagandist for war crimes" and suggesting that inviting him to speak was "akin to the Equality Forum inviting a white South African ambassador as a keynote speaker during the apartheid era."[97] Following the PQBDS call for a boycott, Franke withdrew from speaking at Equality Forum and worked with local activists to organize an alternative event at Philadelphia's William Way LGBT Community Center to educate the community about LGBTQ rights in Israel/Palestine. In an article for *Tikkun* magazine, Franke and Rabbi Rebecca Alpert (who also withdrew from the conference) wrote,

> To uncritically celebrate Israel at a conference organized around notions of *equality* and *liberty*, and have Michael Oren serve as the keynote speaker at the "international" *equality* dinner, is taken as a slap in the face by our queer brothers and sisters in Palestine as well as by the queers within Israel who are actively seeking a just resolution to the Israeli/Palestinian conflict. By avoiding any programming that offers a balanced view of the human rights record of its "featured nation" the Equality Forum lost an important opportunity to

be a leader in the international gay human rights movement, and instead allowed itself to be used as a part of Israel's larger efforts to deflect criticisms of its human rights record (emphasis in original).[98]

Although the Equality Forum went forward as planned, spotlight on Israel and all, the speaker withdrawals and generally robust discourse and high energy level surrounding the protests and alternative event buoyed activist spirits.

Because Franke had played such a vital role in the queer Palestinian solidarity movement, it was surprising when she became the target of public critique from radical purists the following year. It was the private gathering at her home—the one I was invited to along with a diverse group of fifteen other individuals whose work connects Israel/Palestine with queer issues—that drew the purists' ire. The meeting brought together centrist Zionists, leftist Zionists, and anti-Zionists, both Jewish and non-Jewish, and received some financial support from Columbia University merely to cover travel costs for certain participants. A number of BDS supporters and fierce critics of pinkwashing were among the overall roster of participants, having agreed to have a conversation with people who do not share their perspective in recognition of how polarized the discourse in this domain had become. I shared with Franke my concern about the letter of invitation, which referenced Israel without mentioning Palestine (although Franke's email invitation did include a reference to Palestine). I also shared this concern with the group during the gathering and was met with warmth and heartfelt support from Franke and the other attendees. In fact, much of the conversation that day centered around how to respond to queer Palestinian calls for solidarity in ethical and strategic ways.

I trusted Franke and was open to meeting her co-organizer for the gathering, Frederick Hertz, even though I already knew that he and I did not see eye to eye on the question of Zionism. The gathering was productive, and it was the first time in my life that I engaged in a robust, face-to-face discussion of queer Israel/Palestine issues with people who espoused different ideological positions but still treated one another with respect. Franke had accepted our invitation to join the LGBTQ delegation to Palestine, and I reciprocated by accepting her invitation to be part of the conversation. I did so both as an expression of solidarity with her and as someone who recognizes the immense pressure felt by academics who work on these issues to find the language and space to engage with people who disagree with us. It does not serve social change for educators to isolate themselves in intellectual silos.

On the eve of our gathering, someone leaked the email invitation, prompting a fellow queer Palestinian to urge me to withdraw. The individual in question believed that the gathering constituted normalization and would legitimize a Zionist organization represented there, J Street. J Street is a liberal Zionist lobbying group that describes itself as the "pro-Israel, pro-peace" alternative to the hawkish American Israeli Public Affairs Committee (AIPAC). While J Street is to the left of AIPAC, it is to the right of Jewish Voice for Peace. Palestinians define *normalization* in a variety of ways, but the concept has taken on an increasingly negative valence within the Palestinian solidarity movement, most commonly referring to initiatives in which Israelis and Palestinians meet without due acknowledgment of the asymmetry in power between occupier and occupied. When this happens, the occupation is invisibilized and normalized, not forthrightly presented as a human catastrophe demanding urgent redress.

I responded to my colleague that I could not withdraw from the New York gathering in good conscience. My presence was meant precisely to ensure that normalization would not occur, and I made sure to place the Israeli occupation front and center in the conversation. I was puzzled by the objections to my attendance, because there were no Israeli state funds or institutional linkages involved; our private meeting, held in Katherine's home, was not a violation of BDS. US-based, BDS-supporting academics such as Katherine Franke need to have opportunities to engage with others as individuals, including those on the J Street side of the spectrum. One cannot build a movement without engaging with people who hold different views.

Shortly after the gathering began, right-wing groups started attacking liberal Zionist participants through messages online for meeting with pro-BDS individuals. A far left, pro-Palestinian website published an article criticizing Franke for facilitating a meeting with anti-BDS individuals. The article included a statement from Haneen Maikey, speaking in her capacity as a leader in the queer Palestinian movement, accusing Franke of "anti-solidarity." Franke had organized a separate event for Maikey to speak at Columbia University, and Maikey subsequently canceled her participation, publicly announcing, "I don't want to be associated with an 'ally' who is promoting any kind of dialogue about Palestine with Zionist organizations."[99]

Franke has persisted ever since in her Palestine-related teaching and activism and her desire to contribute to conflict transformation. But this persistence has come with consequences. Israeli forces detained Franke at the Tel Aviv airport during what would be her last trip to the region; they deported and banned her from Israel/Palestine for her Palestinian solidarity advocacy. Her experiences reveal just how emotionally and physically draining queer Palestinian solidarity activism has become for so many activists and their allies. These events also demonstrate some of the mechanisms that restrict the growth of the queer Palestinian movement and have contributed to the movement's recent plateau. They reflect the social life of critique: the way critiques from differently positioned actors intersect and subsequently constrain the types of discourse that are possible. This highlights the difficulties that queer Palestinian solidarity activists face when engaging with multiple audiences under the empire of critique.

Summer 2017 and the Intensification of Conflict

The conflicts between queer Zionist and queer anti-Zionist activists over pinkwatching and BDS have only intensified with time. The summer of 2017 brought three tumultuous episodes that caused deep pain for everyone involved. These events received substantially more attention than did the gathering at Katherine Franke's home. These three events, which occurred during the Celebrate Israel Parade in New York, the Chicago Dyke March, and Slut-Walk Chicago, received national media attention and were closely followed by the global queer Palestinian solidarity movement as well as by queer pro-Israel advocates. They echo the Franke episode to the extent that they highlight the ambiguities of boundary policing and the necessity of balancing principled stands against normalization with interactions (such as the one Franke successfully orchestrated) that use dialogue as a tool for transforming conflict.

In June, LGBTQ activists with Jewish Voice for Peace decided to disrupt the Celebrate Israel Parade in New York City by infiltrating the LGBTQ contingent, comprised primarily of Orthodox Jewish youth. The activists initially blended in with the group before unfurling signs and chanting slogans against Israeli oppression and in support of Palestinian human rights. Organizations such as the LGBTQ Jewish group Keshet condemned the JVP activists for purportedly "targeting" vulnerable LGBTQ youth, many of whom had been using the parade to publicly come out for the first time.[100] In an article for the *Forward* titled "Shame On You, Jewish Voice for Peace, for Targeting Pro-Israel Gays," Jay Michaelson alleged that the teens were made to feel unsafe by JVP, which is ultimately not an LGBTQ organization.[101] Mordechai Levovitz, head of the nonprofit Jewish Queer Youth (JQY), accused

JVP of "distortions and dishonesty" and "an unbelievable lack of empathy" for the teens.[102] Another article in the *Forward* later retracted the sexually suggestive claim that a "14 year old watch[ed] the JVP disrupters reveal themselves" and subsequently fled.[103] JQY demanded an apology from JVP and characterized JVP's actions as "censorship," "cowardice," "antisemitism," and "homophobia."[104]

The queer anti-Zionist JVP protesters and their allies were shocked by the accusations. One of the participants, Craig Willse, wrote, "We came together to proclaim loudly and unequivocally that apartheid and occupation are nothing to celebrate." He added, "There are real losses when Jewish people take a stand against Israel—often we lose our relationships with family and some of our friends. . . . But there is so much to be gained, and there is a whole wide world ready to welcome you into its complex, beautiful, difficult, painful and joyous struggle for freedom."[105] Rabbi Alissa Wise, JVP's queer deputy director, responded indignantly: "To be absolutely clear: JVPers did not target vulnerable youth; they targeted a jingoistic, nationalist parade to defend and celebrate a state that denies equal rights for all its citizens, brutally controls Palestinian life and land and fits the international definition of an apartheid state."[106] Wise characterized responses to the protest as "cruel," "homophobic," and "hyperbolic."[107] This episode was painful for Willse and Wise to experience as queer Jews. Wise was also later denied entry by Israel and banned from Israel/Palestine for her Palestinian solidarity activism.

On the blog *Jewschool*, a queer organizer with the Jewish free-speech group Open Hillel wrote, "Only when Jewish communal institutions make the choice to support their LGBT constituents regardless of donor dynamics or communal politics can they truly say that they stand for their most vulnerable members."[108] Queer and trans members of the American Jewish protest movement IfNotNow likewise rejected the accusations against JVP, noting that they "erase the identities of the queer and trans JVP members in question" and neglect "the truly violent hate crimes that queer and trans people face every day in this country, in Israel, and in Palestine. JVP's action was an intentional choice by queer Jews to challenge other queer Jews to acknowledge and reject the Occupation."[109] Trans Jewish anti-Zionist activist Stephanie Skora affirmed the "proud Jewish [and] proud queer history" of agitation and direct action. "The goal of protest is to open conversations," Skora wrote, "especially those that have been avoided or shut down, and to assert the humanity of oppressed peoples.[110]

Also in June 2017, organizers of the Chicago Dyke March, an LGBTQ parade, ejected three Jewish participants who were carrying LGBTQ pride flags emblazoned with the Star of David. The story went viral, with mainstream news outlets such as the *New York Times, Washington Post, Newsweek,* and *Fox News* covering the story, in addition to the Israeli newspaper *Haaretz* and LGBTQ outlets like *Advocate, Out,* and the *Windy City Times.*[111] Mainstream sources generally framed the altercation as an anti-Semitic act targeting Jewish individuals for displaying a Jewish symbol. But Jewish Voice for Peace, leftist LGBTQ activists, and Palestinian solidarity groups[112] reported a completely different version of events. In their telling, a principled radical group ejected people carrying a Zionist symbol that represents imperialism and a system of oppression. Whereas mainstream accounts identified the LGBTQ flag bearing the Star of David as a Jewish symbol, activists insisted that the position of the star in the center of the flag was intended to evoke the Israeli flag. The interpretive ambiguity revived debates about anti-Semitism and pinkwashing. Queer anti-Zionists identified the three individuals as pinkwashing provocateurs, and queer Zionists pointed to the controversy as evidence of anti-Semitic problems with the pinkwashing argument.

The Chicago Dyke March organizers, for their part, maintained their commitment to anti-Zionism, arguing that Zionism is a form of white supremacy. They recalled that they had been in communication with the ejected paradegoers before and during the march to make clear their anti-Zionist position and that the individuals in question had asserted their support for Zionism, thus triggering their ejection. They also revealed that one of the ejected individuals was the regional director of the queer Israel advocacy organization A Wider Bridge. Queer Zionists responded by arguing that Judaism and Zionism cannot be separated and that any exclusion of Jewish people and their symbols constitutes a hateful and anti-Semitic act, even when perpetrated by fellow queer Jewish people. These passionate reactions revealed a deeper issue—namely, that queer Jewish Zionists had begun to feel unjustly excluded from progressive and intersectional spaces, much as queer Jewish anti-Zionists have long felt unjustly isolated from mainstream Jewish institutions for their antiracist and anti-imperialist politics.

In July, not long after the Chicago Dyke March, the organizers of Slut-Walk Chicago, a march aimed at addressing sexual violence, courted controversy by announcing a ban on Zionist displays at their August parade. The predictable uproar against this decision, coupled with an outpouring of support, overwhelmed the organizers. After two weeks, they resolved to welcome religious symbols and discourage national symbols but backtracked on their explicit prohibition of Zionist iconography. Zioness, a group that identifies itself as progressive but exists mainly to advocate Zionism in left-leaning spaces, sent a dozen activists to the march. Anticipating this move, the SlutWalk organizers issued a preemptive disavowal.

> SlutWalk Chicago does not support the "Zioness progressives" planning on coming to the walk Saturday. We at SlutWalk Chicago stand with Jewish people, just as we stand for Palestinian human rights. Those two ideologies can exist in the same realm, and taking a stance against anti-Semitism is not an affirmation of support for the state of Israel and its occupation of Palestine.[113]

At the march, Zioness activists participated but were shunned by a number of marchers, who attempted to block their signs. When a queer Palestinian marcher gave a speech proclaiming that "you cannot be a Zionist and feminist," the crowd "broke into a spontaneous chant of 'Free Palestine.'"[114]

The controversies surrounding the Celebrate Israel Parade, the Chicago Dyke March, and SlutWalk Chicago in the summer of 2017 revealed the strongly held views of queer Zionist and anti-Zionist activists on the types of voices, symbols, and ideologies considered admissible in queer spaces. These episodes heightened critique fatigue for antagonists and onlookers alike, and it is true that the majority of queer Zionists and anti-Zionists are uninterested in boundary policing. But most members of the queer Palestinian solidarity movement, at least, would agree that the purpose of such actions is specifically to bring Palestinian suffering into focus in the face of Zionist attempts to render it invisible. Many activists likewise feel that waging internal struggles around the question of Zionism within the Jewish community is a worthy political project, one suited to the unique positionality of Jewish pro-Palestinian solidarity activists. At the same time, it is also important for movement discourses and strategies, in Palestine and abroad, to make room for robust resistance to Palestinian homophobia. A central aim of this book is to advance the case for holding multiple, interconnected struggles together at once and to welcome a variety of differently positioned actors into the movement.

Toward Peace and Justice

Queer Palestinian solidarity activists typically respond only to local events, but the reverberations of these social dramas have traveled widely as activists share their perceptions and experiences with transnational solidarity networks on the left and the right. They celebrate victories thousands of miles away and commiserate in the challenges of pinkwatching campaigns near and far. Some campaigns are transnational in nature, demanding coordinated responses to globally dispersed pinkwashing initiatives or discourses. A critical audience for pinkwatching activists is comprised of individuals and organizations, primarily in the West, that have not taken a position on how queerness intersects with Israel/Palestine. Queer activism in Palestine cannot so easily ignore the question of Palestinian homophobia, and yet the fact that pinkwatching has become a central paradigm of the global solidarity movement has effectively elevated Zionism over concerns about antiqueer oppression. The fight against Palestinian homophobia should be waged by Palestinians and reside primarily in Palestine, but queer international solidarity with Palestinians also has a role to play in this struggle, particularly in not rendering invisible (or in silencing) the voices of queer Palestinians who aspire to address both Zionism and homophobia as systems of oppression. As we have also seen throughout this chapter, the weight of Israel-aligned institutions in the empire of critique remains overwhelming and formidable, continuing to subject queer Palestinians and their allies to surveillance, criticism, and counterresistance. Despite the cracks in the system that pinkwatching activism has opened, the underlying structures of ethnoheteronormativity endure.

To celebrate Israel's LGBTQ record without reference to the struggles of Palestinians (in Israel and the Occupied Territories) is to exhibit what Bakhtin called monoglossia. This chapter has drawn on Robinson and Lederach's work on conflict transformation as conceptual tools for envisioning future relationships between individuals who care about how queerness intersects with Israel/Palestine. Pinkwashing exemplifies monoglossia in that it is a self-reproducing discourse that unfolds in a hermetically sealed conversational bubble. Pinkwatching and other forms of engagement by queer Palestinian solidarity activists offer queer advocates of Israel an opportunity for a social heteroglossia in which a more nuanced discourse on queer Israel/Palestine can take shape. Such "insurrectionary acts" by pinkwatching activists are most effective when waged in the spirit of conflict transformation. Lederach's typology accounts for conflict *escalation* as one of several indispensable paths to constructive change and ultimate transformation, authorizing confrontation with pinkwashing's support for racism and oppression such that those elements might be addressed and dismantled. But queer Palestinian solidarity activists must also recognize that de-escalation is a critical component of change as well, one without which there may be temporary resolution but never lasting transformation of the dynamics we hope to alter, whether in Israel/Palestine or in the Diaspora. This chapter has revealed how radical purists also seek to advance their own form of monoglossia. Simultaneous attention to long-term relationship building and to laying the foundations for peace are essential, even (or perhaps especially) when confronting one's adversary. As in so many social justice struggles, winning allies from the dominant and even oppressive group is invaluable to the success of the movement. The gathering in Katherine Franke's home embodied the spirit of dialogism and conflict transformation without normalizing Israeli oppression.

The queer policing of boundaries and purity we have encountered in this chapter reveal the place of confrontation in struggles against oppression and injustice. Much is at stake when the queer Palestinian subject is rendered legible only through the politics of pinkwatching and boycotts. Boycotts have served as a form of discursive enfranchisement and political empowerment that queer Palestinians have, in many ways, used to globally reclaim their voices from the Israeli state and its satellite institutions and their formidable resources. In turn, boycotts have become a primary form of transnational queer Palestinian solidarity activism. Augmenting them with openness to differences in ideology and strategy is critical for movement growth. Radical purism has created conditions in which activists often wind up just preaching to the choir. Avoiding this trap requires a commitment to deep listening, the formulation of means that mirror the ends we seek, a generosity of spirit, and a fierce kindness toward ourselves and others. Such steadfastness is essential, even in the face of cruelty, if the movement is to achieve peace and justice.

4   Media, Film, and the
Politics of Representation

W. E. B. DU BOIS ARGUED that the Black American experience under postemancipation white supremacy generated a "double consciousness,"
a bifurcated sense of self arising "from the double life every American Negro must live, as a Negro and as an American."[1] The experience of an all-
encompassing racial hostility alongside official declarations of civic equality
and democratic freedom wrought painful and persistent psychological consequences. Double consciousness, in Du Bois's poetic expression, "is a peculiar
sensation, the sense of always looking at one's self through the eyes of others, of measuring one's soul by the tape of a world that looks on in amused
contempt and pity."[2] The social conditions that subject Black Americans to
oppressive standards of self-assessment are familiar to the queer Palestinian living as a racialized subject under Israeli apartheid. Queer Palestinians
must endure both physical and psychic violence as Palestinian victims of Zionism as well as the conflicted affections and loyalties caused by a Palestinian nationalist project that reifies homophobia. Their sense of self is consequently shaped by the persistent gaze of ethnoheteronormativity. Although
that conflicted selfhood manifests in different ways, queer Palestinian double
consciousness underscores the ambivalence seen in race relations, competing
nationalisms, religious struggles, and conflicts over sexuality among other
forms of contested consciousness that exist at the individual and group levels.

Du Bois's fiction and autobiographical writings aimed to capture the lived
experience of Black double consciousness. Film has served a similar pur-

pose for queer Palestinians; in this domain they can grapple with and represent their own experiences of split consciousness. Just as there is no singular queer Palestinian consciousness, no single representation can capture the wide range of subjectivities that queer Palestinians internally and externally inhabit. Only by highlighting a variety of queer Palestinian voices can films and news outlets come closer over time to accurately representing the ambivalence, love, pain, and individual and collective experiences that characterize queer Palestinian life.

This chapter examines the relationship between the global queer Palestinian solidarity movement and representations of queer Palestinians in film and journalism. Significant mistrust of the global mainstream media has arisen among movement leaders. Activists concerned with the politics of representation have demanded that media discourse on Queer Palestine reinforce a radical purist viewpoint. I recognize the difference between journalistic and cinematic representation, and thus the first part of this chapter is devoted to the former and the second to the latter. It opens with a description of how the mainstream Western press tends to prioritize the most sensational stories about queer Palestinians. The media occasionally features more nuanced representation, but I nonetheless underscore movement leaders' enduring mistrust of the way the news media narrates queer Palestinian experiences and subjectivities. The second half of the chapter outlines the movement's critique of pinkwashing films produced by Israelis and internationals and the movement's attendant calls to boycott those films. It is important to note that what constitutes a pinkwashing film is contentious. This chapter delineates examples of cinematic tropes that clearly reinforce pinkwashing and analyzes films that feature queer love between Israelis and Palestinians. In addition, I discuss a number of queer Palestinian films, highlighting their importance and controversy. The chapter concludes with the story of an as-yet-unreleased documentary on the first US LGBTQ delegation to Palestine.

Al-Qaws, the largest queer Palestinian organization, emerges as highly significant in shaping critical discourse around this media and film landscape. Three particular Al-Qaws interventions that publicly critiqued media representations are highlighted in this chapter; these reveal the extent to which the empire of critique has turned inward and the implications of this for the global queer Palestinian movement. Radical purist activists have used social media and other organizational means to criticize attempts to cover queer Palestinian subjects; this battle of words between purists and others has had a chilling effect on reporting that might have otherwise captured multiple voices and provided analysis of a range of queer Palestinians. These conditions have increased the difficulties facing those queer Palestinians who wish to explore the contradictions of identity and shifting allegiances they experience. I argue that getting past the movement's current plateau requires transcending the impulse to exclusively promote representations that align with a purist politics. In place of a self-defeating search for an archetypical queer Palestinian subject, space must be created for a multiplicity of voices that capture the heterogeneity of queer Palestinian experiences, subjectivities, and ideologies.

Privileging the Sensational

Although queer Palestinian voices have occasionally been heard and debated in radical activist, civil society, and intellectual spaces around the world, it is rare for the Western mainstream media to directly represent them. As we have seen, queer Palestinians and their allies do occasionally appear as problematic minorities that nefariously "single out" Israel with charges of pinkwashing. Beyond this, Western news outlets tend to feature queer Palestinians only when the context is highly sensational. Thus, some of the most devastating experiences with Palestinian homophobia are disproportionately amplified for Western audiences.

For example, one widely circulated article from Georgetown University's student newspaper quotes a young gay Palestinian man who spoke at the university in 2004 at an event organized by the Zionist Organization of America (a right-wing organization) in partnership with a pro-Israel student group. The speaker, identified only as "Ali," describes Palestine as an oppressive place where he lacked the freedom to discuss his homosexuality and lived in constant fear of "random arrests, torture and random killings."[3] Ali is quoted as lauding Israel's record on LGBTQ rights, praising "the legal situation for homosexuals in Israel, [and] pointing out that homosexuals have the freedom to serve openly in the army and that Israeli courts have been issuing legislation protecting equal benefits for gay couples similar to those of married couples. None of these rights exist under the Palestinian government."[4]

In another article that attracted considerable attention, the Israeli journalist Yossi Klein Halevi wrote in the *New Republic* about "Tayseer," a young gay Palestinian man from the Gaza Strip who is said to have been beaten by his family and tortured by Palestinian police. Tayseer's "dream," wrote Halevi, "is to move to Tel Aviv."[5] The article also profiles a young gay man from the West Bank, identified as "Salah," who describes being in a Palestinian Authority prison in which "interrogators cut him with glass and poured toilet cleaner into his wounds."[6] We hear Salah's voice as mediated by Halevi's journalism: "I've tried to kill myself six times already. . . . Each time the ambulance came too quickly. But now I think I know how to do it. Next time, with God's help, it will work before the ambulance comes."[7]

The juxtaposition of Israeli legal tolerance and Palestinian homophobia is misleading to audiences outside of Israel/Palestine. The reality is that Israelis, including Israeli settlers in the Occupied Territories, are governed by Israeli civil law, while Palestinians in the Occupied Territories are governed by both Palestinian Authority law and the legal regime of the Israeli military occupation. These sets of laws do not criminalize homosexuality. Nonetheless, a factual error published and then retracted by the Associated Press (AP) highlights how pervasive this pinkwashing trope has become. The AP article initially claimed that homosexuality is illegal in the Palestinian Territories, asserting that Israel "has emerged as one of the world's most gay-friendly travel destinations, in sharp contrast to the rest of the Middle East where gay people are often persecuted and even killed."[8] The error was later retracted as a result of advocacy by queer Palestinian solidarity activists, with the AP issuing the following correction: "The Associated Press reported erroneously that homosexual acts are banned by law in the West Bank and Gaza Strip. While homosexuality is largely taboo in Palestinian society, there are no laws specifically banning homosexual acts."[9] There is indeed no antihomosexual legislation in the West Bank, but this is not exactly the case in the Gaza Strip, where the British Mandate Criminal Code Ordinance No. 74 of 1936 remains, prohibiting "sexual intercourse with another person against the order of nature."[10] This ordinance can be deployed to criminalize homosexuality in Gaza.

Mainstream media outlets that dismiss the positions of Al-Qaws, Aswat, Pinkwatching Israel, and PQBDS as fringe voices in Palestinian society tend to amplify the most devastating narratives about queer Palestinians. In June 2015, the popular gay magazine the *Advocate* reported on a twenty-four-year-old unnamed gay Palestinian man who converted from Islam to Christianity in Canada and worried that he would be killed by his family were the Canadian government to deport him to the West Bank. Describing his family's connections to Hamas, he asserts, "Converting to Christianity! That is a death penalty. Being open about my sexuality! Again, that is certain death. If I am deported, sent back to where I was born and raised, it's only a matter of time before I am found dead."[11] In an interview with CNN, he states that his father "planned it so I was to be put to death."[12] CNN interviewed the father, who is reported to have said, "What he did is offensive to honor and to religion. . . . And the family has the right to retaliate against him."[13] In a June 2016 article, the *Times of Israel* reported on the same case, noting that the man fled to Israel before arriving in Canada, where his request for asylum was denied because of his familial ties to Hamas. He then sought asylum in the United States, where a court ruled that he could remain in the country because deporting him "would contradict the UN Convention Against Torture."[14]

Another case that became salient in the Western press was that of Talleen Abu Hanna, a trans Palestinian Christian woman from Nazareth. In May 2016, Abu Hanna, a citizen of Israel, won the Miss Trans Israel competition, the country's first transgender beauty pageant. *Time* magazine quoted her as saying, in "perfect Hebrew, . . . I wouldn't be alive if I grew up in Palestine. . . . Not as a gay man, and definitely not as a transgender woman."[15] She added, "I got really lucky to live in a country where they bring everything to you on a silver platter," and, at the same time, "there is still room for improvement, and still some rights we deserve."[16] Although Abu Hanna is reported to have some supportive family members, her father stopped speaking with her, she had to flee her home for fear of violence, and "much of her extended family cut off relations with her years ago."[17] The article also connected the story of another Palestinian pageant contestant:

> Caroline Khouri, a 24-year-old from the Arab-Israeli village of Tamra, fled her home after her male relatives threatened to kill her for transitioning from man to woman. Her father, uncles and cousins chased her to Tel Aviv, where they tied her up inside an apartment, beat her, cut her hair, and starved her for three days. Israeli police rescued Khouri and imprisoned her attackers. She now has no connection to her family.[18]

The *Times of Israel* quotes Talleen Abu Hanna as saying, "If I had been in Palestine or in any other Arab country, I might have been in prison or murdered."[19]

Some queer Palestinian activists were incensed by Abu Hanna's and Khouri's statements to the press, labeling them opportunists and advocates of pinkwashing. A *New York Times* article addressed the controversy:

> Leading Palestinian groups for gay, lesbian, bisexual and transgender people declined to comment on Ms. Abu Hanna's activities. But gay and transgender

activists say the groups see her decision to represent Israel as "pinkwashing," a term that critics use to describe how Israel markets its gay-friendly reputation to shift focus from military occupation.

Lilach Ben David, 26, a transgender woman and activist, said she was "torn."

"Talleen Abu Hanna will most definitely be used by the Israeli propaganda machine in order to justify horrendous crimes against Talleen Abu Hanna's own people," Ms. Ben David said.

But "if Palestinian society was accepting of Talleen Abu Hanna as a trans woman," she said, "then she wouldn't have to go and work with the Israeli establishment."[20]

Ben David's remarks here acknowledge the difficult options that queer and trans Palestinians are limited to. Those committed to viewing the Abu Hanna story through the lens of pinkwashing will find additional evidence in her acceptance of $20,000 from the Israeli government to represent Israel in the Miss Trans Universe competition. They will find even more evidence in her appearance in a video, promoted on an official Israeli government Facebook page, that celebrates her trans and Israeli identities.[21]

In my conversations with other queer and trans Palestinians, a few expressed compassion for Abu Hanna as a young trans Palestinian woman acting strategically to survive and realize her dreams in a deeply racist Israeli society and transphobic Palestinian environment. In noting that "Israel's universal health service covers the costs of sex-reassignment surgery" and that "[Israeli] law is on your side" when it comes to "changing one's gender and name on government-issued documents," Abu Hanna raises concerns that are urgently relevant to the health and safety of trans Palestinians, concerns that should not be blithely dismissed even as her language reinforces damaging Israeli propaganda narratives.[22] Attempts to delegitimize voices such as Abu Hanna's in a personally and emotionally damaging manner reflect the tendency in activist circles to police who can and cannot speak as a queer and/or trans Palestinian and to decide who is or is not considered an authentic voice. But Abu Hanna's subjectivity is part of the rich heterogeneity of LGBTQ understandings and experiences in Palestinian contexts, and her concerns, along with the concerns of other LGBTQ individuals, must be acknowledged if we are to secure more freedom for all Palestinians. Such acknowledgment could happen in the media if there were, among other things, quotations by more thoughtful experts, coverage in a wider range of publications, and moderation of social media excesses.

Between Media Mistrust and Nuanced Representations

Slowly but surely, queer Palestinian voices are being heard in the global sphere beyond those belonging to victims of the most sensational Palestinian homophobic violence and to radical purist activists. Ziad "Zizo" Abul Hawa is one such rising queer Palestinian voice. While many queer Palestinians believe that participating in Israel's deeply contentious annual gay pride parade helps reinforce pinkwashing, others, like Zizo, feel differently. Lihi Ben Shitrit writes for the Carnegie Endowment think tank:

> Ziad Abul Hawa, a well-known Palestinian gay rights activist whose family lives in East Jerusalem, explained that he rarely participates in these pride parades because of pinkwashing, but he made an exception this year. "I cannot separate my sexual identity and my national [Palestinian] identity . . . but I decided that I will go to this parade," he said after the rally. "After all the incitement from religious and political leaders, I couldn't sit at home. . . . I am glad I went, because it was a protest. Last year a girl [Shira Banki] was murdered there; you can't pinkwash that." Even Orthodox religious persons, who don't usually come to such events, were present to show their rejection of intolerant interpretations of Judaism. Perhaps the most significant part of the event was a speech by the father of Shira Banki. In his statement, he linked different forms of intolerance, racism, and Israel's growing culture of violence against minorities, stressing that the LGBT struggle in the country is ongoing and cannot be isolated from other communities' struggles.[23]

With his speech, Banki's father demonstrated the potential for allies of the Israeli LGBTQ community to link the struggle against homophobia to other important struggles in Israel/Palestine.

Moreover, and contrary to the prevailing view among some queer Palestinian activists, Abul Hawa conceives of his participation in the Jerusalem Pride parade as a form of resistance to pinkwashing. He presents himself as intentionally choosing to participate in a forum that, at least on certain occasions, acknowledges the need to address multiple oppressions from an intersectional perspective. Abul Hawa has been disavowed by some leaders of the queer Palestinian activist community, but his voice has been one of the few to receive significant attention from mainstream media outlets around the world. More compelling media representations of queer Palestinians would engage the question of why Abul Hawa's views fail to resonate with radical purist queer Palestinians. At the same time, the global queer Palestinian movement would likewise benefit from deeper engagement with—rather than the rejection of—queer Palestinian individuals and activities that do not perfectly align with purist politics.

Abul Hawa is certainly not alone, as there are many other queer Palestinians with nuanced positions of their own. Such voices can be heard, for instance, in Haifa at Dar al-Raya, a cafe that doubles as a publishing house. They recently published *The Book of Desire*, believed to be among the first volumes of modern erotica by Palestinian authors.[24] Dar al-Raya has also published the work of queer Palestinian writer Raji Bathish, whose books include queer eroticism and who articulates a desire for his provocative texts to "unsettle both liberal Zionists and Palestinian nationalists." Bathish takes pride in the "breaching of boundaries and the transgression of unshakeable Palestinian nationalist tenets" through his queer writing.[25]

A January 2016 *New York Times* article signaled that representations of queer Palestinians beyond the binary of the victim of Palestinian homophobia and the dogmatic activist may be gaining traction. The article sheds light on how young Palestinian citizens of Israel are cultivating a cosmopolitan ethos in Haifa in which social taboos around homosexuality and other traditionally transgressive behaviors are rejected. Diaa Hadid, the Arab-Australian *New York Times* journalist, quotes Ayed Fadel, a Palestinian who runs the Kabareet bar in Haifa: "We want a gay couple to go to the dance floor and kiss each other, and nobody to even look at them. . . . This is the new Palestinian society we are aiming for."[26] Hadid adds, "That society was on display late last year, when some bars and cafes held screenings for Kooz Queer, the first Palestinian gay film festival."

In an almost predictable fashion, some queer Palestinian activists were alarmed by Diaa Hadid's article on queer Palestinian life in Haifa, labeling it a form of pinkwashing. Ayed Fadel, the bar owner, was criticized by radical purists on social media for his appearance in the article. Fadel then posted his own critique of the article on Facebook, pointing to its failure to convey the arguments he had made during the interview, such as his identification of Haifa's queer Palestinian scene as a form of resistance to Israel. Instead, Fadel wrote, the *New York Times* article "portrays the modern Palestinian in a 'Western' image that comforts white readers and makes them say, "Oh, they're just like us!" Well no, we're nothing like them, in fact, we're very different and deep into the shit, and having to portray us in this image is insulting."[27]

Following a "social media storm," *New York Times* public editor Margaret Sullivan published a response to the many complaints she had received about the piece from a "small but relentless group of critics."[28] The way the paper framed the criticism of the piece was to a large extent an example of classic "both sides" journalism that elides the profound power differential between Israelis and Palestinians.

Sullivan quoted Fadel, who derided the article in question as "shallow, offensive and degrading," as well as a pro-Israel critic who sarcastically asserted that "in the midst of violence against Israelis, Ms. Hadid finds it timely to report on how wonderfully liberal the Palestinians in Haifa are for promoting gay rights."[29] Another respondent, reproducing a popular Zionist critique, "objected to the characterization of those interviewed as Palestinians; they should have been called Arab Israelis." A voice from the left wrote:

> This article was orientalist—it made it seem like Israel is the one who "allows" Palestinian culture and resilience to thrive, and Palestinians would otherwise be repressive and drab. To the contrary, Palestinian musicians, artists and queer activists in Haifa (and Jaffa, Jerusalem, Ramallah, and in refugee camps around the region) struggle despite apartheid.[30]

Still another reader expressed frustration that Hadid did not include the common pinkwashing trope that "in the entire Middle East, it is only in Israel, protected by the Israeli army and Israeli police and Israeli laws and Israeli courts, that Arabs can enjoy Western levels of tolerance, freedom and security."[31] Even Sullivan criticized her own paper for neglecting local and geopolitical context. Just hours after the initial response, Sullivan followed up with a second editorial, this time quoting Hadid's reaction to the criticism. As Hadid put it, "I wrote this story really because I wanted to pay tribute to Haifa's unique culture, and particularly how Palestinian citizens of Israel had carved their own dynamic, liberal scene in the city."[32] Hadid added, "I would also note that in the many interviews I . . . conducted, people had quite differing views of what Haifa was to them. I somehow sense that the objections of some readers boil down to the fact that what I represented disagreed with their own political beliefs about both Palestinians and Israel."[33]

The breadth and passion of the criticism that this Arabic-speaking journalist received as a result of her high-profile reportage on increased openness to homosexuality among a subset of Palestinian citizens of Israel in a particular city is a microcosm of the tremendous pressure bearing down on queer and trans Palestinians. Even as Hadid undermined notions of a Palestinian pathology of homophobia, some saw her piece as exacerbating homophobia by failing to highlight the contributions of gay activists to the broader Palestinian struggle against Israeli oppression. Critiquing discourse on queer Palestinians for failing to provide sufficient context has become de rigueur among radical purists, debilitating queer Palestinian activism with the demand that every article, every interview, every film, every press release, and every talk that represents the human experience of queer and trans Palestinians adhere to a rigid set of ideological parameters delineated by some self-proclaimed authority. Even though Zionist activists will always attempt to discourage positive portrayals of queer Palestinians with a barrage of spurious criticism, queer Palestinian movement leaders and allies should not reinforce the tactics of their adversaries by disincentivizing the production of humanizing portraits. The queer Palestinian cause, I suggest, is not served by chastising journalists such as Hadid. Instead, appreciation for Hadid's initiative in broaching these sensitive and important issues could be accompanied by an invitation to consider other perspectives in a follow-up piece. The empire of critique and the rush to knee-jerk criticism of all things Queer Palestine ends up silencing potential allies and movement builders rather than cultivating additional voices and encouraging meaningful action for social change. My own communication with Hadid for this book revealed how challenging the aftermath of this article was to confront, particularly given the criticism she faced from radical purists even though she is very sympathetic to the Palestinian struggle. Hadid left the *New York Times* Jerusalem bureau shortly thereafter.

It is easy to understand why so many queer Palestinians have grown mistrustful of mainstream media accounts of queer issues related to Israel/Palestine. They have grown accustomed to narratives that pinkwash Israel as a gay haven, represent queer Palestinian solidarity activists as ideological extremists, and amplify the most sensational stories of Palestinian homophobia. At the same time, the queer Palestinian movement has largely refused to proactively engage the Western press, instead responding with frustration and reactive criticism once seemingly problematic narratives have been published.

In 2013, Kevin Naff, the editor of the *Washington Blade*, "America's oldest and most acclaimed LGBT news publication," described being denied meetings with queer Palestinian organizations and then accused of pinkwashing for participating in an LGBTQ delegation of leaders from the United States to Israel. He wrote,

Our group was sensitive to pinkwashing from the outset and several of us requested meetings with gay Palestinians and their representatives. Project Interchange worked hard to provide a balanced view of the issues and invited two Palestinian LGBT groups—alQaws and Aswat—to meet with us. Officials at the Tel Aviv and Jerusalem LGBT centers were also asked if they could assist in persuading those groups to meet our delegation or knew of other Palestinian LGBT representatives who would be willing to meet us. Sadly, the groups refused to meet with us. Change is simply not possible without dialogue and I deeply regret this lost opportunity the Palestinians had to engage with an open-minded group of visitors seeking nothing more than understanding and education.[34]

Activists from both groups took issue with Project Interchange's legitimization of Israeli LGBTQ organizations and state-led projects as well as its call for balance, something that cannot exist in the context of such a profound power differential between Israelis and Palestinians. The missed opportunity for American LGBTQ leaders to hear from queer Palestinians may have pushed those delegates further toward internalizing the discourses of the Israeli state and its supporters. It is thus not surprising that Naff employs standard pinkwashing rhetoric in that same piece, writing, "Located in the heart of the Middle East, where homosexuality can be punished by jail time or even death as in Iran, Israel has emerged as one of the world's most pro-LGBT nations."[35] Had queer Palestinian activists taken the time to engage Naff, an influential journalist, he might have produced a more nuanced and accurate account of the queer dimensions of Israel/Palestine for his many readers. Although responsibility rests primarily with such foreigners to be cognizant of the pressures under which queer Palestinians find themselves, the absence of much-needed engagement with external stakeholders is a missed opportunity. Relationship building with the media is essential if the movement is to garner favorable coverage and appeal to constituents beyond the most radical members of its own political camp. Such work can be emotionally and materially draining in a context of finite resources and entrenched ethnoheteronormativity. Approaching it cautiously makes sense, but the task cannot be abandoned altogether.

Mistrust of the mainstream media has not only led to considerable disengagement from the Western press but also served to alienate allies from the movement. A US-based Palestinian American journalist who wanted to write a sympathetic article on the queer Palestinian movement shared with me her experience of being scolded by an Al-Qaws activist because she had previously published in a news outlet that had once featured pro-Israel material from other contributors (she had no connection to those contributors or articles). The journalist was subsequently unable to access any LGBTQ activists in Palestine and could not complete her piece as a result of being considered too politically impure.

This mistrust has also led to queer Palestinian activists issuing public critiques of allies from the progressive, pro-Palestinian press. An incident in September 2014 had a particular chilling effect on the movement. The *New York Times*, which is not generally known for its sympathetic treatment of Palestinian voices, published an article on forty-three veterans of the Israeli clandestine military intelligence Unit 8200 who decided to stop "tak[ing] part in the state's actions against Palestinians." According to the *Times*, the veterans complained that "Israel made 'no distinction between Palestinians who are and are not involved in violence' and that information collected 'harms innocent people.' Intelligence 'is used for political persecution,' they wrote, which 'does not allow for people to lead normal lives, and fuels more violence.'"[36] The article explained that "Unit 8200 veterans described exploitative activities focused on innocents whom Israel hoped to enlist as collaborators. They said information about medical conditions and sexual orientation were among the tidbits collected. They said that Palestinians lacked legal protections from harassment, extortion and injury."[37] That same day, the *Guardian* also reported on the extortion of gay Palestinians, quoting a member of Israel's intelligence services, who said, "If you're homosexual and know someone who knows a wanted person—and we need to know about it—Israel will make your life miserable."[38] The Unit 8200 story was likewise covered by the progressive Israeli online magazine +972, by the pro-Palestine website *Mondoweiss*, and on the widely read blog of American political theorist and Palestine solidarity activist Corey Robin.[39]

In September 2014, Al-Qaws responded to the coverage of the Unit 8200 story in outlets affiliated with the Palestinian solidarity movement, specifically singling out *Mondoweiss* and Robin for censure. The Al-Qaws statement included the following:

> Capitalizing on Israel's gross mistreatment of queer Palestinians by bolstering mainstream LGBT rights discourses is a further colonization of Palestine and queer Palestinians. Concentrating on sexuality alone, no matter how

well-intentioned, ultimately shores up Zionism by re-entrenching the connection between Israel and LGBT/queer, even if it is supposedly to call out Israel's hypocrisy in its exploitation of queer people to serve state interests.[40]

Given that *Mondoweiss* is dedicated exclusively to Palestine solidarity content and that Corey Robin's blog covers Israel/Palestine from a critical anti-
Zionist perspective, the Al-Qaws response struck many as counterintuitive.
Accusing these pro-Palestine allies of being complicit in the "colonization" of
Palestine was severe. One might expect Al-Qaws to have welcomed increased
awareness of Israel's entrapment of queer Palestinians, as the story provides
a powerful argument against pinkwashing. Instead, the response sent activists into a crisis over whether they had "singled out" sexuality in their activism and whether it is ever truly possible to properly contextualize everything
that is happening to Palestinians. The fact that a public critique was leveled
against individuals so deeply committed to Palestine—a critique that charged
them with reinforcing pinkwashing and colonialism when in fact they had set
out to oppose exactly those phenomena—highlighted the shift toward radical
purism and illustrated the harmful effects of the inward turn of the empire of
critique. It is of course not surprising that queer Palestinians would struggle
with trust when they are under so much surveillance from so many quarters.
But without trust-building and outward engagement, social movements cannot secure the additional support they need to overcome the challenges resulting from that very surveillance.

Having long been attacked by pro-Israel groups for singling out Israel,
Palestine solidarity activists must now increasingly contend with critiques
from radical purists within their own movement who accuse them of singling
out Palestine over other places or of singling out the sexual dimension of Palestinian oppression over other issues, as did the Al-Qaws response to the Unit
8200 news reports. The point here is not that such critiques are inherently in-
accurate. In a world that German sociologist Max Weber describes as rid-
dled with unintended consequences, it is legitimate to ask whether movement
practices intended to define, advance, or protect Palestinian rights in fact end
up undermining them. But the crowded jumble of so many internal and external critiques creates a high emotional and discursive barrier for political
activists to overcome as they seek to enter the field and sustain their activism once inside it. Critique on multiple fronts is now leveled for its own sake
as the movement's modus operandi, and that has the effect of weakening solidarity. Too often the result is not empowerment but paralysis.

Film Boycotts

The media representations described thus far have not been as fraught as those in queer Israel/Palestine–related films. The screening of such films has led to some of the most contentious episodes of the global queer Palestinian solidarity movement, with activists adopting boycotts as their preferred mode of intervention. My experience has been that most films dealing with the intersection of queerness and Israel/Palestine have been labeled pinkwashing by movement activists, particularly the radical purists among them. Although numerous films do in fact reinforce pinkwashing, the threshold for what constitutes pinkwashing is very low for radical purists. Many pinkwatchers point to the fact that Israeli films receive state funds and are often screened around the world with the coordination of Israeli embassies and consulates. Support from Israeli state institutions enables LGBTQ films and filmmakers in Israel to appear at international queer film festivals. Israel also hosts its own international film festivals, which the queer Palestinian solidarity movement typically calls on supporters to boycott in protest of the state's violations of Palestinian human rights. In 2009, Queers Undermining Israeli Terrorism (QUIT) spearheaded boycott efforts against the Tel Aviv International LGBT Film Festival (TLVFest), calling on LGBTQ filmmakers not to submit films or accept invitations.

That same year, John Greyson, a gay Canadian filmmaker and academic, declined an invitation to premiere his film *Fig Trees* at TLVFest. In his letter to festival organizers, he wrote that during a conversation with the journalist Naomi Klein, he came to the realization that he "must join the many Jews and non-Jews, Israelis and Palestinians, queers and otherwise, who are part of the growing global BDS (Boycott, Divestment and Sanctions) movement against Israeli apartheid. . . . To not take this stand is unthinkable, impossible."[41] Citing "the devastating Gaza massacre," Greyson also pulled his documentary *Covered* from the Toronto International Film Festival (TIFF) to protest the festival's "City to City Spotlight on Tel Aviv." [42] In an open letter, Greyson referred to the Israeli consul general in Toronto, who in 2008 announced the launch of a "Brand Israel Initiative"[43] targeting TIFF and the City of Toronto. According to Ron Huldai, the mayor of Tel Aviv, "while the City to City program was initiated by the festival, the Israeli ministry of foreign affairs was involved as part of its Brand Israel media and advertising campaign." A group of filmmakers, including the Israeli filmmaker Udi Aloni, wrote a letter in support of Greyson's withdrawal from the festival, criticizing TIFF's "complicity in the Israeli propaganda machine" and noting that in 2008 the Israeli government had partnered with various Canadian entities to launch "a million dollar media and advertising campaign aimed at changing Canadian perceptions of Israel."[44] Judy Rebick, a Canadian Jewish feminist journalist, characterized Greyson's act as "courageous" and "a significant contribution to the Palestinian solidarity movement and the Boycott Divestment and Sanction strategy that it has adopted to shine a light on the inexcusable aggression of Israel against the Palestinian people."[45]

In 2010, queer Palestinian solidarity activists protested the San Francisco LGBT Festival on the opening night of the Out In Israel LGBT Cultural Festival because of the collaboration between the two entities, which the activists linked to the Brand Israel campaign and pinkwashing. The following year, solidarity activists successfully petitioned Queer Lisboa, Portugal's international queer film festival, to decline financial support and sponsorship from the Israeli government. In 2014, Sins Invalid, a justice-based disability performance project centering disabled artists of color and queer/gender-nonconforming disabled artists, pulled their documentary from the 2014 Vancouver Queer Film Festival. In their statement, Sins Invalid urged the festival to "agree to refuse 'pinkwashing' funding in the future, and to stand in solidarity with all queer and gender non-conforming peoples, wherever they may live."[46]

Queer Palestinian solidarity activists have been unsuccessful in their efforts to convince other festivals—including the San Francisco LGBT Film Festival (Frameline), the world's largest LGBTQ film event—to decline funding from the Israeli government. Years of protests, meetings, dialogue, disruptions at Frameline screenings and events, and correspondence with festival organizers have not resulted in what Palestinian solidarity activists consider an end to the festival's complicity with pinkwashing. In 2016, Frameline's board of directors and executive director affirmed that they will continue to accept financial support from cultural organizations and consulates, including the Israeli consulate, to cover costs associated with screening international films. The response came after Frameline had represented itself to the press as "nonpartisan" even as it was coordinating with an Israeli government entity: the consulate in San Francisco.[47] At a 2012 Frameline screening of an Israeli film, queer Palestinian solidarity activists interrupted the introductory remarks by Frameline director KC Price to protest the festival's official partnership with the Israeli consulate. QUIT activists coordinated by Kate Raphael, the group's queer Jewish cofounder, presented festival organizers with the Pink Sponge Award, a symbol for pinkwashing, and accused Frameline of "silencing queers who want their film festival to stand up for the human rights of Palestinians."[48]

May 2017 was particularly significant for the global queer Palestinian solidarity movement in its struggle against the pinkwashing of films and film festivals. That month, award-winning South African filmmaker John Trengove announced his intention to boycott TLVFest, which was scheduled to screen his film *The Wound* on opening night. Trengove wrote, "While I appreciate that the organizers of TLVFest may be well intentioned and progressive, it is impossible to look past the fact that the festival (and my participation in it) could serve as a diversion from the human rights violations being committed by the state of Israel."[49] He added that he was following the cultural boycott and that "with the pain of the Apartheid struggle still fresh in our collective consciousness, the issue is, as you can imagine, a very sensitive one for many South Africans."[50] In a follow-up letter, Trengove added,

> I have however come to believe that as long as current circumstances in Israel prevail, a rigorous boycott against ALL government funded initiatives is necessary. As a South African, I have first-hand experience of how boycotts helped bring about democratic transformation and therefore have decided to add my name and voice to the boycott Israel initiative.[51]

Festival organizers rejected the notion that their efforts constituted a form of pinkwashing and emphasized their commitment to including films that address Palestinian struggles. "We do not deny being partially sponsored by the [Israeli] Ministry of Culture," they wrote, "but no international film festival in Israel can be held without their support. Unlike other countries it is impossible to have a festival without government support."[52]

Meanwhile, right-wing members of the Israeli government threatened to withdraw funds from TLVFest because it included submissions by filmmakers who support BDS. These events highlight the precarious position in which progressive Israeli artists find themselves. Progressive Israeli filmmakers who produce work critical of the Israeli occupation risk being boycotted and accused of pinkwashing for accepting funds from the Israeli state in a context in which financial support for the arts is very limited. Yet if they reject such funds and speak openly about their reasoning, they are likely to face boycott calls from the right. TLVFest ultimately proceeded, and three other filmmakers with featured films joined Trengove in boycotting the festival, leading to a wave of cancellations. Today, contestation around the screening of queer Israel/Palestine films continues apace at film festivals and more intimate venues around the world.

In October 2012, I received an invitation to speak at the United Nations in New York as part of an event on gay Palestinians and asylum. The event organizers planned to screen the film *Invisible Men*, a documentary featuring the struggles of three gay Palestinian men hiding in Tel Aviv. Yariv Mozer, the Israeli filmmaker, had agreed to speak after the screening, and the organizers invited me to present alongside him. After preliminarily agreeing to attend, I conferred with queer Palestinian colleagues, making the case that the forum presented an invaluable opportunity for UN diplomats and others to hear from me as an empowered gay Palestinian. The gay Palestinians featured in the film, whose voices are mediated by an Israeli filmmaker, have faced heartbreaking adversities from Palestinian and Israeli societies. I appreciated the opportunity to attend the event and contribute additional data points to the heterogeneous mosaic of queer Palestinian experiences. But fellow queer Palestinian activists dissuaded me from participating. My colleagues were concerned that my presence would lend legitimacy to what they viewed as a pinkwashing film (which had benefited from Israeli state funds) and that the event would portray Israelis as essentially queer friendly and Palestinians as inherently homophobic. Because it was important for me to avoid being perceived as perpetuating such pinkwashing discourse, I withdrew from the event, explaining to the organizers the various pressures I was feeling. One of the organizers kindly agreed to read my statement at the event. I did feel a sense of loss, though, that the audience did not have the opportunity to engage with a queer Palestinian voice that had a very different set of experiences than the ones they saw onscreen that day.

Pinkwashing Film Tropes

Such experiences have led me to the realization that what constitutes a pinkwashing film is deeply contested and that what is ultimately at stake in these debates is the politics of representation: who is allowed to speak for queer Palestinians, and who determines how their lives and struggles are represented for local and international audiences? It is also a way of using the publicity of the cultural event or product to raise political questions and to draw attention to institutional hegemony through funding. Efforts to police this domain risk marginalizing certain queer Palestinian voices and flattening the heterogeneity of queer Palestinian experiences. The emergence of a queer Palestinian movement in Israel/Palestine has elevated particular activists as leaders of the community, but their empowerment as the primary authorities on queer representation has foreclosed constructive conversations about pinkwashing in film. Although there is a set of enduring tropes that reinforce pinkwashing, we must be more careful how we attach this label to queer Israeli/Palestinian films. Otherwise we risk undermining pinkwashing in detrimental ways. In this section, I will analyze recent prominent examples of pinkwashing in Israeli films, from those that are the most obvious in their pinkwashing to those that are the most subtle.

The most offensive and straightforwardly pinkwashed film genre is the subset of Israeli gay pornographic films known as "desecration porn."[53] Coined by queer Palestinian solidarity activist Nadia Awad, the term indicates a grotesque merging of supremacist ideology, colonized landscapes, and pinkwashing. Michael Lucas, a gay man who left Russia for the United States and eventually obtained Israeli citizenship, has become a leading gay porn entrepreneur through his company, Lucas Entertainment. In an interview, Lucas described his background.

> I experienced a great deal of anti-Semitism when I was growing up in Russia. Part of my family was killed in the Holocaust. . . . That's why I understand the need for Jews to have their own state where they can defend themselves and never be exterminated again. My great-grandfather was a rabbi and was killed in his own synagogue by Nazis. . . . I believe in the state of Israel and the history of my people, which was very tragic. The contributions Jews have made to the world are great, and all the Jews were getting back was discrimination and extermination.[54]

Motivated by his support for Israel, Lucas produced *Undressing Israel: Gay Men in the Promised Land*, a documentary celebrating LGBTQ life in Israel, as well as the gay porn film *Men of Israel*, which Lucas described as the first pornographic film with an all-Jewish cast.

Men of Israel is two hours long and showcases much of Israel/Palestine's beautiful geography. As journalist Mitchell Sunderland notes, "If not for all the hardcore gay sex, it could have been made by the Israel Ministry of Tourism."[55] In an interview with Sunderland, Lucas stated, "I totally wanted to bring attention to Israel and bring tourists and it was a success."[56] After publishing a pro-Israel opinion piece in the *Advocate* during the 2014 Israel-Gaza War, Lucas told the *Times of Israel*:

> I'm sure people will comment on my article and say, "Oh, yeah, you're having fun in Israel while babies are dying, you're going dancing while Israel murders, whatever." They will say what they want and I will explain very clearly how Israel was well-prepared with the Iron Dome for this, and that this whole idea of proportionate response is ridiculous. . . . Whatever they say, I don't care. My thoughts are always with Israel.[57]

Lucas is not only indifferent to or actively supportive of the suffering of Palestinians, but his films also contribute to the ongoing erasure of Palestinian bodies, voices, and experiences from the landscape of Israel/Palestine and the historical record.

In an interview with *Try State* magazine, Lucas commented on *Men of Israel*:

> The next day we went to an abandoned village just north of Jerusalem. It was a beautiful ancient township that had been deserted centuries ago. . . . However, that did not stop our guys from mounting each other and trying to repopulate it. Biology may not be the lesson of the day but these men shot their seeds all over the village.[58]

The inhabitants of the Palestinian village to which Lucas was referring and in which a portion of his porn film was shot were forcibly uprooted from their homes during the establishment of Israel in 1948. Viewers of *Men of Israel*, however, are led to believe that an unknown people "abandoned" their village "centuries ago" and that what is significant is the ability of Israelis to film gay porn amid the site's natural beauty. Many Palestinians are painfully aware of this video, and this has, at times, sharpened homophobia within Palestinian society. One queer Palestinian shared with me that he was asked by a straight acquaintance, "Oh, you are gay, like Michael Lucas gay?" Mortified, the queer Palestinian replied, "No, absolutely not. He is one kind of gay, and I am a completely different kind of gay."

Lucas's desecration porn has thus been established as the most egregious form of pinkwashing, but the question of whether pinkwashing is present in other kinds of queer Israel/Palestine films is typically much less straightforward. It is difficult for any queer film on Israel/Palestine to emerge without being labeled pinkwashing by at least some activists. *Yossi & Jagger*, the 2002 film by Israeli film director Eytan Fox, features a love affair between two male Israeli soldiers stationed on the Lebanese border, troubling queer Palestinian solidarity activists for what they viewed as the normalization of Israeli militarism through gay representation. Fox's 2006 film, *The Bubble*, follows a group of friends in Tel Aviv, including a gay male Israeli soldier who meets his Palestinian lover at a checkpoint. The Palestinian, Ashraf, loses his sister when she is killed by Israeli soldiers conducting a search in the West Bank for the perpetrators of a bombing in Tel Aviv. His brother-in-law, Jihad, a Hamas militant, puts pressure on Ashraf to marry his female cousin and sets out to avenge the killing of his wife. Ashraf then chooses to take his brother-in-law's place, blowing himself up along with his Israeli lover in Tel Aviv. The film's representation of Israelis and Palestinians was reductive, sensationalizing Palestinian violence and reinforcing anti-Palestinian stereotypes, thus earning it a pinkwashing designation from many activists.

In the 2012 film *Out in the Dark*, Israeli filmmaker Michael Mayer also explores love between an Israeli and Palestinian. The Palestinian's mother and sister are portrayed as deeply religious and his brother as an angry militant. Ella Taylor, in a review for National Public Radio (NPR), writes:

> Paving the way for a brand-new subgenre—the gay romantic thriller—the atmospheric neo-noir *Out in the Dark* tells of a Palestinian university student who seeks refuge from the homophobia of his traditionalist West Bank village in the more gay-friendly atmosphere of metropolitan Tel Aviv.
>
> There Nimr (Nicholas Jacob) falls in love with Roy (Michael Aloni), a privileged Jewish lawyer from a seemingly liberal family. Israeli-born director Michael Mayer handles their love affair with sexual candor, but his heroes' godlike physical beauty also, somehow, projects a blazing, innocent purity.[59]

For Palestinian solidarity activists, this juxtaposition of Israel and the West Bank is a marker of the film's pinkwashing. Purists consider the Palestinian actor to have betrayed his people by accepting a role in this film.

The Israeli "hero" embodies the figure of the white savior that also bothered queer activists in Yariv Mozer's filmmaking. Like Mozer's *Invisible Men*, though, *Out in the Dark* provides a forceful critique of Israel's treatment of Palestinians. A gay friend of Nimr's is killed by Palestinian militants who accuse him of collaboration after Israeli intelligence agents exploit his vulnerable position to extract information before ultimately deporting him back to the West Bank. Nimr is likewise blackmailed by Israel to spy on his Palestinian classmates. Yet as with *Invisible Men* and *The Bubble, Out in the Dark* reinforces the simplistic binary that Palestinian men are either violent militants or forced to seek refuge in Israel. All three films deliver the message—true in certain contexts—that it is not possible for openly gay Palestinians to exist at home as a result of both Israeli state oppression and Palestinian society's rejection of their sexuality. Queer Palestinian solidarity activist Brady Forrest describes *Out in the Dark* as a pinkwashing film because "it overtly and covertly perpetuates racism, apartheid, and the excusing of the Israeli occupation."[60] This is a serious accusation that implicates Mayer's intentions in producing the film and reduces it to mere propaganda in support of the Israeli regime. But the criticism of Israeli policies in this film undermines the notion that Mayer is simply an apologist for Israel. *Out in the Dark*'s portrayal of contemporary Israel was overall quite damning. Pinkwatching activists are correct to problematize certain reductive representations of queer Palestinians, but they are ill-served by denying the legitimacy and authenticity of every aspect of the queer Palestinian experience depicted in this film and others like it. Furthermore, pinkwatching activists fail to recognize the textuality of such films, which asks for a reading and analysis along multiple axes.

Although it is far-fetched to portray gay Palestinians as imminently susceptible to becoming suicide bombers or even to portray them as living in such close proximity to militant activity, as the plots of many of these films require, other experiences depicted in this body of work—such as vulnerability, familial homophobia, and societal rejection—resonate with many, though surely not all, queer Palestinians. In his film review, Forrest recognizes the existence of Palestinian homophobia, attributing it "in large part . . . to outside influences from the West, of which Israel must be included."[61] Forrest does not acknowledge, however, the way *Out in the Dark* so poignantly illustrates how Israel's entrapment of queer Palestinians exacerbates homophobia in Palestinian society. That said, it is clear that Mayer critically interrogates neither the savior complex he reinforces nor the moral equivalence he establishes between occupying and occupied societies. In an interview, Mayer described his intention not to take political sides and distanced himself from what he called the "radical" Israeli activists who protest, in solidarity, alongside Palestinians in the Occupied Territories.[62]

Similarly, *Invisible Men* traced the struggle of three gay Palestinian men escaping the homophobia of their families and society in the West Bank

as well as anti-Palestinian persecution within Israel. The Israeli film director Yariv Mozer describes these men as being "hunted"[63] by the Israeli authorities as they hide in Israel and plan their escape from Israel/Palestine.
Louie had been hiding in Tel Aviv for eight years, Abdu was "exposed as gay
in Ramallah and accused of espionage and tortured by Palestinian security
forces,"[64] and Faris's family in the West Bank tried to kill him, precipitating
his escape to Tel Aviv. Abdu says, "The Palestinians won't accept us because
we are gay, and the Israelis won't accept us because we are Palestinians without permits." At the end of the film, after the trio receive asylum in Europe,
the pain of being uprooted from their homeland and separated from their
families is represented in a palpable manner.

In 2012, queer solidarity activists protested outside of the Vancouver
Queer Film Festival's screening of Invisible Men, charging the film with pinkwashing on the basis that it had received Israeli government funding. One
activist, Arielle Friedman, charged that "Israel's attempt to pinkwash apartheid includes its funding and support for movies like 'The Invisible Men,'
which fail to portray the realities of Israel as a settler colonial state." Friedman equated the festival's decision to screen the film with "perpetuat[ing] the
silencing of Palestinian queers who resist colonization as queer minorities on
a daily basis."[65] Other commentators, meanwhile, took issue with the characterization of Invisible Men as a pinkwashing effort. Citing the film's clear criticisms of the way Israel treated the gay Palestinian men it featured, journalist Sigal Samuel wrote, "As the film went on to depict checkpoints, barriers,
and the thousand indignities visited upon Palestinians every day, it became
increasingly hard to see how this film could rightly be accused of pinkwashing."[66] After hearing from Yariv Mozer, Samuel wrote, "Mozer, meanwhile,
emphasized that he did not believe there was an 'official' Israeli program of
propaganda underlying the government's decision to finance his film."[67]

In a subsequent interview, Mozer laments the reduced funds for progressive Israeli cultural production under the country's increasingly right-wing
government. He goes on in that interview to describes Palestinians as "prim-
itive"[68] and claims that queer solidarity activists in San Francisco tried to silence him just as right-wing prime minister Benjamin Netanyahu attempted
to silence the Israeli left. Expressing his desire to "help" gay Palestinians at
risk of being killed, he compares what he considers the relative openness of
Israeli society to the dangers of being queer in Palestinian society. For many
queer Palestinian solidarity activists, Mozer's discourse clearly expresses
both the logic of pinkwashing and a condescending white-savior complex.

Queer Israeli-Palestinian Love

Such films raise important questions about the possibility of queer love across the Israeli-Palestinian divide. Queer Palestine activism does not always account for the different forms of solidarity—and, yes, love—that sometimes exist between queer Israelis and Palestinians. I have engaged with radical purists who believe that the cinematic representation of queer Israeli-Palestinian love is always a form of pinkwashing. My view is that in many cases the transgressing of boundaries imposed on Israelis and Palestinians in such an intimate manner is also a transgression of Israeli apartheid and the ideological project that undergirds pinkwashing.

Tablet Magazine once featured an interview with two twenty-nine-year-old men, one Israeli and one Palestinian, who were dating but then had to break up as a result of constraints on their travel and the inability to be physically present with one another due to the geographic separation imposed by Israel. They described an instance of being stopped by Israeli police because the Palestinian was "illegally" in Jerusalem. The former couple discussed the affection they had for each other. The Israeli, crying, said, "We had a very big love," and the Palestinian said, "I thought it would last forever." The latter described introducing his Israeli partner to his family, who was accepting of the relationship, but then he explained that he could not be out in Palestinian society, where people say that gays should be killed. He expressed his desire to leave the country, saying, "I really don't feel like Palestine is my home, I feel like a stranger in this place." The Israeli also expressed his intention to leave. "I had enough," he said. "Everything is against you. The law is against you. . . . This separation is so deep, and when individuals try to break it, they wear out. I'm all worn out."[69]

Gay Israeli-Palestinian relationships are not common, but the stories that surface demonstrate how challenging it is for these couples to navigate so many complications. In 2012, Amira Haas, an Israeli journalist who has devoted her life to exposing the Israeli occupation, reported in the Israeli newspaper *Haaretz* on a gay Israeli-Palestinian couple who had been together for two years when they were stopped in Jerusalem by Israeli police. As in the *Tablet* story, the Palestinian, a West Bank resident, was traveling "illegally" in Jerusalem. The police questioned his Israeli partner and recommended "charging him with transporting a person illegally in Israel."[70] The Israeli security services later attempted to recruit the Palestinian as an informant, threatening to out him to the Palestinian Authority. Haas writes,

Shaul Ganon, an activist with the Israeli National LGBT Task Force, who specializes in requests for temporary legal status for Palestinian partners in gay Palestinian-Israeli couples, says the sensitive position of gay people in Palestinian society puts them at risk of blackmail by both Israeli and Palestinian intelligence agencies. "The Shin Bet tries to draft almost every gay Palestinian that gets arrested," he told Haaretz.[71]

Another *Haaretz* article highlights the story of Majed Koka, a Palestinian man who had been living with his Israeli partner for eight years when it became known that he was gay. He began receiving threats and left the West Bank, eventually going to live with his partner in Israel. On a rare trip to visit his family, Koka "was arrested by the Palestinian police on suspicion of collaborating with Israel and subjected to severe torture—which he believes was prompted by his sexual orientation."[72] Koka contextualizes his experience. "There have been cases of people like me who went back to visit their families and were attacked," he said, adding that in such cases, "the assailants usually begin by saying they heard the victim is gay and only then move on to accusing him of collaboration with Israel."[73]

In 2002, Koka and his Israeli partner registered as a married couple with the local municipality, which proved to be futile because Israel does not fully recognize gay marriages. In 2009, Koka requested legal residency from the Israeli interior ministry and did not receive a response. This was despite an interior ministry decision the previous year to grant a gay Palestinian from the West Bank a temporary residency permit to live with his partner in Tel Aviv. The lawyer in that case successfully argued that the applicant "faced death threats from fellow Palestinians who disapproved of him being gay."[74] The decision was a rare exception. In a 2012 interview with the *Daily Beast*, Sabin Hada, spokesperson for the interior minister, falsely stated that "according to international law, being gay is not a reason for granting asylum" and then asserted that "anyone can say that they're gay in order to get asylum. How can we know for sure?"[75] Such skepticism of homosexual claims is reflected in the routine rejection of gay Palestinian asylum seekers. Koka, for his part, also applied for refugee status with the UN High Commissioner for Refugees (UNHCR) but was turned away because UNHCR cannot serve Palestinians. Deemed "illegal" by the Israeli state, "he is subject to frequent arrests; his lawyer is constantly fighting for his release."[76] As a result of these legal conditions, it is challenging to ascertain the number of queer Palestinians from the Occupied Territories living in Israel, with or without Israeli partners.

The Israeli regime of control, separation, and subjugation has a devastating impact on queer Palestinian lives. At the same time, it is important to understand Palestinian homophobia on its own terms and in the context of Palestine's own cultural logics and social norms of heteronormativity and patriarchy. For queer Palestinians, homophobia and Zionism operate in both parallel and intersecting ways. The empirical reality is that some queer Palestinians, in precarious and sometimes dangerous circumstances, do seek support from Israeli institutions, including the National LGBT Task Force (Aguda). Others become activists with the queer Palestinian movement, calling for a boycott of Israeli institutions. The solution to the limited representations of queer Palestinian voices in existing films and other domains is the production of more artistic works, films, and documentaries and the undertaking of more research and knowledge so that audiences can be exposed to a bigger mosaic of queer Palestinian subjectivities. One part of this mosaic captured by film is intimate queer Israeli-Palestinian relationships across apartheid divides.

Certainly, some films have succeeded in capturing queer Israeli-Palestinian love alongside rich and nuanced depictions of queer Palestinian experiences. Canadian-Jewish filmmaker Elle Flanders, who grew up in Israel, produced a powerful documentary, *Zero Degrees of Separation*, that juxtaposes images from her family's archive of their settlement in Israel with interviews and footage of two mixed Israeli-Palestinian couples. Ezra, an Israeli antioccupation activist, and Selim, his Palestinian partner, are stigmatized in their respective societies and struggle to live together in Jerusalem with the constant threat of deportation for Selim. They passionately describe their resistance to the occupation, the struggle of life under the Israeli regime, and the harassment, homophobia, and continual arrests that Selim faces at the hands of the Israeli police and security services.

Samira is a nurse and Palestinian citizen of Israel who is also an antioccupation activist. Her girlfriend, Edit, is a progressive Jewish Israeli who works as a social worker at the rape crisis center in Tel Aviv. As they try to bridge the cultural divides between them and cultivate their love for each other, Samira and Edit are articulate in describing their reality. Edit asserts, "I have no problem saying that we are to blame. Zionism did not take into account that there was another nation here. It could have been done differently, but it was not done differently." Later in the film, she says that the Israel she knew was far from the dream of Zionism that she was raised with and that "the entire lesbian agenda has been abandoned and the feminist agenda is about to be abandoned, and we will be left with a militaristic country with acute problems of unemployment and hunger, with Arabs as scapegoats."[77] Further images and narration by Flanders allow the viewer to analyze her positionality as the filmmaker: her Zionist familial background contrasted with the anti-Zionist queer Israeli and Palestinian subjects of her film sheds light on her use of cultural production to support the global queer Palestinian solidarity movement.

Samira also appears in the documentary *City of Borders* by Korean American filmmaker Yun Suh. Suh features five queer patrons of Shushan, a gay bar in Jerusalem, including Sa'ar, the Israeli bar owner; Adam, a young Israeli living in an illegal settlement north of Jerusalem; Boody, a religious young Palestinian man from the West Bank; and Samira and her girlfriend at the time, Ravit, a Jewish Israeli doctor. Samira and Ravit had met at the hospital where they both work and had been living together for four years at the time of filming. They describe the taboos of family and society that they confront as an Israeli-Palestinian lesbian couple. Both Sa'ar and Adam are activists, with Sa'ar having been the first openly gay man elected to public office in Jerusalem. He describes the violence and death threats he faces from fellow Israelis as a result of his public identity. Adam built a home with his male partner in the settlement and worked to secure a civil union in Israel. He describes being stabbed three times by an Israeli extremist while marching in the 2005 Jerusalem Pride parade. Most devastating, though, is Boody's situation. He puts everything at risk to sneak into Jerusalem to perform in drag at Shushan, an exhilarating and affirming experience given the harassment he encounters from Palestinian society because of his effeminate demeanor. After receiving threats of violence, he processes the realization that he may have to leave Palestine, remarking, "I think I'm going to be losing myself." He still has love and affection for Palestine as well as a strong faith in Islam. *City of Borders* captures the different tensions, contradictions, creativity, and resilience that queer Palestinians and Israelis embody.

Queer Palestinian Films

Radical purists in the queer Palestinian movement sometimes insist that queer Israel/Palestine cinema should focus exclusively on Palestinians in order to avoid the juxtaposition component so central to pinkwashing. This section examines two queer Palestinian films to highlight the important development of queer Palestinians playing leading roles in the production and circulation of films relevant to their lives.

The title of queer Palestinian filmmaker Raafat Hattab's *Houria* is a double entendre that deliberately combines the Arabic words for "freedom" and "mermaid." Colleen Jancovic and Nadia Awad write that "Hattab performs a kind of in-between state—queerly embodied as neither male nor female, human nor fish, and positioned between the resort beaches of Tel Aviv and the shores of the Old City of Jaffa."[78] Scenes include Hattab as a mermaid lying on the shore of ethnically cleansed Manshiye as well as footage of his aunt describing the forced displacement of their family from Manshiye, which lies at the meeting point between Palestinian Jaffa and Israeli Tel Aviv. The film also shows Hattab receiving an Arabic tattoo that reads "Jaffa, Bride of Palestine." Jancovic and Awad observe that *Houria*'s "queer and feminist perspective reframes a predominantly masculinist narrative of Palestinian national loss and struggle for return through the emphasis on listening to Hattab's aunt's voice."[79] Hattab, the mermaid and tattoo bearer, remains silent throughout, accompanied by a queer Palestinian playing a traditional Arabic song with a violin.

The queering of Palestinian film also emerges in Palestinian visual artist Sharif Waked's *Chic Point*. In this seven-minute art film, images of Palestinians lifting their clothes for Israeli soldiers at checkpoints to demonstrate that they are not carrying weapons are juxtaposed with a fashion show of Israeli and Palestinian men that Waked curated. These men reveal flesh, primarily hairy, toned abdomens. Omar Kholeif writes,

> Waked queers his subjects by fetishizing them and their ensembles. Fashion garments are cropped into such revealing items as crocheted tank tops akin to S/M fetish attire. The sexualization of the act of inspection is enhanced by the postures adopted by Waked's players. As the men gaze at the camera, lifting their shirts with taunting call-boy seduction, the artist shifts the video's focus; the silent second half of the work consists of a series of photographic stills from Gaza and the West Bank that evoke starkly violent counter realities.[80]

Those counterrealities, the routine humiliations endured by Palestinian men forced to publicly disrobe in front of occupying soldiers, quickly temper the seduction for a homosexual male gaze.

Gil Z. Hochberg also offers a queer lens through which to understand Waked's work:

The film's critical impact relies heavily on its effective mobilization of queer desire as a way to make "the invisible" visible, calling attention to the central role of homoeroticism— its enactment, repression, displacement, and redirection— in both sustaining and potentially transgressing the national or racial borders engraved by the toxic Israeli occupation and played out as stripping rituals at the checkpoints.[81]

According to Hochberg, *Chic Point's* message is that the Israeli national security justification for strip searching is "a mere pretext for an explicitly 'perverse' and sexually charged exchange in which Israeli soldiers 'check out' Palestinian men, who are in turn ordered to (un)dress for the occasion."[82] Although the oppressive nature of this practice is clear, Hochberg also recognizes the agency of the Palestinian men highlighted in Waked's footage. Analyzing the behavior of one man at a checkpoint who commands the attention of the soldiers, Hochberg writes, "His gesture of opening the jacket and exposing his chest no longer conveys the predictable message of submission or humiliation. Rather, it seems confrontational and teasing, if not explicitly seductive."[83] This is not to say that Waked intended to portray some Palestinian men as literally seducing the occupying soldiers degrading them. Instead, he seems to hope that viewers will recognize that amid the tragedy and brutality of Israel/Palestine there also exist conscious and unconscious, latent and overt, and expected and unexpected forms of homosociality and irreducibly human homosexual desire.

An alternative form of queer Palestinian activism is emerging outside of the formal structures of queer Palestinian organizations (Al-Qaws, Aswat, PQBDS, and Pinkwatching Israel), catalyzed by individuals such as Khader Abu-Seif, a queer Palestinian activist and citizen of Israel. Predictably, Abu-Seif has received public criticism from radical purists among his fellow queer Palestinians. His writing and activism is trilingual, integrating Arabic, Hebrew, and English, and he is open about living in Israel and falling in love with Jewish Israeli citizens, even as he recognizes the anti-Palestinian and anti-Arab racism endemic to Israeli society. Abu-Seif relates deeply personal experiences and their attendant complexities but does not shy away from describing emotions such as the "humiliation of being asked to undress by two Border Policemen in the middle of Tel Aviv" for the crime of carrying a large backpack while Arab.[84] His wide following among Jewish Israelis enables him to raise consciousness about the systematic discrimination that he and other Palestinian citizens of Israel endure as they attempt to make lives for themselves in that difficult social milieu.

In 2015, Abu-Seif appeared in the documentary *Oriented*, which explores the intersection of the national and sexual struggles experienced by Abu-Seif and two other gay Palestinians living in Tel Aviv, Naeem Jiryes and Fadi Daeem. The three friends are very close, as is apparent in the footage captured by the British filmmaker Jake Witzenfeld. Abu-Seif is shown navigating the alienation he feels as a Palestinian in Israel living with his Jewish Israeli partner. Daeem finds himself falling in love with a Zionist, a painful and bewildering experience exacerbated by the guilt he feels for not living under military occupation alongside his Palestinian compatriots in the West Bank and Gaza Strip. Jiryes, for his part, negotiates coming out to his family while finding his own voice and independence. Some queer Palestinian activists have labeled *Oriented* a pinkwashing film; others have pointed to the director Jake Witzenfeld's non-Palestinian identity as a reason to suspect his intentions; and still others have rushed to discredit the trio's legitimacy in speaking for queer Palestinians. Yet, the fact that the documentary contains very little editorializing and is mainly devoted to showcasing the perspectives of its queer Palestinian protagonists—who speak for themselves and on their own terms—is reason enough to regard their experiences as authentic and worthy of representation. They express one set of subjectivities in a broad universe of queer Palestinian experiences.

No one can speak for all queer Palestinians, of course, but that impossibility should not discredit any particular voice from being heard, especially when it is based on real experiences. *Oriented* has done tremendously well at securing global audiences, with screenings at film festivals, universities, LGBTQ centers, and other venues across the world. The fact that this group of friends speaks openly about their Palestinian identities; that they refer to Tel Aviv as part of Palestine; that they draw attention to anti-Arab racism and discrimination in Israel; and that they use the language of apartheid to describe Israeli policies all help undermine critiques of the film. The overriding focus on Palestinian voices and the potential for this film to challenge the logic of pinkwashing belies the charge that the film constitutes a form of pinkwashing. During my interview with the protagonists in Tel Aviv, they emphasized their agency as queer Palestinians in their responses to the radical purist critiques of the film.

At the same time, they disapproved of Witzenfeld's decision to screen *Oriented* at TLVFest in 2016. Daeem, who had once been an activist with Al-Qaws but left the organization after experiencing alienation, released the following statement on his Facebook page.

3 years ago I took part in a documentary called "Oriented." Over the last year the film has spread through cinemas around the world, from New York to Bucharest.

I feel proud of what my closest friends and I accomplished but somewhere along the way the message I tried to bring got lost. Now the film is set to open the TLV Fest (an LGBTQ film festival that takes place during Pride Week in Tel Aviv) and I couldn't be more ashamed.

In my opinion, the film was made to highlight a new struggle that the occupation has created, the struggle of clashing identities and discrimination. Screening the film during TLV Fest, a festival sponsored by the Israeli government, is a direct act of Pinkwashing and represents the opposite of what I tried to accomplish with the film.

An occupying country cannot celebrate freedom while denying it from a whole nation.

A racist country cannot celebrate diversity.

I will not take part in these screenings and celebrations. I hope you won't either.[85]

Daeem called for a boycott of a screening of the very film in which his life experiences had been highlighted, and he publicly expressed his sense of betrayal at Witzenfeld's decision to showcase the documentary in that venue. Some of the film's earliest critics felt that Daeem's post had vindicated their concerns about it being a form of pinkwashing, while others saw Daeem's principled stance as evidence of the sound moral compass and antipinkwashing underpinnings that had guided his decisions all along, including his initial decision to take part in the film project.

In his critique of *Oriented*, queer Palestinian writer Fady Khoury notes that the documentary was shot during the 2014 Israeli war in Gaza and that it did not represent the suffering of Palestinians in Gaza. The exclusion of voices from Gaza, Khoury writes, makes "clear what the film . . . left out, and what Israeli Pride events conceal when it comes to the challenges facing Palestinians, including LGBTQ Palestinians."[86] This critique reveals the immense burden placed on queer Palestinian activists such as Abu-Seif and Daeem. Although they live in Tel Aviv and work in Israeli society, they are expected to provide a window into life in Gaza and to speak for people there. When they don't accomplish this, their activism is rendered suspect because it does not represent every Palestinian experience. They have been criticized for not amplifying a range of other voices and perspectives: What about the

West Bank? What about the Diaspora? The "whatabouts" are endless. But the real question we should be asking ourselves is: how constructive is it to critique activists for "singling out" their own voices, experiences, locales, and positionalities?

Abu-Seif has developed a particularly thick skin. Despite the enormous resistance he has faced from the right and the left, he believes in the power of his own authentic expression of self. Nonetheless, it was painful for Abu-Seif, Daeem, and Jiryes to read the public statement released by Al-Qaws denouncing the film as pinkwashing and labeling it an "unfortunate erasure of Palestinian queer narratives." The statement reads:

> Perhaps the main danger of the film's discourse is its purportedly "sophisticated" framing, which the film adopts in an alleged effort to avoid promoting clichéd, pinkwashing stories about queer Palestinians as victims of society and Israelis as saviors, etc. Despite good intentions, we think this film and the media discourse around it nevertheless reproduce these same mistakes. The film's aim to promote "stories about strong queer Palestinians" is based in the same dehumanizing racist assumptions that also lay at the heart of "queer Palestinians as victims" movies. It is a pity to define our stories within an unfortunate racist and binary choice—we are "strong" or we are "victims"—promoted by the Israeli and Western audiences who are this film genre's primary consumers.[87]

Abu-Seif, Daeem, and Jiryes were puzzled by the assertion that the film featured Israeli "saviors" (of which they could not identify any). They were likewise perplexed by the argument that, by highlighting their strength and resilience as queer Palestinian citizens of Israel, the film was somehow reproducing pinkwashing or promoting false binaries (with their understanding that one of pinkwashing's goals is the denial of queer Palestinian agency).

The Al-Qaws statement also chastised the film for purporting to be "universal" and claiming that its protagonists purport to represent "a new generation of queer Palestinians."[88] Just as Al-Qaws has spoken for queer Palestinians writ large despite now representing the small fraction of queer Palestinians who adhere to a very particular set of radical political positions, so too do the *Oriented* protagonists represent a specific generational current among queer individuals living in historic Palestine and navigating their sense of identity and belonging amid the regimes of control and societal homophobia that shape their lives. The Al-Qaws statement positions queer Palestinians in Tel Aviv as somehow completely disconnected from—and in cir-cumstances utterly different than—those living in other cities in Israel and the West Bank without recognizing the parallel conditions and experiences that unite queer Palestinians across geography. There is a contradiction in ac-cusing *Oriented* of both falsely universalizing a local experience *and* repro-ducing the pinkwashing logic of Tel Aviv as exceptional. In reality, by fram-ing Tel Aviv as completely separate from historic Palestine, the Al-Qaws statement itself advances the pinkwashing image of Tel Aviv as a gay ha-ven. The deeply personal testimonies presented by the documentary are very much grounded in Tel Aviv *and* in the protagonists' identification as queer Palestinians—their sense of belonging to struggles against both racism and homophobia in what they consider historic Palestine. This, coupled with their connection to other queer Palestinians, undermines pinkwashing in ways the Al-Qaws statement is unable to recognize.

The statement also disregards other examples of the film's opposition to pinkwashing, such as when the friends attend a concert in Amman. They speak about their positive experiences as gay Arab men visiting Jordan and enjoying a concert by an Arab band whose lead singer is openly gay and inte-grates lyrics that address gender and sexual diversity. The friends push back against the common pinkwashing trope that says that only Israel, and none of the Arab countries surrounding Israel, could ever make such an experi-ence possible for gay people. In its online blog, "Palestine Square," the Insti-tute for Palestine Studies explains precisely how the film contests the logic of pinkwashing.

> In one scene, Khader relates he's often told *if you don't like it here, go to Jordan and see how they treat gay people.* As he looks around the hipster concert in . . . Amman, Jordan, he says with a smirk *well, here I am.*
>
> The trio of friends shy neither from Israeli discrimination nor Palestinian homophobia: They are proud and expressive of their culture, live openly as a right in their homeland and not a privilege bequeathed by their conqueror, and they need no caveats in their identity as gay Palestinians. They remind us that gay rights and queer liberation are not discrete causes, but only realize their full potential within a broader securement of individual and collective rights.[89]

Although some gay Palestinians do feel alienated from their nationality as a result of Palestinian homophobia, *Oriented* demonstrates that it is possible to embrace both your sexual and national identity as a queer Palestinian despite tremendous societal efforts to constrain that.

While Abu-Seif is passionate about his activism, his media interviews make it clear that he hopes the film will serve as a tool for the empowerment of other gay Palestinians; he encourages them to celebrate both aspects of who they are. In a June 2015 interview with *Out* magazine, Abu-Seif recalls,

> The second screening in L.A., that was the time I cried. Like, I died on the stage, I couldn't speak. Because, from the beginning, I always told Jake that I want just one gay Palestinian to watch this. And at the end of the movie, there was this guy sitting in the crowd, and he said, "I don't have any questions, but I want to tell you that, I'm American, and I'm gay, and watching this movie, this is the first time that I'm also proud to say that I'm Palestinian." And I was like, [wiping his hands] bye. Because for me, this was the purpose. For me, it was always to represent Palestine; it was to represent the LGBTQs inside of Palestine.[90]

Elsewhere, he adds, "We're fighting two fights here. On one side, we're fighting our fight in front of our communities, in front of Palestinians, to show that we're gay and we're allowed to be gay and to change the perception of what a gay Palestinian is and what a Palestinian is inside this country. The second fight is for your national identity."[91]

In another interview, Abu-Seif identifies an additional struggle that he and other queer Palestinians face: the battle against religious fundamentalists in Palestinian Christian and Muslim communities.

> While I am Muslim and Fadi and Naeem are Christians, we don't talk about it inside of our relationship because we are not those kind of boys. We are human. We are not religious people. But for me, it's super-important for me to say I'm Muslim because I want to show the world, the sheiks, the Muslim fanatics, that we have LGBTs and gays inside our community, to understand that we are here and we are not afraid.[92]

Whereas hegemonic pinkwashing discourses erase the voices of queer Palestinians who are challenging social norms within their cultural and religious communities, Abu-Seif intentionally defies that erasure. He recognizes the importance of non-Palestinian audiences as well. In yet another interview, he says, "I have no idea how much the global audience cares or wants to know more about the Israeli-Palestinian issue. . . . But I hope that people recognise us and our desire to be recognised, and just know that we exist in this big mess."[93] Considering the Palestinian belief that "existence is resistance," Abu-Seif's desire for queer Palestinians to be visible and acknowledged at home and around the world is a powerful form of resistance to both homophobia and Israeli domination, and it sends an inclusive message of inspiration to queer Palestinians across the world. This message and its medium may not resonate with all queer Palestinians, such as some Al-Qaws activists, but dismissing Abu-Seif through reductionist caricatures of his work as pinkwashing only further divides queer Palestinians and those in solidarity with them.

As new screenings of *Oriented* take place around the world, some zealous queer Palestinian solidarity activists, with the Al-Qaws statement in hand, continue to decry the provision of platforms for the film. In fact, after I announced a screening of *Oriented* at my institution and invited Abu-Seif to speak on our campus as part of it, an external activist pressured me to cancel the event. He pointed to the Al-Qaws press release as the reason the film should be boycotted. I responded, sharing the decision to proceed with the screening. I also explained to this activist how ironic it was that Abu-Seif and I, as queer Palestinians, were being asked by a non-Palestinian to censor a film about queer Palestinians because of the solidarity activist's belief that the film is pinkwashing and does not "properly" capture the experience of queer Palestinians. The empire of critique has reached a point at which activists feel entitled to serve as arbiters of which queer Palestinian voices should be considered the most authoritative and archetypical. This impossible endeavor also has the potential to contribute to the dehumanization (through caricatures) of a heterogeneous population, all of whom grapple with double consciousness in their own deeply personal ways, even as community and collective solidarity are possible.

Although *Oriented* has not gained traction in radical purist spaces, it has done very well in broader circles. Abu-Seif has described the film as "the first LGBTQ movie featuring Arab people that doesn't portray them as victims [and] people like to see strong figures fighting for their rights inside of their communities."[94] Abu-Seif is resisting the singular representation of victimhood, whether that is the right focusing on Palestinian oppression of homosexuals or the left focusing on Israeli oppression of Palestinians. By centering the joy, strength, love, pleasure, and friendship of queer Palestinians in the face of so much hardship, *Oriented* destabilizes the pinkwashing/pinkwatching debates from all sides.

Filming the LGBTQ Delegation to Palestine

Debates within the queer Palestinian solidarity community about filming the first LGBTQ delegation to Palestine brought the controversies surrounding pinkwashing and the role of critique very close to home. The queer Palestinian solidarity movement is certainly not monolithic and includes an array of experiences and political worldviews. As transnational solidarity networks have broadened their global reach, queer Palestinian solidarity activists in Palestine and abroad increasingly level critiques against each other. These critiques are both public and private, and because it remains challenging to respond to critiques from external actors, addressing individuals from within the movement has become more common. Proximity facilitates this engagement in ways that can be constructive at times and counterproductive at others.

The increasingly inward gaze of critique has intensified its corrosive, demoralizing effect on movement building. This became evident at several critical moments in the Homonationalism and Pinkwashing Conference at CUNY in April 2013. Nadia Awad, a queer Palestinian American filmmaker based in the United States, presented at a panel on "The Queer Arab Imaginary." She explained that she had filmed the US LGBTQ delegation to Palestine and that she would present a brief excerpt of her in-process documentary for the audience.

As discussed earlier in this book, Sarah Schulman was integral in organizing the delegation to Palestine for sixteen prominent American LGBTQ figures.[95] The tour was initiated at the invitation of Aswat and Al-Qaws, and I served as coleader of the delegation along with Dunya Alwan, who had been director of the Palestinian solidarity tour organization Birthright Unplugged.[96] The delegation was an exhilarating moment for the global queer Palestinian solidarity movement. Queer figures from the United States traveled to Israel/Palestine to bear witness to Palestinian suffering and resilience, discuss how they might display solidarity with the struggle for equal rights between Israelis and Palestinians, and strategize about future activism. In the article I coauthored with one of the delegates, Darnell Moore, we describe how the delegation brought us together, forged a friendship, and advanced one strand of our work: Black-Palestinian queer reciprocal solidarity.[97] Such work reflects the intersectional commitments of the queer Palestinian solidarity movement.

After returning to the United States, I attended the queer film panel at the CUNY conference and was able to hear Awad present about our delegation.

In a clip from her documentary, we watched the delegates walking through the Dheisheh refugee camp in Bethlehem. Two delegates seemed to fall behind, attempting to communicate in broken English with a local Palestinian tour guide. One of them, appearing exhausted, tried respectfully to follow the guide's remarks as he explained the meaning of Handala, a Palestinian artistic symbol that was painted on the wall in front of them. The guide asked whether the delegate was familiar with Handala, and the delegate responded with a no. Shortly thereafter, the second delegate approached a local Palestinian woman standing on her doorstep in the camp, shook her hand, and said to the smiling woman, "Thank you for saying hello." A number of conference attendees began to laugh, creating a deeply unsettling feeling in the room. The symbol of Handala, a prisoner refugee boy famously rendered by acclaimed Palestinian cartoonist Naji al-Ali, was never explained, not to the delegates or even to the audience watching the clip in New York. Handala appears barefoot, his back to the world, fated never to grow old or reveal his face until Palestine is free. Israeli anthropologist Guy Shalev calls Handala "a symbol of Palestinian resistance and defiance" who "silently observ[es] a world dominated by Arab corruption, Israeli repression, and American imperialism."[98] No explanation of Handala as a quintessential form of Palestinian meaning making was communicated to the delegates featured in the film clip, and Awad did not convey that explanation to conference attendees. By presenting communication between the locals and internationals as stunted and awkward, Awad's clip seemed to convey a deep critique of the LGBTQ delegation for failing to make this type of learning possible.

Sarah Schulman, who was present for the panel, asked the first question during the question-and-answer session. Schulman graciously directed it to Awad, saying, "Is it possible to have delegations without colonialism? And to what extent can it still be valuable?" Awad then proceeded to reply as follows:

> I think being a delegate to a place that's suffering from apartheid, and that's under occupation, comes with a lot of personal responsibility, and I think that you really need to do a lot of decolonization work on yourself before you can go there, and go there with a level of humility.[99]

As a coleader of the delegation who had been on the ground in Palestine throughout, it was important for me to hear the filmmaker speak. It was also my first opportunity to view an excerpt from the film and the first time since returning from the delegation that I was able to gather more information about the premise of the documentary. The organizers and queer Palestinian groups that had instigated the delegation welcomed Awad's New York–based film crew to capture the work we were doing in large part because they knew the filmmaker to be an activist in the queer Palestinian movement in the United States. On that basis, we reasonably presumed that she would be in solidarity with our work. It was our belief that she wanted to help further diffuse that solidarity through her filmmaking.

In Palestine, I was the only queer Palestinian who agreed to be filmed for the documentary. The vast majority of my colleagues did not want to be publicly outed. It required a level of trust in the film crew that I was willing to extend because I assumed that we shared a mission. The excerpts screened at the CUNY conference were thus disconcerting. They clearly critiqued the delegates, and I wrote the filmmaker to ask whether the central aim of her documentary was to critique the solidarity delegation as a political project. I also asked whether the upshot of the film was to present the delegation as a form of colonialism. Awad's response to Schulman had left the audience to infer that the delegation was colonial without specifically clarifying Awad's own view. And in fact, her reference to the need for preliminary decolonization work echoed internal critiques that delegation organizers had received—namely, that we had not sufficiently educated and briefed the delegates before they arrived in Palestine. The question of preparation became a contentious matter throughout the experience. Preparatory work is essential, and there definitely is always more that can be done. At the same time, nothing can adequately prepare people for the first time they witness and experience life under military occupation.

My communication with Awad was to discern whether she intended for the thrust of her documentary to be a critique of the delegation as a form of colonialism. Despite pressing her for an explanation of what she was trying to accomplish, I was provided with almost no information. As though the vulnerability I felt as a queer Palestinian welcoming a filmmaker into my world was not reason enough for anxiety, I was now concerned about a possible failure of mutual understanding and an erosion of trust. It was likely that I and my colleagues would be represented as complicit in a colonial project. With no reassurances to the contrary, I explained that I did not want them to use the footage of me. After learning about this, a number of delegates withdrew their consent to be featured in the film. At the CUNY panel, Awad had offered the audience no context, such as the fact that the delegation had traveled to Palestine at the invitation of queer Palestinian groups or that the over-whelming majority of Palestinians encourage international solidarity groups to help break the siege they experience, bear witness to their suffering, support the local economy, and return to their countries to raise consciousness about the Palestinian cause. She did not explain that the language gaps between delegates and locals did not prevent profound forms of communication. The audience was not made aware that we pushed delegates to their limits as a result of our nonstop itinerary, one that they embraced from a place of deep empathy, concern, and solidarity.

The delegate who shook the hand of the local refugee woman did so out of tremendous respect and love. It was therefore painful for me to hear audience members laughing at this delegate and to hear a number of individuals speak disparagingly about her afterward. The sixteen participants took precious time and resources away from their homes and loved ones to join this historic LGBTQ delegation to the Occupied Palestinian Territories. The filmmaker may not have been able to convey all of this at the panel. But that none of it was conveyed and that my concerns were not subsequently addressed signaled to me that her project was in all likelihood just another example of how critique has become the primary lens through which much left-leaning activism around Queer Palestine is conceived and enacted.

At the same Homonationalism and Pinkwashing Conference, Haneen Maikey delivered a keynote address with content that came as a surprise for a number of queer Palestinian solidarity activists. Maikey devoted her address to a series of critiques of the movement. She reiterated the concern that Jewish groups, individuals, and activists were "dominating" movement spaces. She also critiqued some members of the LGBTQ delegation that Al-Qaws had invited to Palestine. Maikey's address reified the East/West binary, framed Palestinian oppression as mutually exclusive to and more urgent than homophobia, and labeled delegates who wanted to discuss homophobia and sexuality in particular as having "sexual privilege."[100] Her critique was communicated to the hundreds of individuals in attendance, the thousands who would receive transcripts of the talk, and the countless other individuals connected to the broader movement.

Although the request that delegates be sensitive to local context in the Occupied Territories was reasonable, the fact that queer Palestinian organizations had invited queer and trans activists made it only natural for delegates to want to connect discussions of the Israeli occupation to sexuality. Delegates asked to misrepresent their relationship status were understandably concerned. Maikey's address did not give voice to queer Palestinians who view Zionism and homophobia as equally central and intertwined in their experience of oppression. And it is not clear why that kind of public critique of international delegates would serve to bolster the movement; in fact, I observed how it created a situation in which queer activists were even more reluctant to engage openly on the topic of Palestine for fear of being charged with reproducing imperialism. A number of the delegates have subsequently withdrawn completely from global Palestinian solidarity activism.

Toward the end of her address, Maikey delineated the three groups with which Al-Qaws refuses to partner: Jewish Israeli groups, LGBTQ groups narrowly focused on sexuality, and groups that are complicit in or take no clear position against Zionism. For queer Palestinians and other queer activists who take a more open approach to political engagement or who believe in the politics of visibility, such messages make it clear that Al-Qaws is not a space in which they are able to invest their time and energy. Maikey's powerful reminder that international activists must be in solidarity not only with queer Palestinians but also with Palestinians more generally was well received by most participants. It is useful to remember that queer Palestinians face many of the same struggles as straight Palestinians and that the fates of queer and straight Palestinians are tied together. But the delivery of that crucial message can be alienating if framed as merely a rebuke of individuals who have spent significant time and resources and taken big risks to engage on Palestinian human rights in the face of formidable opposition from the pro-Israel camp. Maikey's and Awad's public critique of the delegation contributed to a documentary film on the historic LGBTQ delegation to Palestine not seeing the light of day.

Embracing Double Consciousness

In exploring depictions of queer Palestinians in the news media and film, this chapter has illuminated the damaging nature of the controversies generated by the empire of critique and underscored the need for greater interpretive nuance when it comes to the politics of representation. Journalism and filmmaking have contributed to the heightened surveillance and criticism that queer Palestinians face. An excessive focus on the most sensational examples of queer Palestinian vulnerability and the integration of pinkwashing tropes into journalistic reports and narrative films have contributed to the palpable mistrust that leading queer Palestinian activists have of the mainstream media. Yet journalism and film can also offer platforms for solidarity, venues for complex representation, megaphones that amplify a diversity of queer Palestinian voices, and cultural outlets for the expression of queer Palestinian double consciousness.

The leadership of the most globally visible queer Palestinian organization has adopted an ethic of radical purism that effectively denies queer Palestinian double consciousness and promotes distanced relationships with news and film outlets, allies in the movement, fellow queer Palestinians who do not subscribe to radical purist politics, and many others. This chapter examined three of Al-Qaws's public critiques and demonstrated how its interventions served to further alienate queer Palestinians and internationals who otherwise might have enthusiastically embraced Al-Qaws's mission. These include Al-Qaws's criticism of Palestinian solidarity media outlets for their coverage of the Israeli security services' blackmailing of queer Palestinians in a manner that "singles out sexuality"; its criticism of the queer Palestinians featured in the documentary film *Oriented* for being "complicit in pinkwashing"; and its criticism of members of the first LGBTQ delegation to Palestine for "furthering sexual-colonial privilege." Such interventions reveal a pattern that illuminates how the empire of critique has turned inward and thus contributed to the global queer Palestinian movement entering its current plateau phase. Radical purists whose public interventions lambaste media and film representations of queer Palestinians whenever those representations fail to conform to a rarefied ideological model (meant to elevate anti-imperialism above all else) consequently elide the anxiety and ambiguity of double consciousness that characterize much queer Palestinian experience.

The ensuing impasse that has taken hold of the global queer Palestinian solidarity movement can be overcome by radically rethinking how critique is operationalized in the movement, recognizing the need for national and sexual liberation, including a wider variety of queer Palestinian voices through a reduction of ideological policing, and making concerted efforts to partner with journalists and filmmakers in order to broaden rather than constrict solidarity and the range of queer Palestinian perspectives that circulate in the global public sphere.

5 Critique of Empire and the Politics of Academia

DURING OUR PLANNING AND ORGANIZING of the LGBTQ delegation to Palestine, queer Palestinian solidarity activists informed me that they had received an inquiry from a US-based academic. The academic requested one of the sixteen spots on the delegation and inquired about whether the organizers would fundraise to cover that person's specific costs. The person added, "I am interested in being part of this so that I can critique the delegation in my writing upon my return." We were astonished and declined the request. How, we wondered, could anyone expect queer Palestinians to welcome a person into their lives and inner worlds who vows *in advance* to publish academic criticism of the queer Palestinian movement for public audiences abroad? Most surprising was the idea that such a critique would be naturally understood as a form of solidarity by its subjects—and that queer Palestinians should be grateful that someone from the academy abroad was interested in them in this capacity.

The relationship between academic theoreticians and the queer Palestinian solidarity movement is the subject of this chapter. As an entrée into this terrain, consider another anecdote from my time working at the intersection of academia and activism. In March 2015, during a postdoctoral fellowship at Brown University's Watson Institute for International Studies, I organized an Engaged Scholarship conference for the Middle East Studies program with a significant grant from the (Soros) Open Society Foundations. The conference brought together twenty-three scholars and practitioners committed to LGBTQ movements in the Middle East. Entitled "Sexualities and Queer Imaginaries in the Middle East/North Africa," the symposium drew over one hundred participants who were eager to bridge the divide between theory and praxis on these issues. It was exhilarating to behold the range of themes we covered from across the region and the academy, including work by queer artists, religious figures, journalists, filmmakers, human rights advocates, and NGO leaders.

One of the seven panels focused on Palestine. Jason Ritchie, an American anthropologist who works on queer Palestinian activism (and whom I referenced in the first chapter of this book), opened his comments with what he described as a "provocative critique." He asserted that "queer Palestinians do not exist." Ritchie linked this hypothesis to the remarks delivered at Columbia University by former Iranian president Mahmoud Ahmadinejad, who notoriously claimed that there are no homosexuals in Iran. It is undeniable, Ritchie clarified, that Iranians and Palestinians who engage in queer acts exist. Yet the *category* of the queer Palestinian or queer Iranian is discursively produced in the West, he posited. As such, this category is less relevant to Palestinian and Iranian experiences than it is to ascertaining Western queer "spaces, bodies, and lives."

As Ritchie spoke, Ghadir Shafie—a fellow panelist, queer Palestinian feminist, and codirector of Aswat (Palestinian Gay Women)—was clearly exasperated by the analysis she was hearing. When it was her turn to speak, a smiling Shafie retorted, "Let me just start by affirming that there are Palestinian queers. We do exist. If you have any doubts, and happen to be a woman, I'm staying at the Biltmore Hotel, room 318." The audience erupted into laughter and applause.

To be sure, Ritchie raised important points at the symposium, and his scholarship has enriched this academic field. But Shafie's response highlights a broader question about the difficulties of academic theorizing when confronted with the lived experiences of nonacademics. We must ask to what extent our conceptual tools speak to those experiences and serve the needs of activists on the ground who are engaged in the contentious social movements we study and write about.

It is often difficult to gauge the impact of academic writing on the trajectories of the social movements it analyzes. In the case of global queer Palestinian activism, I argue that some influential Western academic paradigms, in their efforts to oppose imperialism, have inadvertently contributed to the empire of critique, adding yet another layer of surveillance and critical scrutiny to the struggles of queer Palestinian solidarity activists. Pressed to respond, queer activists either resist the accusations leveled against them, reshape their activism in light of these academic critiques, or attempt to demonstrate that they are "innocent" of the infractions with which they are charged. Those infractions revolve around the concern that queer Palestinian activism, both in Palestine and elsewhere, is complicit with imperialism.

This chapter examines two theoretical frameworks elaborated by Western-based scholars—the gay international by Joseph Massad and homonationalism by Jasbir Puar—as they have been applied to the global queer Palestinian solidarity movement. I reveal the debilitating effects that these academic critiques have had on the Queer Palestine movement and raise the possibility for academics and activists to formulate a new mode of scholarly engagement aimed at supporting queer social movements in Palestine and across the Middle East. As in previous chapters, I compare contributions that are corrosive, placing activists in the cross fire between left- and right-wing criticisms of their efforts, to those that raise difficult intellectual, ethical, and practical questions while protecting those who struggle for justice from paralysis.

Although there are Western academics who have made invaluable contributions to the global queer Palestinian solidarity movement, I have nonetheless encountered a pervasive skepticism among queer Palestinian activists in Israel/Palestine about Western academics who shift their scholarly gaze onto queer Palestinians. Even when academics are of Palestinian heritage and/ or queer themselves, the disciplinary approach to understanding sexuality-based activism tends to emphasize critique over solidarity. When that critique emanates from academics who live abroad and not have forged meaningful relationships with queer Palestinians on the ground in Palestine, it can be particularly dispiriting for the latter. A type of epistemic coercion attends the process of turning the struggles of people under colonial domination into objects of analysis and critique in service of Western theoretical frameworks. Such frameworks participate in the empire of critique: a discursive apparatus that, without invitation, without consent, and often without giving locals an opportunity to respond, subjects people around the world to its gaze, analysis, expertise, and critique.

Self-authorized and leveled from afar, these critiques exert a form of power and control over the individuals and movements that are their subjects, contributing less to ending their struggles and more to building the personal academic reputation, career, and livelihood of the Western-based scholar. Although read by a limited profile of individuals and frequently inaccessible to anyone who is not well versed in these theoretical modes of writing, such critiques can at times proliferate widely within academic and activist circles, taking on a life of their own and ultimately causing harm to the marginalized people on the receiving end of the critique.

In my academic and activist work with the global queer Palestinian solidarity movement, both in Palestine and the United States, I have witnessed the disheartening effects of such critiques on movement building. I have also experienced the challenging task of navigating tensions between academics and activists. My reflections here represent my own efforts to balance the production of scholarship with the moral imperative to support social movements for human liberation. Furthermore, the particular context at the center of this book is connected to a larger phenomenon on the left of critique (and not only related to Palestine) focused on dismantling with limited attempts to offer alternatives.

The Gay International

Several years ago, I received a phone call from a former student I had been mentoring ever since he was an undergraduate in Boston. He was gay, smart, American, and passionate about Palestinian rights, and he later gained admission to a top graduate school. I was thrilled to support him. Because our previous interactions had been pleasant and rewarding, I was surprised when it turned out that the purpose of his call that day was to berate me. He proceeded to scold me for my participation in the queer Palestinian movement, accusing me of being involved with groups that were "inciting to discourse," "introducing LGBTQ subjectivities in Palestine where they had not previously existed," and serving as a "native informant" for the "Western sexual imperialist project" in the Middle East. Even though I was baffled, I remained patient, explaining my positions and making it clear that I expected us to treat each other with mutual respect. He was not ultimately persuaded by my refutations of those criticisms of the queer Palestinian movement—criticisms I had heard many times before—but we ultimately agreed to disagree. He later sent me a message apologizing for his behavior, but the experience nonetheless saddened me deeply.

A major objective of this book is to think through how it is that we—queer

Palestinians and their allies—as well as academics and activists, have gotten to this point. How could the ties between an academic mentor and mentee—both of whom identify as part of the same global social movement—become estranged as the result of disagreements over linguistic and analytic categories, movement organizing strategies, and the ethics of intellectual and political engagement related to Queer Palestine? Answering this question requires a closer look at some of the academic frameworks that have helped debilitate queer Palestinian solidarity work over the last decade. In that time, no accusation has done more damage to the movement than the charge of cultural imperialism—and no academic framework has conveyed that charge more effectively than Joseph Massad's theory of the gay international.

In this section of this final chapter, I discuss the relevant arguments that Massad makes mainly in his book *Desiring Arabs* and his article "Re-Orienting Desire: The Gay International and the Arab World."[1] I analyze his line of reasoning about gay rights advocacy, state repression, and the notion of "native informants" for imperialism. My analysis illustrates how such argumentation is undergirded by victim blaming, Orientalism, and the naturalization of oppressive power relations. This section ends with a call for paradigmatic alternatives beyond the impasse in thought on LGBTQ social movements in the Arab world.

In his work on the intersection of queer issues and Middle Eastern societies, Massad claims the following:

1. The vast majority of Arabs who have same-sex sex do not think of themselves as homosexuals or organize around a gay identity.

2. Those who do have a gay identity are a small minority of middle- or upper-class and Western-educated individuals.

3. Representatives of Western-based gay rights NGOs sometimes utilize civilizational discourses that depict the Arab/Muslim world as "backward."

4. Those NGOs incited the creation of a negative discourse on homosexuality in the Arab world where none previously existed.

5. That incitement precipitated state violence against practitioners of same-sex sex.

6. The middle-class Arabs with gay identities mentioned earlier are transmission belts ("native informants") for the processes of negative discourse on homosexuality and state repression.

Gil Z. Hochberg describes Massad's thesis, saying "that the difference between 'Western' homosexuality and the desire for same-sex sex within the Arab world is that 'one is an identity that seeks social community and political rights, while the other is one of many forms of sexual intimacy that seeks corporeal pleasure.'"[2] Massad maintains, in Hochberg's words, that homosexuality is a "Western cultural product imposed on the colonized society," one that "reflects ongoing Western imperial dominance, particularly that of the United States."[3] According to Massad, "homosexuality is located at the heart of these cultural wars," and the "international gay rights movements (along with the 'white Western women's movement') are singled out as prime representatives of the Western cultural episteme violently imposed on the Arab world."[4] Massad derisively refers to this global coalition of organizations opposing gender and sexual oppression as the "Gay International."

Massad subsequently extends these criticisms to groups such as Al-Qaws, which have an explicitly anti-imperialist politics. Lama Abu-Odeh, scholar of gender and law in the Middle East, has emerged as one of the most vocal critics of the gay international framework. Abu-Odeh references an interview in which Massad critiques Al-Qaws, and she problematizes his implication that queer Palestinian activists are "already commoditized" locals as a result of capitalism.[5] She challenges his assertion that they are being "used" by gay international proponents to advance (whether intentional or not) sexual imperialism, that they have "abandoned" their cultural contemporaries, namely, same-sex-practicing Arabs not tainted by Western sexual categories and political agendas, and that they have become "the Trojan horse for Empire."[6] In Massad's writing and speaking on Al-Qaws, he emphasizes that the organization is "Israeli-based,"[7] mentioning this three times in one interview alone. As a scholar who is already so strongly critical of Israeli colonialism, he adds with this statement another dimension to his critique of queer Palestinian activism.

I do not deny that Massad has put forward legitimate points. He does not provide evidence for his analysis of same-sex identifications in the Arab world, but one must acknowledge that some aspects of Western human rights and LGBTQ rights discourse have helped authorize imperial interventions. Pinkwashing is a prime example of this. Furthermore, being identified as a member of a social category can make one vulnerable to state repression on the basis of that category—a potentially real fear for Arab same-sex sex practitioners.

At the same time, Massad's framework includes claims that do not necessarily align with realities on the ground in contemporary Arab contexts such as Palestine. For instance, his assertion that Western gay rights advocacy has stimulated Islamists and the state to develop a negative moral discourse about homosexuals is put forth with little evidence. In fact, his evidence would seem to prove that a discourse on homosexuality as "sexual deviance" long predated international gay rights advocacy. He also makes no distinction between the globalization of Western cultural representations of homosexuality, the behavior of sex tourists, and the political work of gay rights NGOs—these are all collapsed as the gay international in his analysis.

Furthermore, Massad believes that Middle Eastern state violence against gays was a response to NGO activity. Yet he denies that international NGOs respond to acts of state violence, instead claiming that their primary goal is the aggressive and imperialist goal of universalizing Western gay subjectivities. This reading relies on Massad inverting the order of events. While he acknowledges that the Iranian Revolution stimulated a reactionary Islamist discourse on sexuality that predated gay NGO activity, he labels the execution of gays in Iran in the 1980s (to which gay rights NGOs responded) an imperialist fabrication. In the case of Egypt, he ignores the broader political-economic context surrounding the Queen Boat raid and contradicts himself by arguing that the Egyptian state was punishing the Boat people for their public gay identities while also telling us that those same Boat people *denied having gay identities*.[8]

It is puzzling that Massad would ascribe the label of "native informants" to imperialism when groups in the region such as Al-Qaws have refuted that claim, indigenizing Western LGBTQ terms and engaging in what are primarily anti-imperialist politics. This ascription then leads to a form of victim blaming. Even if the gay rights response to state violence triggered a further backlash, the question with any social justice struggle stands: why should people protesting their mistreatment be blamed for the backlash caused by their protestations? Would we blame other oppressed populations advocating for their rights for causing backlash from the oppressive structures?

In his most recent book, *Islam in Liberalism*, Massad critiques Al-Qaws for their acceptance of international funding:

AlQaws's funders include such liberal luminaries as the Ford Foundation Israel Fund, the US gay internationalist Astraea Lesbian Foundation, and liberal Zionist Organization the New Israel Fund. The director of alQaws went on a

fundraising trip to the Netherlands in 2009, which is arguably the most Islamophobic and anti-Palestinian country in Europe, whether at the level of government policy, the press, or civil society and NGO discourse. No radical funders,
whatever those may be, are anywhere in sight! . . . More recently alQaws' funds
have also come from such organizations as the Euro-Mediterranean Foundation of Support to Human Rights Defenders (EMHRF), the Global Fund for
Women, the Open Society Foundations, the Heinrich Boll Stiftung, and the
Arcus Foundation.[9]

Massad does not recognize how international aid in Israel/Palestine, as my
own forthcoming research has revealed, can both facilitate Israeli settler-
colonial processes and equip Palestinians with tools to resist those processes.

Although Massad has persuasively illustrated how categorization is an exercise of power and that we must interrogate how we create certain subjects,
at no point does he delineate how he expects queer Palestinians to remain
pure from Western epistemologies and Western institutional funding. This
situation heightens activist concerns about academics who themselves are not
morally pure (is anyone on earth morally pure?), and yet these academics recognize neither their own positionality nor the impossibility of purity. Such
academics employ Western epistemologies to level critiques against subaltern
populations in the Global South for the pursuit of their financial livelihoods.
Yet these academics often do not connect this fact to a consciousness of their
own financial benefits from Western institutions invested in such realms as
the transnational security-/prison-/military-industrial complex that harm
vulnerable populations in the Global North and South. This lack of awareness
raises ethical questions about building careers on critiques of activists in social movements thousands of miles away who engage in material pragmatism
under tremendously challenging conditions.

Massad's analysis does not take into consideration Al-Qaws's attempts
to minimize their reliance on international aid (entrance fees each month to
the Al-Qaws parties comprise a significant portion of the annual budget of
the organization), the limitation of paid staff to very few individuals, the rejection of funds from donors who attempt to impose an agenda that is not
aligned with the Al-Qaws mission, and the clear articulation of their values,
including an unwavering commitment to BDS.

The BDS call was issued by Palestinian civil society—a civil society largely
dependent on international aid. From the perspective of Al-Qaws activists,

strategic use of international aid to fund programs supporting queer Palestinians locally, to help add a queer contingency to the BDS civil society coalition, and to sustain pinkwatching activism globally is considered a form of subversion and resistance. These activists are cognizant of Black South Africans benefiting from the resources of South African institutions under apartheid while waging their anticolonial struggle, and activists also remember the call for an international boycott of those same institutions. Massad's critiques fail to acknowledge that Palestinian society in general is increasingly connected to globalized, internationalized, and transnational institutions, communities, and networks and that these networks are shaping everyday lives and subjectivities. Such an approach is seen as consistent with, not contradictory to, Al-Qaws's radical purist agenda. The Al-Qaws leadership, however, still attempts to appease external radical critics (who can never be fully appeased), even at the expense of alienating fellow queer Palestinians who comprise the vast majority of the population and who do not share those ideological commitments as fully.

In addition to his criticisms of queer Palestinian organizations receiving Western sources of funding, Massad's objections are directed at ideology or identity related to homosexuality. His argument that homosexuality is socially constructed and has a Western etiology mirrors an objection that could be leveled against the Foucauldian paradigm that he used to formulate his argument in the first place. According to his logic, both could be characterized as Western imperial epistemology. Foucault specifically criticizes this kind of essentialism of 'origins' in his work on genealogy. In his essay "Nietzsche, Genealogy, History," Foucault writes, "What is found at the historical beginning of things is not the inviolable identity of their origin; it is the dissension of other things. It is disparity."[10] According to Foucault,

> A genealogy of values, morality, asceticism, and knowledge will never confuse itself with a quest for their "origins," will never neglect as inaccessible the vicissitudes of history. . . . History is the concrete body of a development, with its moments of intensity, its lapses, its extended periods of feverish agitation, its fainting spells; and only a metaphysician would seek its soul in the distant ideality of the origin.[11]

Thus, Massad's commitment to a unidimensional understanding of LGBTQ categories and their spatial and temporal origins defies what Foucault intended in his work on genealogy.

Massad's logic coupled with his lack of ethnography or engagement among queer communities in Palestine causes him to miss the richness of queer Palestinian experiences on the ground. He does not see how terms such as *gay* are borrowed, and in some ways no longer Western, as they are translated into new contexts, and all the while they are interacting with preexisting Arabic concepts in Palestine. Queer Palestinian activists are surprised when Massad naturalizes national categories of Arab and Palestinian (even as these activists face Zionist critiques that their Palestinian identity is also merely a socially constructed category in the service of a nefarious political project). Massad does not recognize how LGBTQ categories and identities are deployed, internalized, reconfigured, and indigenized by queer Palestinians.

In denying agency to LGBTQ Arabs, the gay international paradigm reinforces Orientalism. Massad portrays Arab culture as static and Western influence in the region as inherently coercive. He also romanticizes the place of men who are outside the fold of LGBTQ movements and who have sex with men in Arab societies and are able to remain strictly private about it.

Queer Arab researcher Samir Taha problematizes Massad's distinction between the Arab world and the West, considering this distinction a form of Orientalism in how it views the East and Occidentalism in how it essentializes the West. Taha writes that it presumes that the

West is always positively defined as possessing certain epistemic categories, primary among them the category sexuality with everything that it contains from homophobia and heteronormativity to gay rights and queer resistance, while the non-West is also always contrastively and negatively defined as lacking both the categories and the need for the politics they contain and generate.[12]

According to Taha, Massad represents the non-Western as "socio-sexually *invisible*" and says that it "does not have sexuality, public socio-sexual identities nor sexual politics."[13] Therefore, there is no room in this framework for homosexuals "to complain about their stigmatized and demonized condition"[14] without the risk of taking on homosexual identities and therefore eliciting societal repression against them from local forces resisting sociosexual identities.

Taha argues that Massad therefore exonerates local homophobia by representing it merely as a response to Western sexual imperialism, and Taha reveals that Massad holds not the homophobic perpetrators but local queer activists responsible for inciting that violence against their own community. This line of thought thus maintains that gay and lesbian categories *"can only* be universalized by the epistemic, ethical, and political violence unleashed on the rest of the world by the very international human rights advocates whose aim is to defend the very people their intervention is creating."[15] Taha juxtaposes Massad's approach with the antiessentialist and humanist scholarship of Edward Said, writing that

> in the face of such separatist and nativist identitarianism—such occidentalist orientalism, masquerading as "critique," which degrades those it purports to defend just as it does those it attacks, what becomes urgently needed is an articulation of the utopian emancipatory universal that we all, as human beings, can globally and "contrapuntally" strive for, as Said's phrase once had it.[16]

I share Taha's concern that this work reproduces elements of Orientalist scholarship.

In *Orientalism*, Said delineated "dogmas" of Orientalism, including "the absolute and systematic difference between the West . . . and the Orient," "abstractions about the Orient . . . based on texts" rather than on "direct evidence drawn from Oriental realities," and the notion that "the Orient is eternal, uniform, and incapable of defining itself."[17] All three of these dogmas undergird Massad's representations of queerness in the Arab world. This chapter demonstrates that the West and East are not absolutely and systematically different categories, queer Arab movements cannot be understood through websites online, and queer Arabs are perfectly capable of defining themselves. Academics positioned in the West cannot assign themselves to be the ultimate authorities on analyzing and representing the "passive Orient" and making it legible for itself and others.

Additionally Massad, who himself is US-based, has written falsely that "there are indeed indications" that Palestinian Queers for Boycott, Divestment, and Sanctions (PQBDS) is "US-based and not Palestine-based."[18] In fact, PQBDS was based in Israel/Palestine, with central organizing in Lebanon and with only two US-based queer Palestinian activists, who served in a secondary capacity on the steering committee. This was before PQBDS dissolved during the peak of the empire of critique. Massad also wrote about queer Palestinian activists in English to his English-speaking audience; he said that the "entire website" of PQBDS "is in English,"[19] as if that language choice could be an indictment. He also added that Al-Qaws's "website is in English with the less numerous Arabic webpages sounding for the most part like translations from English than as texts originally written in Arabic."[20]

Massad's critique, relying on web presence rather than on meaningful engagement with living, breathing queer Palestinians themselves fails to recognize that Al-Qaws activists who publish in Arabic are native Arabic speakers and that every Al-Qaws member I have ever met has been a native Arabic-speaking Palestinian. The Arabic rolling off the tongues of volunteers as they take turns with shifts on the Al-Qaws hotline or of queer Palestinians gathered in one space after the other in Palestine cannot be so easily dismissed. As we saw in chapter 1, it is these ordinary acts on the ground in historic Palestine that sustain the queer Palestinian movement.

The Orientalist strand at work in this context naturalizes oppressive power, particularly as deployed against women and effeminate queer men. The sexual subjectivity Massad posits is in fact the product of patriarchal power relations that Massad is apparently unconcerned with. This is surprising for a scholar who identifies as Foucauldian in his analysis, supposedly attuned to the ways every regime of knowledge is created by (and creates) a regime of power. He is not interested in who wins or loses under the current power configuration; he is concerned only with warding off challenges that seem to emanate from or be influenced by the West.

Regarding the absence of patriarchy from Massad's analysis, Hochberg writes,

> Massad's view of "authentic" Arab sexuality is limited to his understanding of male sexuality, however, for in his account, Arab women are situated outside these authentic cultural formations and outside sexuality altogether. Arab (male) sexuality is organized around sexual roles and discussed in terms of passivity and activity defined in relation to penetration.[21]

The exclusion of women and focus on male homosexuals that Hochberg identifies in Massad's analysis was also explicated by Lama Abu-Odeh. Abu-Odeh draws attention to "two social groups" that are denied "social entitlements and privileges that are socially associated in Arab culture with masculine men."[22] They are "women married to men who practice same sex contact, who are kept in the dark about their husbands' sexual shenanigans; and the practitioners of same sex contact who are visibly effeminate and who are derogatorily hailed as *khawal*, unable to enjoy the privilege of invisibility."[23] Abu-Odeh elaborates, saying, "Gay rights, I contend, is the vengeance of the feminine exacted over the masculine poking the eye of misogyny that undergirds the hatred of women/*khawal*. And that is why, to my mind, import or not, they are a good!"[24] By examining how attention to women complicates notions of the gay international, Hochberg and Abu-Odeh highlight the struggles, erased by Massad, that queer rights activism in Palestine helps facilitate, for queer women, straight women married to queer men, and effeminate queer men already vulnerable in their society for being read as womenlike.

Hochberg considers Massad to be engaging in a "kind of paranoid criticism" and believes that his analysis fails to realize that "every and any local cultural 'style' is in itself always already an outcome of mixing, comparing, contrasting, and rewriting of multiple influences and styles."[25] Similarly, Abu-Odeh writes, "It is a paranoia that is directed against cultural invaders, that sniffs collaborations and complicity everywhere, and one that is mobilized to protect and safeguard an authentic cultural self/sex that is viscerally resistant to the feminist motto: the personal is the political."[26]

Abu-Odeh captures the consequences of a nonfeminist approach to sexuality as promulgated by Massad.

> Theoretic/political formulations about the Arab world that evoke the sexual and sexuality have to be handled with utmost care. Not only should hetero/homo normativity be shunned, but everything that resides within its conceptual scheme as well. The closet, homophobia, discrimination against the homosexual, gay rights—all should be treated with an overdrive of suspicion. Indeed the very question of the sexuality of the Arab should not altogether be posed, for to posit the category "sexuality" is to already be "complicit" in a knowledge/power conglomerate that wants to take you over.
>
> Since "difference" is what is to be protected, Massad appoints himself as its spokesman: "It *is* same sex act, it is *not* homosexual," while also erecting a wall of "defense" around it, essentially prohibiting any expression of difference (from Massad) about the truth of the difference (of the Arab).[27]

Abu-Odeh's reference illustrates how Massad disavows entanglement in regimes of knowledge/power while functioning as an advocate of a different, more patriarchal regime of power in the name of anti-imperialism.

Whereas Abu-Odeh refers to Massad's self-appointment as spokesperson, Hochberg problematizes Massad's critique of Arab LGBTQ activists as spokespeople.

> How and why the West has been so successful in imposing its notions of sexuality on the Arab world is a question Massad fails to answer, the Arab world apparently a passive victim in these imposed cultural transactions driven

completely from the "outside" via capitalism and cultural globalism and serving U.S. and other Western needs. As for the existence of Arab LGBTQ activists, Massad has only patronizing things to say: "While there is a small number of upper class and upper middle class westernized Arabs who are seduced by gayness and the American example of it, they are not representative of, nor can speak for, the majority of men and women who engage in same-sex practices and do not identify themselves in accordance with these practices." This small group of "seduced" individuals (note the connotation of fallen sexual behavior), who are but an insignificant "minority of Arab same-sex practitioners who adopt [Western] epistemology," are further and most explicitly undermined by Massad as sellouts.[28]

For queer activists in Palestine, the concern about being considered a local informant of the gay Western sexual imperialist agenda has been omnipresent. This fear is also a result of the degree to which voices such as Massad's have been heard among radical purist academics and activists over the voices of those such as Abu-Odeh and Hochberg.

It is critical to acknowledge the alternative approaches to understanding the intersection of LGBTQ rights and the Arab world. We can simultaneously critique overt usages of human rights discourse for imperialist purposes and remain sensitive to the fact that globalization and routine cultural contact have engendered hybrid subjectivities that are no less authentic or worthy of respect and protection than the subjectivities created by earlier configurations of power. Massad's separate writing and advocacy regarding nonqueer and non-gender-related Palestine material are examples of the way Western institutional resources can be redeployed for anti-imperialist purposes. Yet this is something that Massad forecloses on when it comes to queer Palestinian activists. The fact that queer Palestinians and their allies abroad are subjected to this layer of the empire of critique represents one of the greatest challenges to the global queer Palestinian solidarity movement. Whereas some activists resist the charge of complicity in Western imperialist sexual epistemological projects, radical purist leaders work tirelessly to demonstrate their imperialism-free credentials, leading to conflicts within the movement.

While Massad charges queer Palestinian organizations with "complicity at the level of epistemology and ontology,"[29] there is no way for LGBTQ activists in the Middle East to be immune from being characterized as engaging in "incitement to discourse" and serving as "native informants"[30] to Western sexual imperialism and the gay international. Considering that queer Palestinian activists must already contend with the reality that LGBTQ Palestinians are suspected of being Israeli informants within Palestinian society and considering that these activists have often already prioritized anti-Zionism and anti-imperialism over homophobia in their work, such charges emanating from the left of complicity with imperialism are particularly devastating. Massad's academic critique has, more than any other, served to demoralize many members of the global queer Palestinian solidary movement. As one queer Palestinian activist shared with me, "Massad's criticism of our work is like a cloud that always hovers above me. How do I prove a negative? I am tired."

Homonationalism

In August 2012, *Jadaliyya*, a Middle East–focused online magazine edited mainly by Western-based academics, published a critique of the queer Palestinian solidarity movement by South Asian American queer theorist Jasbir Puar and Lebanese American anthropologist Maya Mikdashi. As with Massad's intervention, Puar and Mikdashi's widely circulated article "almost instantly threw activists based in Europe and North America working within the queer Palestine movement into a crisis over their solidarity," in the words of one activist.[31] Just as many queer Palestinian solidarity activists in Palestine and around the world had to ask whether they had been implicated by Massad's theory of the gay international, the *Jadaliyya* article forced those same activists to struggle to respond to yet another damning charge. In this case, it was the charge of reproducing "homonationalism," or the linkage between a country's treatment of homosexuals and its moral-civilizational value.

Whereas Massad singles out specific queer Palestinian organizations as his objects of derision, Mikdashi and Puar level their critique at "pinkwatchers" in general, declining to provide even a single example of an intervention that would illustrate the allegations they put forward. In their article, the authors charge pinkwatchers with accepting and reproducing in their antipinkwashing work some of the underlying premises of Israeli pinkwashing. They argue that pinkwatchers believe that Israel's occupation of Palestine contradicts its otherwise stellar record on gay rights. Pinkwatchers, according to Puar and Mikdashi, thus reinforce the homonationalist premise that protection of gay rights is a marker of moral virtue, one that can be distinguished from the broader political systems in which it is embedded. Pinkwatching discourse, they argue, treats "gay rights as if they operate in a legal vacuum, separate and separable from the legal system as a whole."[32]

Puar and Mikdashi list many additional charges against pinkwatchers, all of them stated abstractly and without evidence. They accuse pinkwashers of "ignoring" ongoing US settler-colonialism and US complicity in Israel's occupation of Palestine, thereby "colluding with US imperialism."[33] They claim that pinkwatchers do not sufficiently problematize the deployment of homophobia as a "political whip" by the homonationalist West.[34] They accuse pinkwatchers of failing to recognize that Palestine predated the existence of Israel. They assert that pinkwatchers reduce the question of Palestine to a matter of "segregated human rights abuses that can be ameliorated piece by piece by state entities."[35] They claim that pinkwatching discourse does not address issues such as the plight of Palestinian refugees, the annexation of Jerusalem, or the occupation of the Golan Heights. They chastise pinkwatching activists for their supposed adoption of the two-state solution and refusal to affirm the right of Palestinians to "militarily resist occupation."[36] And they charge pinkwatchers with remaining silent on the war on terror, the invasion and occupation of Iraq, the demonization of Iran, Islamophobia, Arabophobia, and domestic US racism.

Puar and Mikdashi describe pinkwatching activism as a form of "lowest common denominator politics" aimed at forging identity-based solidarities between queer Palestinians and "Euro-American gays" by "recovering the queer Palestinian voice."[37] The authors describe attention to the emergence of queer Palestinian groups as merely a response to the Western call for "authentic LGBT activists in the Arab world."[38] In an oblique reference to Massad, they write that pinkwatchers therefore "mimic the identity politics of the gay(s) internationally" by attempting to isolate Palestinian queers "from the fabric of Palestinian society."[39] The authors characterize the movement as speaking "almost exclusively to an American queer audience," thus obfuscating the complicity of "*all* American citizens [with] the continued settling of historical Palestine."[40] As a result, they write, "pinkwatching has become the primary, myopic lens through which queer youth (but not only youth) are asked to (and allowed to) be politicized around the issue of Palestine" and around US foreign policy more generally.[41] The authors conclude that "pinkwashing and pinkwatching [both] speak the language of homonationalism. One does so in the name of Israel, the other does so in the name of Palestine."[42]

In the wake of Puar and Mikdashi's article, Haneen Maikey, director of Al-Qaws, and Heike Schotten, a US-based academic and pinkwatching activist, published a response in *Jadaliyya* in October 2012 aimed at debunking the unsubstantiated allegations leveled against the movement. They questioned Puar and Mikdashi's "virtually exclusive reliance on homonationalism" as a lens through which to evaluate pinkwatching activism, noting that it "pushes their criticisms dangerously close to a rehearsal of academic critique at the expense of . . . movement building." In any event, "the lack of a single example" in Puar and Mikdashi's article "renders their argument impossible to actually assess, leaving us grasping at straws."[43] Maikey and Schotten elaborated:

> Our fellow activists felt blamed, humiliated, or singled out by this piece. Some were unsure if they were the target of critique, given that the authors did not cite any examples. The authors may have been legitimately cautious about naming specific people or organizations in an already small movement. However, the lack of concrete evidence for their claims leaves us wondering just where the finger is pointing. And it is clear that finger-pointing is going on. Although the authors are careful to specify that their argument about the homonationalist structure of pinkwatching is not a normative one, by the end of the article, pinkwatchers' alleged complicity with homonationalism emerges as an egregious intellectual, political, and strategic error. This error needs to be called out, but apparently lacks any solution or productive mode of address (or at least none the authors care to offer). Such finger-pointing is, we believe, very different from invitation or constructive critique.[44]

These queer Palestinian solidarity activists raised invaluable questions about the fetishization of critique in the American academy and the relationship between Western academics and the activists they critique.

With the release of Maikey and Schotten's response, *Jadaliyya* simultaneously published a rejoinder by Puar and Mikdashi, thereby privileging the voices of the academic coauthors by ensuring their critiques were heard first and last.[45] In their rejoinder, Puar and Mikdashi charge Maikey and Schotten with "misreading"[46] their article, thus echoing Joseph Massad's claim that his critics "misquote" him as a result of their "egregious theoretical illiteracy."[47] The exchange underscores an all-too-common occurrence: academics will publish abstruse theoretical critiques of social movements, and when activists from those movements push back on those critiques, they are dismissed as too unsophisticated to grasp the academics' original insights. Even when the activists in question are themselves well versed in theoretical writing and fully capable of comprehending the critique, the academic critics refuse to treat them as intellectual equals. My concerns should not be read to suggest that academics, who are situated in a professional field that rewards abstract theorizing and are often living beyond the immediate reach of political oppression, have nothing of value to contribute to the struggle for justice in Palestine. The problem in such cases is not the academy per se but rather the assumption on the part of individual scholars that their superior knowledge must always prevail over the subaltern's definition of their own situation and that people living in the conflict on a daily basis are not competent to name their own reality.

Although it was not at all clear to activists in the global queer Palestinian solidarity movement, Puar and Mikdashi later claimed to have been "very clear that [they] were discussing pinkwatching activism in the United States only."[48] They explained further, saying, "We trusted our readers to find themselves in the critique. Had we named names, we would have restricted the freedom to relate to the critique on one's own terms. If the critique resonated, perhaps uncomfortably so, then there might be something there to think about."[49] The statement astonished many queer Palestinian solidarity activists I spoke with in Palestine and the United States, causing further alienation from Western-based academics who publicly berate the vulnerable with no sense of accountability. Some queer Palestinian activists agreed with aspects of the critiques that Puar and Mikdashi leveled, but the overwhelming majority of those I interviewed felt that the totalizing character of the claims and endless litany of critiques were far from constructive for the movement. There was a near consensus that academics were more deeply invested in cultivating their own platforms—in which queer Palestinian solidarity organizing was merely an object of analysis for Western audiences—than in contributing to the empowerment of queer Palestinians in Palestine. The fact that activists in Palestine issued the call for global solidarity and that queer solidarity activists around the world have become parts of their political, social, and intimate networks meant that any widely circulating academic critique of non-Palestinians in the movement, if taken seriously, could have consequences for activists in Palestine. Indeed, transnational networks have been invaluable to the reach of the queer Palestinian movement. On the flip side, many non-Palestinian activists abroad felt paralyzed as the result of Puar and Mikdashi's article, worrying that their solidarity work was under scrutiny from radical purists as well as from the Zionist right. These queer Palestinian solidarity activists were aware that they could be publicly attacked by people whose leftist, academic credentials gave them authority, and this inhibited the growth of the movement.

Natalie Kouri-Towe, a queer theorist and solidarity activist living in Toronto, described the near crisis that Puar and Mikdashi's critique produced among activists in Toronto—and this demoralizing effect quickly became evident to me in other cities as well. Kouri-Towe captured the paralysis that resulted from the authors' charge that pinkwatching activists "replicated the conditions of homonationalism and settler colonialism."[50] As Kouri-Towe wrote, although the intent of Puar and Mikdashi's article may have been to stimulate self-criticism in a movement rapidly gaining momentum in the United States, "their conclusion, 'that both pinkwashing and pinkwatching speak the language of homonationalism,' functioned to destabilize a movement that was only just beginning to develop a network and basis for transnational solidarity."[51] She continued,

> Against the backdrop of an upcoming attempt to generate a cohesive transnational movement of activists working on anti-pinkwashing and Palestine solidarity activism, Puar and Mikdashi's critique couldn't have come at a worse time. In Toronto and on international listservs, I witnessed and participated in countless discussions about whether it was even ethical for Western-based activists to continue working on anti-pinkwashing organizing if our work served to reinforce homonationalism—the very function our efforts aimed to contest.[52]

While affirming the value of constructive critique, Kouri-Towe noted the flattening of relevant distinctions between a powerful settler-colonial state and the "resistant discourses of a decentralized and shifting social movement." Indeed, global queer Palestinian solidarity activists were puzzled by how homonationalism as an analytic framework could subsume the activism of both. "Were anti-pinkwashing activists and the Israeli state's pinkwashing tactics *inherently* the same," Kouri-Towe wondered, "or was there a way of recuperating Western solidarity while still maintaining the critique of Israeli state practices?" The absence of clarity on this question left self-critical activists without a way forward and "risked unravelling the early momentum" of what Kouri-Towe calls "an emergent movement without central leadership or basis of unity."[53] I join Kouri-Towe in recognizing the defining moment that came with the publication of this *Jadaliyya* piece on homonationalism. Indeed, it helped mark what I identify as the movement's plateau that same year in 2012.

The queer Palestinian solidarity activists with whom I spoke also articulated frustrations with Puar and Mikdashi's article. Having opened their worlds and hearts to Jasbir Puar during her time as part of the LGBTQ delegation to Palestine, the queer Palestinian activists she met with did not expect her to publish such an article lambasting their global solidarity movement soon after her return to the United States. Of course my colleagues recognized the potential of productive critique to strengthen social movements. When developed within activist circles, however, that critique typically assumes a very different form than that of Puar and Mikdashi's article. There was a palpable sense that the authors were attempting to expand the theoretical frontiers of Puar's framework of homonationalism, which was sound when applied to settler-colonial states such as the United States and Israel. But subsuming the queer Palestinian solidarity movement under this framework was not productive. Activists felt strongly that it was inappropriate, given the immense asymmetry in power, to place efforts at solidarity with a stateless and colonized population in the same analytical frame with supporters of a colonial state, with all its discursive and material resources.

Puar and Mikdashi did not acknowledge the agency of queer Palestinians in ethically and strategically leading their global solidarity movement, and they did not recognize that almost all queer Palestinian solidarity activists in the United States are simultaneously part of local movements for justice. Many of these activists come from social justice backgrounds and have long been struggling against militarism, imperialism, neoliberalism, mass incarceration, and transphobia. These activists also work in the domains of AIDS, immigration, Latinx rights, Native American populations/settler-colonialism, queer liberation, poverty alleviation, racial justice, and South African freedom, among many other causes. Many draw connections between those movements and Palestine; at the same time, however, many are vigilant about the nature of collapsing all subaltern populations into one homogenous mass, and they instead recognize important contextual differences between the United States and Israel/Palestine.

As previous chapters of this book have demonstrated, queer Palestinian solidarity activists around the world have largely recognized that US-based activists must confront Western complicity in the oppression of Palestinians, particularly given US financial and diplomatic support for Israel. They also link their analyses of Western culpability in Palestine to the situations of other marginalized populations. Be it through opposition to global processes of settler-colonialism, to the military-industrial complex, to the prison-industrial complex, or to other far-reaching oppressive systems, queer Palestinian solidarity activists are fully cognizant of the way transnational social justice frameworks have shaped the political culture of the queer Palestinian solidarity movement. Like Massad, Puar and Mikdashi neglected the full range of interlocutors and varied forms of engagement with which queer Palestinians and their allies abroad interface.

In processing Puar and Mikdashi's intervention, queer Palestinian solidarity activists around the world debated a number of additional critiques that the academics raised. The claim that the movement is premised on identitarian commitments could not be addressed simply, because queer Palestinians have indeed requested solidarity from queer activists abroad, and recognizing the existence and voices of queer Palestinians is central to resistance against pinkwashing. The term *identity politics*, which has assumed a negative connotation in some academic circles, does not necessarily carry the same associations for activists addressing the intersection of Palestine and queer liberation.

Many queer North Americans in the movement are motivated not only by affinity with Palestinians but also by opposition to a system of domination in which the United States and, to a lesser extent, Canada are complicit. Solidarity with Palestinians and a sense of responsibility for what the Israeli government does are not mutually exclusive and, in fact, are key features of global queer Palestinian solidarity activism. Dismissing a rights-based discourse and a political agenda based on international law, Puar and Mikdashi charge pinkwatchers with framing colonialism in Palestine as a human rights issue to be addressed by states, sarcastically adding that "after all, indigenous people everywhere would feel much safer under the watchful eye of the United Nations, the International Criminal Court, and entities such as the United States and the 'western' world."[54] Such radical purist and elitist academic disavowal of international institutions runs contrary to global queer and nonqueer Palestinian solidarity work that is largely responsive to the Palestinian civil society–led call for BDS. The BDS call is predicated on rights claims rooted in international law. At best, Puar and Mikdashi remind us that, even when human rights are embedded in international legal institutions, their implementation will always require political struggle.

Many global queer Palestinian solidarity activists celebrated Haneen Maikey and Heike Schotten's response to Puar and Mikdashi. It was empowering to witness the increased opportunities for activists, especially those living under settler-colonial conditions, to respond directly to the academics
who had authorized themselves to critique movements built by subaltern activists. As a queer activist in Palestine and a Jewish antipinkwashing activist
in the United States, Maikey and Schotten observed that Puar and Mikdashi
were "implicitly presenting activist work as less thoughtful or intellectually
sophisticated than academic work, and thus needing to 'learn from' the les-
sons being taught in [their] piece."[55] Maikey and Schotten wondered, "As 'ob-
servers' of pinkwatching, are the authors claiming a (solely?) academic perspective? Is academia (or are academics) outside of or beyond activism? Do
the authors (or academics more generally) have an analytical framework that
activists lack?"[56]

This exchange in *Jadaliyya* raised additional questions among queer Palestinian solidarity activists about who can and should create litmus tests
for the ethical and political acceptability of activist tactics, what such a list
should consist of, and why Puar and Mikdashi cautioned against the use of
homophobia as a "political whip" against Palestinians while they employed
homonationalism as an "academic whip." What, furthermore, is the responsibility of academics toward the social movements they analyze and from
which they derive resulting scholarly capital? What are the conditions that
make critiques constructive as opposed to adding yet another layer of surveillance and policing to social movement work and communities already under
constant scrutiny and repression? To whom are academics accountable when
they level such critiques? How do we distinguish between solidarity and antisolidarity in these contexts? These questions are at the heart of this book.

Left Mirrors Right

Not lost on Maikey and Schotten were the parallels between the debate over
homonationalism and the earlier debates over the gay international. They
wrote,

> Many of us may recall working under the powerful shadow of Joseph Massad's
> work on the Gay International. For many, Massad's work effectively produced
> a straw image of the "Gay Arab" who is, by definition, complicit with cultural
> imperialism and an agent of international gay organizations.[57]

Just as Massad had produced a caricature of the "Gay Arab," Puar and Mikdashi introduced "a new set of straw caricatures—not the Gay Imperialist . . . but the Homonationalist Pinkwatcher and Token Palestinian Queer."[58] Such an exercise, Maikey and Schotten write, appears to be less about "furthering a movement" than about distinguishing "good pinkwatchers" from "bad pinkwatchers" and doing so "from a position of academic observation, analysis, and judgment" rather than from a position of solidarity.[59] Both the Massad and Puar/Mikdashi episodes revealed the power dynamics involved in academic critiques of global queer Palestinian solidarity activism. And as Maikey and Schotten note, these critiques also took emotional, intellectual, and material tolls on pinkwatching activism. In some cases, criticism from the left actually paralleled criticism leveled by the Zionist right. Whereas once it was only pro-Israel advocates who accused global queer Palestinian solidarity activists of turning queer Palestinians into tokens, now radical purists on the left level that charge as well.

Among their many critiques, Puar and Mikdashi also charged the movement with "exceptionalism," leveling the unfounded allegation that "pinkwatching does not take into account [the] broader global context, and instead focuses on the state of Israel as the sole offender of this use of gay rights to demarcate civilizational aptitude."[60] As we saw earlier in this book, supporters of the Israeli state who criticize pinkwatching often voice a similar critique as a form of discursive disenfranchisement. Pinkwashers accuse pinkwatching activists of "singling out" Israel. Global queer Palestinian solidarity activists have grown accustomed to responding to these right-wing critics—citing, for instance, the way the Homonationalism and Pinkwashing Conference in New York applied these frameworks to the United States and other contexts outside of Israel. Having to marshal similar responses to critics on the left has been disorienting.

By characterizing the activism of LGBTQ Arabs as "tiny" and "miniscule," Massad sought to discredit the salience, resonance, and importance of their work. His dismissal echoes the argument made by pro-Israel advocates, intended to discredit the pinkwatching movement, that the number of queer Palestinian activists is insignificant. Massad writes that a "tiny number of gay-identified Arabs organized in Gay Internationalist organizations are complicit with an imperial sexual regime"[61] and that queer Palestinians who identify as such "remain a minuscule minority among those men who engage in same-sex relations and who do not identify as 'gay' nor express a need for gay politics."[62] Again, the fact that queer Palestinian women dominate the leadership of the movement is elided by Massad. It would be surprising for an objective observer to describe these queer Palestinian activists as miniscule after realizing that they have confronted one of the world's most powerful states and its global pinkwashing campaigns. These activists have galvanized a global social movement—based in Israel/Palestine—that has made solidarity with Palestinians one of the most enduring domains of transnational intersectional LGBTQ activism and contemporary politics.

Also often missing from discourses that diminish queer Palestinian activism is the reality of Palestinian homophobia and the fact that Zionism's exacerbation of homophobia in Palestinian society makes it dangerous for many queer Palestinians to openly express their identification as gay and their desire for gay politics. In the previous chapters, we have seen numerous examples of Israeli discourses and actions that continue to exacerbate homophobia in Palestinian society. This includes the entrapment of queer Palestinians by Israeli security services, the discourses on queerness underlying pinkwashing campaigns that weaponize homophobia against Palestinians to justify anti-Palestinian oppression, and the Israeli state's waging of imperialist projects, such the Israeli occupation of the Palestinian Territories, in the name of gay rights and inclusion of gay soldiers. When we consider the realities of ethnoheteronormativity, we can see that this exacerbation complicates the argument that one must choose between opposing Zionism and opposing Palestinian homophobia. I do not think it is a coincidence that Gaza is the region in Palestine in which homophobia is most prominently and aggressively manifested as well as the region facing the most brutal and devastating Israeli occupation policies.

Massad's mirroring of the way reactionary forces stigmatize and render queer Palestinians suspect contributes to the inability of the queer Palestinian movement to reach its full potential in terms of size and scale. The story of the emergence of the queer movement in Palestine reveals that LGBTQ organizing is organic and tailored to the local context. The more that queer Palestinians break the shackles of fear of being labeled gay internationalists or homonationalists or agents of Western sexual imperialism or informants of one kind or another from the left or the right, the more the movement will be able to resume growing.

Massad's claim that Al-Qaws is "based in Israel" also resonates with critiques described earlier in this book of queer Palestinian solidarity activism leveled from the right. Queer Israeli solidarity activists often point to the fact that the two largest queer Palestinian organizations, Al-Qaws and Aswat, are registered in Israel and not with the Palestinian Authority. In so doing, they attempt to undermine pinkwatching activism by highlighting what they see as the gay friendliness of Israel and the endemic homophobia of Palestinians. Queer Palestinians do confront homophobic Palestinians who seek to portray them as alien to Palestinian society, and Massad's rhetoric exacerbates this problem. Massad's reference to Al-Qaws's geographic positioning raises further suspicions about the organization. Massad casts queer Palestinian activists as people whose intentions ought to be regarded with deep skepticism. The implication is that they and their activism are not natural parts of Palestinian society.

Israel/Palestine is already a place in which the politics of space is constantly contested. The fact that the main Al-Qaws office was located in the building of the Israeli LGBTQ organization Open House in Israeli-majority West Jerusalem, that Al-Qaws's director also lives in West Jerusalem (not East Jerusalem), and that Aswat's leadership is based in Israel (in Haifa) opened queer Palestinian organizing to critique from radical purists. This particular critique was shared by some members of Al-Qaws in Palestine. Although they were a minority, those members preferred a complete avoidance of West Jerusalem, which they saw as too Israeli to host the headquarters of a queer Palestinian organization. But pinkwashers and right-wing supporters of Israel, homophobic Palestinians, and critical Western-based academics rarely asked why this geographic positioning was a nonissue for and was even supported by many queer Palestinian activists. The answer is that many of these activists feel the artificial division of Palestinian citizens of Israel from Palestinians in the Occupied Territories is the product of colonial practices and that by further distinguishing between the two populations, critics of queer Palestinian solidarity activism are reinforcing those practices and the fragmentation they are intended to create. Although Palestinian citizens of Israel may have been the ones to launch the queer Palestinian movement (prompting them to register with the Israeli state), their subsequent outreach extended to queer Palestinians in the West Bank. Due to its limited budget, Al-Qaws was able to pay a much-reduced rent by remaining in the Open House building in West Jerusalem. Al-Qaws activists emphasize that starting as a queer Palestinian initiative of an Israeli LGBTQ organization and growing into an independent Palestinian NGO is to be celebrated.

Queer Palestinian citizens of Israel who are active in Al-Qaws and Aswat underscore their Palestinian identity and often remind the world that even if they live in what are today considered Israeli cities—West Jerusalem or Haifa, for example—those cities are part of Palestinians' ancestral lands. For them, every inch of Israel and the Occupied Territories is considered part of historic Palestine, and many believe they should be commended for remaining in their ancestral homes at a time when most Palestinians in those areas were forcibly displaced. Nonetheless, in 2015, Al-Qaws made the decision to vacate its West Jerusalem office and move to a rented office in East Jerusalem. It is difficult for Al-Qaws activists to discuss this trajectory—from their early existence as a Jerusalem Open House project to becoming a separate NGO renting space in the JOH building to having their own office in East Jerusalem—without rendering themselves vulnerable to critique from right and left alike.

Reciprocal Solidarity

After the Puar and Mikdashi article was published, a US-based colleague in the queer Palestinian solidarity movement (who asked not to be named for fear of retribution) said to me,

> When they chastise us for refusing to affirm the right to militarily resist the occupation, do they not realize that Zionists are attacking us and automatically assuming we are violent? I'm in disbelief! I'm a gay brown Muslim American man for God's sake. If I do as they want me to say, I will be immediately sent to prison here in the U.S. or to Guantanamo with the charge of material support for terrorism. [He laughs after the joke of the last sentence and then resumes his serious tone.] I'm in disbelief that they expect us to gloss over the disagreements among Palestinians about how to wage your struggle, with or without arms. That they are expecting me and other outsiders to Palestine to condone one form of resistance—when no such ask has been made by Palestinians to those of us in solidarity abroad in a concerted way. Whereas there is the BDS call and that was a concerted call and a nonviolent one from Palestinians, so that is why I focus on that in opposing this madness of pinkwashing.

He spoke passionately about how detached from reality he felt the homo-nationalism-centered critique of the movement had been.

Meanwhile, in reference to Joseph Massad's critiques, an interviewee who identifies as lesbian and is a Palestinian in the West Bank said to me,

Zionists tell me that Palestinian is a social construct and Massadists tell me that LGBTQ is a social construction or whatever you call it. Honestly, I don't care where these terms come from. All I know is that these words feel right, they are me, and this doesn't make me any less of a Palestinian. I would die for Palestine and my heart breaks every day I wake up to this suffocating life. I want the soldiers gone. I want to see freedom, I mean real freedom in all directions, in my lifetime. It's painful that Massad doesn't know anything about us. He has never been here to see us, to actually talk to queer people in Palestine. If I want to start an NGO one day to spread awareness here so gay men know to use protection, so they understand STDs, so I can start a family with my girlfriend without being afraid of being killed, so that we can talk about sharia law's punishments of homosexuality, so they don't tell me I'm sick in the head, what exactly makes me complicit? He thinks we are trying to be like Americans. Does Massad not see the irony? He's a Palestinian who left Jordan for America. He lives in the belly of the beast. In New York, they can benefit from sexual freedom and gay liberation. He pays taxes in America that go to Israel, to kill us here. . . . He writes in English and he writes about us for people to read all the way there, nowhere near here. It's about us, to disparage us, but not for us. He uses words I don't recognize but I don't need those words to learn about being me. I learn that by living here, by being me. Tell me, who exactly is complicit in what?

Her words moved me deeply and have helped shape my understanding of the queer Palestinian movement.

It is in engaging with activists in Israel/Palestine and queer solidarity activists doing this work around the world and in recognizing the embodied experiences and meaning making of queer Palestinians as an anthropologist that I witnessed the courage it requires to push back against academic critiques of a certain kind. This raises questions of how we normalize academic critiques against subjects in the Global South when these subjects are rarely able to answer to the critiques leveled against them. In the *Jadaliyya* debate, space was provided for such subjects to articulate responses to the criticisms leveled against them. Queer Palestinian activists were thus able to problematize the positionality of the Western-based academics who publicly initiated these debates, which were intended primarily for the consumption of Western audiences. It is also rare to see the subjects of Massad's critiques being able to respond, in similar forums, to the criticisms he has articulated about them.

As this chapter has illuminated, discursive disenfranchisement is one dynamic in effect in this context. While queer Palestinians are directly oppressed by the conjoined forces of Zionism and homophobia, there are attempts to deny them the right to identify with their nationality and sexual orientation and the right to name the central systems of oppression in their lives. Palestinians often confront the denial of their national existence as Zionism's victims and of the right to resist that system of oppression. Similarly, queer Palestinians confront discursive disenfranchisement in the denial of their sexual existence and are labeled epistemic imperialists for identifying as homophobia's victims and resisting that system of oppression. They and their allies in the heart of the world's empire who respond to the queer Palestinian call for solidarity risk being labeled homonationalist. Intersectionality combines struggles against colonialism, racism, classism, sexism, homophobia, ableism, and religiously based discrimination, among other oppressive systems. I consider attempts to isolate and exclude homophobia from this equation—and the impulse to undermine the ethical and political soundness of the mere naming of homophobia—as in and of itself contributing to homophobia. No queer subject can be expected to accept their oppression.

Protecting people from being coerced into assuming LGBTQ identities or engaging in queer activism is a laudable objective, and it is especially important to protect those for whom doing such things would not resonate or for whom it might simply be too dangerous. But that is different from suggesting that we should not encourage those who have significantly less at stake to play a role in helping dismantle homophobia. When such individuals refrain from engaging in this kind of queer resistance, masculine-passing closeted queer men continue to benefit from the privileges of a patriarchal society, because they read as heteronormative and are treated as such, and the burden of queer resistance falls on fewer shoulders. Sensitivity to different needs and vulnerabilities requires that we encourage and empower those with the ability to actively and openly choose to resist homophobia.

All same-sex-loving people have the capacity to resist heteronormativity privately, and many do so all the time. Dismantling the structures of homophobia cannot occur in the private sphere alone, however; it will necessitate the politicization of the private coupled with public resistance. Of course, the private is already politicized, although its politics are of entrenched homophobia and patriarchy in Palestine. Public discourses on what can and cannot be done in bed already exist in Palestinian society, converging and diverging with discourses elsewhere. Yet homophobia must be undermined at the institutional level. Public resistance against homophobia will inevitably incur blowback, but that blowback cannot be a justification for a return to heteronormative complacency. All liberation struggles for equality and justice require some level of sacrifice. External actors can play counterproductive roles, and this should be addressed. But as we live in an increasingly interconnected world, it is more than possible for solidarity from abroad to be productive. We must trust queer Palestinians to lead the way in building transnational solidarity networks based on mutual respect and reciprocal inspiration and in conducting this activism with a democratic and inclusive spirit. This can be done without the burden of radical purism.

Although the situation is slowly changing, there remains a dearth of queer scholarship and scholarship on queer themes in Palestine Studies, Middle East Studies, and Middle East Anthropology. Naming homosexuals, openly condemning homophobia, and calling for the dignity of LGBTQ people in the region poses very serious risks for Western-based Middle East scholars who fear that states and other institutions will deny them access for research or that they will incur even more severe consequences such as surveillance or imprisonment. Middle East Studies scholars are not immune from Middle Eastern homophobia, whether as perpetrators, victims, or bystanders. In that context, reproducing the discursive disenfranchisement of queer people in the region becomes a convenient strategy. Why take the risk of integrating homophobia into a truly intersectional analysis when one can evade the issue altogether by invoking the argument that the homosexual as a category does not exist in the first place? Many Middle East Studies scholars have grown comfortable with eliding the reality of queer bodies, lives, violence, dreams, and struggles, in Palestine and across the region.

When we do pursue work on the queer Middle East but apply one paradigm in a totalizing manner, we help reinforce elements of the patriarchal authoritarianism that has contributed to the endurance of homophobia in the region. I have seen how young academics who want to explore scholarship in this domain can feel trapped intellectually as a result, with their creativity and innovation stifled. Some existing academic work then has the potential to inadvertently contribute to the undermining of real queer liberation struggles on the ground. Instead, we can create more spaces in which to criticize the privileged role of critique in our fields, to question the power underlying who is able to critique whom, to develop new tools for conceptualizing the subjectivities of queer Middle Easterners and others, and to find ways for our scholarly engagement to constructively support queer solidarity movements.

In discussing the Western-based academic work that has contributed to the splintering and demoralization of solidarity activism, we should take care not to view those interventions as representative of the role of scholars in this or any other social movement. The existence of unconstructive criticism perceived as constructive critique does not preclude other academics from engaging productively with global solidarity movements. At the same time, even a mere few academics can help induce a significant crisis of morale among activists. Global queer Palestinian solidarity activists are forced to respond to criticism from so many different quarters, and the divergent frames of reference that divide academics from activists can exacerbate tensions when they arise. Thus, individuals whose work helps bridge the worlds of activism and academia are invaluable to this and other progressive social movements. For example, queer North American professor-activists such as Judith Butler, Angela Davis, and Sarah Schulman have played critical roles in helping to build and sustain the transnational networks on which the global queer Palestinian solidarity movement depends. The movement can harness the intellectual, political, and personal contributions of such Western-based academics whose hearts and souls are deeply invested in reciprocal solidarity.

Conclusion

"we were never meant to survive"

IN APPROACHING THIS BOOK, I have sought to be careful not to assume that I can speak for "the downtrodden." I have also problematized notions of authority and authenticity in academic and activist representations. Questions are raised when individuals from middle-class and elite backgrounds claim to have complete understanding of the needs of "the poor" and other vulnerable populations, assume that these categories of humanity are monolithic, and purport to know what their priorities should be (even when those priorities do not necessarily align with the material and social realities of others). The prisms that scholars and activists bring to these discussions can have as much to do with those individuals and their ideological commitments as with the embodied experiences of the communities on the ground being analyzed. This has the potential to reify hierarchies in the name of redressing inequality. Just as it is a form of epistemic coercion to attempt to impose queer discourses on particular individuals, it is also presumptuous to assume that such individuals must forgo queer politics in the name of anti-imperialism. I am weary when the latter impulse elides the cry for the amelioration of queer suffering. Such neglect contributes to the normalization of structural homophobia and the bolstering of the social and political pressures of heteronormativity.

I hope that this text can assist academics and activists in identifying differences between critique and criticism. Critiques can be constructive, particularly when employed to challenge inequalities, such as those that exist between

Western-based academics and queer individuals in the Middle East. That is why critique of critique is necessary, especially considering that academics, activists, and activist-academics rarely identify their self-regarded critiques as criticisms, even when mere criticism and the policing of thought are clear. We can instead envision a critique intimately linked to ethnography, emancipation, critical thinking, discovery, imagination, and public engagement.

My tracing of the rise of the queer movement in Palestine that resulted from courageous activists there, followed by its global ascendance and subsequent plateau amid the empire of critique, is meant to foreground the ordinary forms of queer resistance in Palestine that take place among extraordinary circumstances. I aimed to bring into relief the many stars that make up the constellation of queer life in Palestine: at once local, Palestinian, and affected by particular types of patriarchy, homophobia, and nationalism; at once binational, interfacing with Israeli occupation; and also transnational, subject to the critique (and sometimes the aid) of actors across the world. This constellation is in many cases flattened into the general and abstract narrative of the Israeli-Palestinian conflict. The terms within which queer Palestinian activists can voice their concerns and critiques, the ways that pinkwashing discourse has emerged, and the forms that pinkwatching critiques take are framed in terms of larger state conflict and the ideologies it has engendered. The local, familial, and personal pathways that sexuality intersects with in these systems are veiled and superseded by the very systems themselves.

Certainly there are rich avenues for further scholarship on queer Palestinians, particularly for ethnographic explorations of the learning and unlearning of Palestinian homophobia, the impact of religion on queer Palestinian subjectivities, and the effects of the relationship between gender and class on queer Palestinian activism and social movement building. In her in-progress book manuscript, *The Gender of Class: Social Inequalities and Daily Life in Urban Egypt*, anthropologist Farha Ghannam argues that scholars should "move beyond intersectionality, which presumes different structures that meet or intersect at one point, and show how class and gender are inseparable and the production of a gendered subject is simultaneously the production of a classed subject."[1] My book has briefly discussed the impact of Christian and Muslim identities on queer Palestinians, the disproportionate role that queer Palestinian women inspired by the Palestinian feminist movement have played in establishing the queer Palestinian movement, and the disproportionate role that urban and middle-to-upper-class Palestinians have played in queer activism in Palestine. Diving deeper into these realms—and properly explicating the inseparability of religion, sexuality, gender, and class—is beyond the scope of this specific project (which is focused on defining, analyzing, and transcending the empire of critique), but research in this area is critically needed, especially from emerging scholars.

Attention to the work of the queer Palestinian movement can enable an analysis that queers the occupation beyond pinkwashing and beyond identity politics and brings queer theory to bear on the idea of Zionism and the splintered identity of Palestine and Palestinians. Thus, we can think not only about queer Palestinians but about how we can provide tools to queer the idea of Palestine itself. For instance, the early political goals for Palestinian nationalism were not necessarily tied to a state-led project for the Occupied Territories.[2] The longing for a state-focused model of liberation was partly a reaction to the Israeli occupation/seizure of land. What became the Palestinian Authority identified the need for a state as their political horizon. This strategy was a symptom of the oppression and constrained agency that Palestinians face. Palestinians therefore sought legibility in terms recognized by their oppressors, just as queer subjects so often seek legibility from the states that oppress them.

The plateauing of queer activism in Palestine reflects the general paralysis of activism within broader Palestinian civil society, largely as a result of the Israeli occupation. This plateau is a symptom and effect of the pain of the occupation itself. Furthermore, the Palestinian Authority has hindered the development of Palestinian civil society—including the labor movement—so that it is very difficult for productive political resistance to grow within the Occupied Territories. The weakness of the Palestinian Authority mirrors the crisis of leadership across Palestine. Queer Palestinian organizing is not immune from this crisis.

My vision for the queer Palestinian movement places it at the intersection of queer futurity and utopia. This articulation is deliberate, inspired by the writing of queer theorist Jose Muñoz. Over the course of his lifetime, Muñoz wrote persuasively on the compelling nature of utopian thought. As he put it, "Although utopianism has become the bad object of much contemporary political thinking, we nonetheless need to hold on to and even *risk* utopianism if we are to engage in the labor of making a queer world."[3] For Muñoz, queerness is utopian, and the utopian is queer. "Queerness as utopian formation is a formation based on an economy of desire and desiring," Muñoz wrote. "This desire is always directed at that thing that is not yet here, objects and moments that burn with anticipation and promise."[4] In addition to the integration of desire in this analysis, Muñoz was also attuned to temporality, saying, "But on some level utopia is about a politics of emotion. . . . And hope, I argue, is the emotional modality that permits us to access futurity, par excellence."[5] Thus "utopia lets us imagine a space outside of heteronormativity. . . . More importantly, utopia offers us a critique of the present, of *what is*, by casting a picture of what *can and perhaps will be*."[6] According to Muñoz, this queer utopian vision links time and space as well. He explained that "it is productive to think about utopia as flux, a temporal disorganization, as a moment when the here and the now is transcended by a *then* and a *there* that could be and indeed should be."[7]

It is possible for the queer Palestinian movement to preserve its radical nature but it should do so without purism. I dream of queer Palestinians overcoming the surveillance and disenfranchisement—both discursive and embodied—that they face from many directions, although I recognize that these forces do not all wield the same power. Such forces include the Israeli state and its supporters, Palestinian groups and institutions, their own families, Western academics and media professionals, Israeli solidarity activists, and activists within the global and local queer Palestinian solidarity movement. The enfranchisement of queer Palestinian subjects can begin with the inclusion of a broader range of voices and activists into the fold of movement organizing. These new agents can then assist in the dismantling of the empire of critique. This breaking-down process requires attention to the resistance against both imperialism and internal systems of oppression. The combined struggle for national and sexual liberation can allow the movement to transcend its current plateau and, through further growth, dismantle the structures of ethnoheteronormativity so that Israelis and Palestinians, straight and queer, can all live together as equals.

If the queer Palestinian movement adopts a more expansive conceptualization of queerness that encompasses the questioning of all normativity, including that which stems from Palestinian nationalism, then this can enable an embrace of pluralism in the movement. This pluralism, replacing attempts to maintain ideological conformity, does not foreclose the possibility of internal critique. When we invite in rather than call out, model self-criticism, practice compassionate and constructive criticism, and improve upon reflection, social movements grow and are strengthened. This work toward internal movement cohesion-building must be accompanied by spaces for joy, plea-sure, and love. This will enable the queer Palestinian movement to democ-ratize by ensuring that no single queer Palestinian can purport to speak for all; that governance boards of queer organizations are larger, more represen-tative, and more accountable; and that decisions are not made in a haphazard or authoritarian manner.

In my view, the threshold for public disavowal of queer Palestinians and their allies must be extremely high. Queer Palestinian activists should free themselves from trying to fulfill the expectations of Western-based academ-ics who are not partners to any queer Palestinians on the ground. Time and emotional labor invested in responding to charges from abroad can instead be reinvested in building more robust programming to serve the most press-ing needs of queer Palestinians in Israel/Palestine. Although there is signifi-cant pain involved when activists whose entire existence revolves around re-sisting imperialism are charged with complicity in that imperialism, the heart of the movement ultimately lies in the everyday lived realities of queer peo-ple under colonization in Palestine. Thus, initiatives such as promoting safe-sex practices, assisting individuals facing significant threats, building further partnerships with feminist collectives, generating a more robust public dis-course on gender and sexuality, and many other forms of queer activism and resistance take priority over enmeshment in the empire of critique and the discursive disenfranchisement it reproduces. It would be useful to expand the repertoire of global queer solidarity with Palestine to encompass tools such as improved local and international media engagement, transnational inter-faith activism, increased LGBTQ physical and mental health resources in the Occupied Territories, and a radical openness to the priorities of the younger generations.

One does not always need to prove one's existence and humanity in the face of political litmus tests, suspicion, and erasure. Queer Palestinians should celebrate their brave efforts to exert their limited political capital to reclaim their voices from the sphere of Israeli statist propaganda that seeks to appropriate the bodies and experiences of queer Palestinians on global stages in order to justify and legitimize the systems that subjugate them.

The debate over who can speak for queer Palestinians is mitigated when queer Palestinians in diaspora communities play more formidable roles in building the movement. Perhaps Al-Qaws and Aswat could consider estab-lishing chapters in parts of the world such as North America and Europe where fundraising and networks can be expanded and where queer Palestinians in the diaspora are thriving. A much more serious conversation about the representation of—and support for—queer and trans Palestinians in the Gaza Strip is critical, as they have receded from collective consciousness while confronting Israel's medieval siege and the suffocating oppressive pressures of Hamas control. Queer Palestinians in the West Bank feel by and large that they have been relegated to second-class status within the queer organizations that are meant to empower them. They increasingly discuss how more social events—and, yes, fun—are needed as they hear their queer Palestinian counterparts in Israel coming together and celebrating life. Queer Palestinian groups could also benefit from more nuanced positions on the varied experiences of queer and trans Palestinian citizens of Israel. Queer Palestinian groups are demanding that their queer Palestinian activists in Israel disavow their connections to Israeli institutions. This is unrealistic and alienating for many of them. The fact that some individuals do turn to Israeli queer institutions instead is sometimes a reflection of the alienation they have experienced in Palestinian society and organizations, including queer ones. One can be critical of the system that has made Palestinians dependent on Israeli institutions and economic structures while treating queer Palestinians who are struggling to survive with compassion.

In fact, the frontiers of queer liberation could be broadened by queer Palestinian organizations strategically partnering with queer Israeli institutions in the processes of decolonization, coresistance to occupation and homophobia, and the enhancement of services for the most vulnerable racialized queer and trans individuals and communities in Palestinian and Israeli societies (including Black and Mizrahi populations in Israel), whose fates are intertwined. In so many liberation struggles around the world, we have seen the power of members of dominant and dominated groups coming together in the march toward freedom. This union must be accompanied by the abandonment of the accusation that one is complicit in one's own oppression unless one engages in the anti-imperialist struggle according to *one* particular formula or by resisting at *all* times.

Queer Palestinian groups have been limited by the urge to remain as morally pure as possible, which has led to an overly restrictive policy on receiving international aid. Being more open to increased funds from a broader set of donors does not mean these groups have to fundamentally compromise their values and mission. For instance, more resources could allow Al-Qaws and Aswat to hire additional staff beyond the current models of only a few paid staff members. There is no shame in being fairly compensated for one's activist and professional labor, in the same way that academics are compensated for theirs. A focus is needed on hiring, training, and empowering young queer Palestinians to make the organizations sustainable so that power is not continuously concentrated among a few leaders. This can be coupled with robust programmatic units to cultivate more amicable and productive relationships with civil society institutions and human rights organizations and a careful openness to foreigners who seek to become at the very least interlocutors and sources of support. Queer Palestinians understandably need to be selective about whom to trust considering the surveillance they face and the limited resources they have, but treating others with automatic suspicion, as queer Palestinians so often are in daily life, contributes to movement plateau.

Non-Palestinian queer activists who are in solidarity with Palestinians can also play an important role in enabling this global movement to return to a period of growth. Even as the recognition of the devastating nature of occupation and toxic masculinity leads to legitimate outrage and frustration, demonstrating empathy for others is an antidote to political paralysis in social movement building. It does not serve the movement well when responses to the callous instrumentalization of Palestinian homophobia to further pinkwashing involve the instrumentalization of Israeli homophobia just to undermine pinkwashing. Recognizing the humanity and suffering of queer and trans Israelis is a powerful form of resistance to the pinkwashing discourse and logic aimed at the dehumanization and erasure of Palestinians. It is essential to be clear that Israeli LGBTQ rights advancements are irrelevant to the illegality and immorality of the Israeli occupation. But that does not mean that the achievements of the LGBTQ Israeli community are never relevant to queer Palestinians, particularly as queer Palestinian citizens of Israel often find themselves betwixt and between Israeli and Palestinian queer civil societies. Queer Palestinian solidarity activists around the world should not feel so impotent that the mere thought of acknowledging the achievements of LGBTQ Israelis is automatically misconstrued as pinkwashing and a threat to Palestinian self-determination.

Expecting others to address the Israeli occupation and apartheid system in one particular manner every time they speak further alienates many people from even thinking about Israeli oppression in the first place. The recognition of Israeli LGBTQ rights accomplishments and discussions of Israel/Palestine that are strategically multidimensional at times and unidimensional at others have the potential to be much more effective tools to contextualize and undermine pinkwashing. Using these tools can help expand the ranks of the movement. Activists should seriously question whether they need to call for the shutting down of every pinkwashing event—or if their energy is sometimes better spent creating alternative spaces and discourses for pinkwatching perspectives to be heard.

Academics in the movement have room to critically question whether they are legitimizing specific queer Palestinian voices over others, lifting some of these voices as authoritative and archetypical while silencing voices whose perspectives and political strategies are not aligned with their own. There is a tendency to minimize the heterogeneity of queer and trans Palestinian identities and experiences while reifying polarized conceptions of the West versus the rest. Too often queer Palestinian discourse is represented in monolithic terms by sympathetic and nonsympathetic Western-based academics, so that there is an assumption of unanimity in rejecting "Western" categories, organizations, and political projects.[8] As we have seen, although many queer Palestinians do not subscribe to the politics of victimhood, visibility, and coming out, others find in these conceptual resources tools for self-realization and political struggle.

Palestinian activists are often unable to point out the homophobia they experience because it is seen as disenfranchising one of their own causes—that of Palestinian national freedom—by legitimating the discourse of the "backwardness" of Palestinians and by using "colonial" sexual terms. And critiques of pinkwashing are normally met with charges that reduce them to repeated ethnonational indices (such as when critiques of pinkwashing are met with false allegations that they are inherently anti-Semitic). It is important to show the social life of critique and the unexpected ways that certain critiques can feed larger ideologies and systems (such as academic critiques feeding Zionist and Orientalist ideologies).

Certainly there is some anti-Semitism among the queer Palestinian solidarity movement, both in Israel/Palestine and globally, and this must be named and resisted. My deep knowledge of this domain tells me that these strands do not represent the vast majority or thrust of this social movement. Countless Jewish members and leaders of the queer and the broader Palestinian solidarity movements take issue with attempts to ascribe internalized anti-Semitism or self-hatred onto them for their solidarity with Palestinians.

In fact, these individuals often articulate their Jewish identity and values as largely underlying their critiques of Zionism and Israeli policies and their motivations to participate in Palestinian solidarity activism. The instrumentalization of anti-Semitism charges in service of the Israeli state makes the important struggle against anti-Semitism more challenging to keep up. Recognition of the struggles for dignity of all Jewish and Palestinian populations in Israel/Palestine and worldwide will always remain imperative for people of conscience.

There are a multitude of homophobias, patriarchies, and forms of governance within which *pinkwashing* becomes a loaded and contested term. By showing these systems in the plural, such as *Israeli* homophobia as well as *Palestinian* homophobia, we are able to zoom in on how these contextual systems affect the everyday lives of individuals navigating multiple realms and structures. We can also refrain from abstracting homophobia, patriarchy, and governance to singular, transhistorical terms that rearticulate the logic of pinkwashing as though homophobia is an ontological given through which one can compare contemporary civilizations. My chronicling of this movement is aimed at countering the flattening discussions about sexuality, empire, colonialism, Israel/Palestine, and utopia.

One cannot emphasize enough the critical importance of working to counsel families on acceptance of their LGBTQ loved ones. For instance, if we do not want Israeli entrapment of queer Palestinians to succeed as a strategy, then familial acceptance of queer relatives would be a great source of protection. In many cases, had that familial support existed in the first place, their queer relative would have been significantly less vulnerable, rendering the threat of being outed to one's family by the occupation forces much less potent. The family is, in many ways, a key to queer liberation, considering the foundational place of the family in Palestinian society and politics. In Palestine, unconditional love from family largely enables love for one's self and others. Although leftist and activist spaces have not always been sources of healing, many of us feel that we can never abandon them for the sake of collective liberation. Thus, transforming activism with loving energy from both familial and fictive kin can enable these spaces to become sites of healing and of personal and collective transformation.

Over the course of my life, I have experienced how many Zionists want to wish away the Palestinian subject and many homophobes want to wish away the queer subject. I have also been a firsthand witness to the radical purist desire to wish away the queer Palestinian subject whose voice and experience does not neatly map onto a single ideological framework. I do not draw moral equivalence between these three forces but instead recognize how they intersect under the empire of critique. Although the intentions underlying these forces are often different, their effects can be similar. This book speaks to the silence and erasure that stems from all of these directions. Queer liberation cannot be realized while colonial subjugation persists, but the movement toward dignity for queer people should not be expected to wait until the realization of national liberation. Decoupling these struggles is ultimately impossible; they are inextricably linked.

In my own mind, I keep returning to the day I was at home in Palestine and sat beside a dear friend—a fellow queer Palestinian—whose life ended before anyone could say goodbye. Together, we read these words by Audre Lorde, the African American lesbian, poet, and activist:

> and when we speak we are afraid
> our words will not be heard
> nor welcomed
> but when we are silent
> we are still afraid
> So it is better to speak
> remembering
> we were never meant to survive

Notes

Preface

1. Audre Lorde, "The Transformation of Silence into Language and Action," in *Sister Outsider: Essays and Speeches* (Berkeley, CA: Crossing Press, 2007), 44.

2. Joseph Massad, "Re-Orienting Desire: The Gay International and the Arab World," *Public Culture* 14, no. 2 (2002): 361–85, https://doi.org/10.1215/08992363-14-2 -361.

3. Michel Foucault, *The History of Sexuality, Vol. 1: An Introduction* (New York: Random House, 1978), 59.

4. Heewon Chang writes that autoethnographers "undergo the usual ethnographic research process of data collection, data analysis/interpretation, and report writing. They collect field data by means of participation, self-observation, interview, and document review; verify data by triangulating sources and contents; analyze and interpret data to decipher the cultural meanings of events, behaviors, and thoughts. . . . Like ethnographers, autoethnographers are expected to treat their autobiographical data with critical, analytical, and interpretive eyes to detect cultural undertones of what is recalled, observed, and told of them." "Autoethnography as Method: Raising Cultural Consciousness of Self and Others," in *Methodological Developments in Ethnography*, vol. 12, *Studies in Educational Ethnography*, ed. G. Walford (Bingley, UK: Emerald Group, 2008), 207–21.

5. Carolyn Ellis and Arthur P. Bochner, "Autoethnography, Personal Narrative, and Personal Reflexivity," in *Handbook of Qualitative Research*, 2nd ed., ed. Norman Denzin and Y. Lincoln (Thousand Oaks, CA: Sage, 2000), 742.

6. Norman Denzin, "Analytic Autoethnography, or Déjà Vu All Over Again," *Journal of Contemporary Ethnography* 35, no. 4 (August 2006): 419–28, https://doi.org /10.1177/0891241606286985.

7. Paul Atkinson, "Rescuing Autoethnography," *Journal of Contemporary Ethnography* 35, no. 4 (August 2006): 400–404, https://doi.org/10.1177/0891241606286980.

Introduction

1. For more information on Israel's violations of international law, see Noura Erakat, *Justice for Some: Law and the Question of Palestine* (Stanford, CA: Stanford University Press, 2019).

2. "East West Global Index 200—2011," Nation Brand Perception Indexes, East West Communications, accessed October 1, 2019, http://www.eastwestcoms.com /global.htm.

3. Sarah Schulman, "Israel and Pinkwashing," *New York Times*, November 22, 2011, http://www.nytimes.com/2011/11/23/opinion/pinkwashing-and-israels-use-of-gays-as -a-messaging-tool.html.

4. Ibid.

5. The term was first used in reference to companies marketing breast cancer awareness while also marketing their products containing ingredients linked to disease.

6. The BDS movement's rise within Palestinian society has included a call for a global boycott of institutions complicit in Israel's denial of Palestinian rights. This boycott is to be promulgated until Israel meets three conditions: ending the occupation of the West Bank and Gaza Strip, providing equal rights to Palestinian citizens of Israel, and promoting and enabling the right of return for Palestinian refugees. Palestinian activists identified this as a nonviolent strategy that is in accordance with international law and was inspired by the global anti-apartheid boycott movement in solidarity with South Africa.

7. Itay Hod, "Tel Aviv: The New Gay Travel Hotspot," *Daily Beast,* January 24, 2013, http://www.thedailybeast.com/articles/2013/01/24/tel-aviv-the-new-gay-travel -hotspot.

8. Ibid.

9. Ibid.

10. Natalie Kouri-Towe, "Solidarity at Risk: The Politics of Attachment in Transnational Queer Palestine Solidarity and Anti-Pinkwashing Activism" (PhD diss., University of Toronto, 2015).

11. Omar Barghouti and Sarah Schulman, "Equal Rights for All in Palestine," video interview posted by the Palestinian Campaign for the Academic and Cultural Boycott of Israel, April 11, 2011, http://www.pacbi.org/etemplate.php?id=1558.

12. "Final Results, Best of 2011," GayCities, accessed October 1, 2019, http://www .gaycities.com/best-of-2011/vote.php?page=10.

13. Oren Yiftachel, *Ethnocracy: Land and Identity Politics in Israel/Palestine* (Philadelphia: University of Pennsylvania Press, 2006), 11.

14. Ibid., 3.

15. Judith Butler, *Parting Ways: Jewishness and the Critique of Zionism* (New York: Columbia University Press, 2014).

16. Michelle Goldberg, "Anti-Zionism Isn't the Same as Anti-Semitism," *New York Times*, December 7, 2018, https://www.nytimes.com/2018/12/07/opinion/rashida -tlaib-israel-antisemitism.html.

17. Omar Kholeif, "Queering Palestine: Piercing Eytan Fox's Imagined Bubble with Sharif Waked's Chic Point," *Camera Obscura* 27, no. 2 (September 2012): 159, https://doi.org/10.1215/02705346-1597249.

18. Daniel Boyarin, *Unheroic Conduct: The Rise of Heterosexuality and the Invention of the Jewish Man* (Berkeley: University of California Press, 1997).

19. Orna Sasson-Levy, "Constructing Identities at the Margins: Masculinities and Citizenship in the Israeli Army," *The Sociological Quarterly* 43, no. 3 (2016): 357, http://doi.org/10.1111/j.1533-8525.2002.tb00053.x.

20. Brandon Davis, "Desiring Israel: Gays, Jews, and Homonationalism" (undergraduate thesis, Princeton University, 2013), 18.

21. See Rhoda Kanaaneh, *Birthing the Nation: Strategies of Palestinian Women in Israel* (Berkeley: University of California Press, 2002).

22. See Meira Weiss, *The Chosen Body: The Politics of the Body in Israeli Society* (Stanford, CA: Stanford University Press, 2002).

23. Emile Durkheim, *The Rules of the Sociological Method* (New York: The Free Press, 1982).

24. See Tom Boellstorff, *The Gay Archipelago: Sexuality and Nation in Indonesia* (Princeton, NJ: Princeton University Press, 2005); Ann McClintock, *Imperial Leather: Race, Gender, and Sexuality in the Colonial Contest* (New York: Routledge, 2005); George Mosse, *The Image of Man: The Creation of Modern Masculinity* (New York: Oxford University Press, 1996); and Nira Yuval-Davis, *Gender and Nation* (London: Sage, 1997).

25. For more on the use of the term *apartheid*, see Sean Jacobs and Jon Soske, *Apartheid: The Politics of an Analogy* (Chicago: Haymarket Books, 2015).

26. I draw on several articles from that issue in this book. For this special issue, see *GLQ: A Journal of Gay and Lesbian Studies* 16, no. 4 (2010).

27. Leila Farsakh, Rhoda Kanaaneh, and Sherene Seikaly, eds., "Special Issue: Queering Palestine," *Journal of Palestine Studies* 47 no. 3 (Spring 2018): 7–12, https://doi.org/10.1525/jps.2018.47.3.7.

28. Sofian Merabet, *Queer Beirut* (Austin: University of Texas Press, 2014), back cover.

29. Ibid., 6.

30. Ibid., 7.

31. Merabet, *Queer Beirut*, 7. Elizabeth Povinelli argues that we are all prisoners of love, queer or not. See Elizabeth Povinelli, *The Empire of Love: Toward a Theory of Intimacy, Genealogy, and Carnality* (Durham, NC: Duke University Press, 2006).

32. Ibid., 67.

33. Ibid., 148.

34. Ibid., 112.

35. Ibid., 113.

36. Ibid., 116.

37. Ibid., 9.

38. Ibid., 78.

39. Ibid., 135.

40. Ibid., 22.

41. I am also alluding to Didier Fassin and Richard Rechtman's *The Empire of Trauma: An Inquiry into the Condition of Victimhood* (Princeton, NJ: Princeton University Press, 2009).

42. Didier Fassin, "The Endurance of Critique," *Anthropological Theory* 17, no. 1 (2017): 8, https://doi.org/10.1177/1463499616688157.

43. Ibid., 5.

44. Ibid.

45. Ibid., 14.

46. Ibid., 18.

47. Ibid., 24.

48. Aeyal Gross, "Where LGBT Rights and Nationalism Meet," *+972 Magazine*, April 20, 2011, http://972mag.com/where-lgbt-rights-and-nationalism-meet/13515.

49. Ibid.

50. Fassin, "The Endurance of Critique," 12.

51. Audre Lorde, "There Is No Hierarchy of Oppressions," in *Homophobia and Education: How to Deal with Name Calling*, ed. Leonore Gordon (New York: Council on Interracial Books for Children, 1983).

52. Fassin, "The Endurance of Critique," 19.

53. Ibid., 18.

54. Ibid., 19.

55. Ibid., 26.

56. Ibid., 25.

57. Queers Against Israeli Apartheid, "Queers Against Israeli Apartheid Retiring," *QuAIA*, posted February 26, 2015, https://queersagainstapartheid.org/2015/02/26/queers-against-israeli-apartheid-retiring.

58. Benjamin Doherty, "Pinkwashing, 2008–2011: Obituary for a Hasbara Strategy," *Electronic Intifada*, November 26, 2011, https://electronicintifada.net/blogs/benjamin-doherty/pinkwashing-2008-2011-obituary-hasbara-strategy.

59. El Jones, "The Coup at the Pride Meeting," *Halifax Examiner*, October 6, 2016, https://www.halifaxexaminer.ca/featured/the-coup-at-the-pride-meeting.

60. Ibid.

61. Sherine Hamdy, "How Publics Shape Ethnographers: Translating across Divided Audiences," in *If Truth Be Told: The Politics of Public Ethnography*, ed. Didier Fassin (Durham, NC: Duke University Press, 2017), 311–12.

62. Ibid., 313–14.

63. Ibid., 315.

64. Ibid.

65. Eve Spangler, personal communication, September 2017.

66. Frances Lee, "Why I've Started to Fear My Fellow Social Justice Activists,"

Yes!, October 13, 2017, http://www.yesmagazine.org/people-power/why-ive-started-to-fear-my-fellow-social-justice-activists-20171013.

67. Stan Grant, "Black Writers Courageously Staring Down the White Gaze—This Is Why We All Must Read Them," *Guardian*, December 30, 2015, https://www.theguardian.com/commentisfree/2015/dec/31/black-writers-courageously-staring-down-the-white-gaze-this-is-why-we-all-must-read-them.

Chapter 1

1. "Palestinian Protesters Whitewash Rainbow Flag from West Bank Barrier," *The Guardian*, June 30, 2015, https://www.theguardian.com/world/2015/jun/30/palestinian-protesters-whitewash-rainbow-flag-west-bank-barrier.

2. Ibid.

3. Sharon Kurtz, *Workplace Justice: Organizing Multi-Identity Movements* (Minneapolis: University of Minnesota Press, 2002), xxvi.

4. Ibid., xxi.

5. Sophia Sepulveda, "Arab Women, Red Lines: The Anti-Sexual Harassment Movement in Egypt" (undergraduate thesis, Brown University, 2015), 53–54.

6. Joel Beinin and Frederic Vairel, "The Middle East and North Africa: Beyond Classical Social Movement Theory," in *Social Movements, Mobilization, and Contestation in the Middle East and North Africa*, eds. Joel Beinin and Frederic Vairel (Stanford, CA: Stanford University Press, 2011), 8.

7. Ibid., 10.

8. Ibid., 14.

9. Phillip Ayoub, *When States Come Out: Europe's Sexual Minorities and the Politics of Visibility* (Cambridge, UK: Cambridge University Press, 2016), 23.

10. Diana Allan, *Refugees of the Revolution: Experiences of Palestinian Exile* (Stanford, CA: Stanford University Press, 2013), 35.

11. Ibid., 8.

12. Ibid., 3.

13. Ibid., 34.

14. Jason Ritchie, "Pinkwashing, Homonationalism, and Israel–Palestine: The Conceits of Queer Theory and the Politics of the Ordinary," *Antipode* 47, no. 3 (June 2015): 616, https://doi.org/10.1111/anti.12100.

15. Ibid., 616.

16. Jasbir Puar, *Terrorist Assemblages: Homonationalism in Queer Times* (Durham, NC: Duke University Press, 2007), 7.

17. Ritchie, "Pinkwashing, Homonationalism, and Israel–Palestine," 616.

18. Ibid., 622.

19. Veena Das, *Life and Words: Violence and the Descent into the Ordinary* (Oakland: University of California Press, 2006), 6–7.

20. Ibid., 54.

21. Ibid., 92.

22. Minoo Moallem, "Violence of Protection," in *Interventions*, ed. Elizabeth Castelli and Janet Jakobson (New York: Palgrave Macmillan, 2004), 17.

23. My transliterations are based on pronunciations according to colloquial urban Palestinian Arabic.

24. "Palestinian Refugees and the Right of Return," American Friends Service Committee, https://www.afsc.org/resource/palestinian-refugees-and-right-return.

25. I use *LGBTQ* consistently throughout this book, unless I'm referring to a title or referencing another individual who uses an alternative, such as *LGBT*.

26. Pseudonym

27. Pseudonym

28. Pseudonym

29. Ghadir Shafie, "Pinkwashing: Israel's International Strategy and Internal Agenda," *Kohl: A Journal for Body and Gender Research* 1, no. 1 (Summer 2015), https://kohljournal.press/pinkwashing-israels-international-strategy.

30. "The Arab World in Seven Charts: Are Arabs Turning Their Backs on Religion?," *BBC*, June 24, 2019, https://www.bbc.com/news/world-middle-east-48703377.

31. "Global Views on Morality," Global Attitudes and Trends, Pew Research Center, accessed October 1, 2019, https://www.pewresearch.org/global/interactives/global-morality/.

32. "Pew Survey Says: Israelis More Open-Minded than Most of the World," *Haaretz*, April 27, 2014, http://www.haaretz.com/israel-news/science/1.587593.

33. Abbad Yahya, "Facing Death Threats and a Ban on His Novel, a Palestinian Author Flees," April 1, 2017, *NPR's Weekend Edition Saturday*, interview by Joanna Kakissis, podcast audio, http://www.npr.org/sections/parallels/2017/04/01/521094950/facing-death-threats-and-a-ban-on-his-novel-a-palestinian-author-flees.

34. Joumana Haddad, "A Palestinian Novel Unearths Dirty Secrets in the Arab World," *New York Times*, July 3, 2017, https://www.nytimes.com/2017/07/03/opinion/a-palestinian-novel-unearths-dirty-secrets-in-the-arab-world.html.

35. "Pride and Prejudice: The Hellish Life of Gaza's LGBTQ Community," *Haaretz*, June 25, 2019, https://www.haaretz.com/middle-east-news/palestinians/.premium-pride-and-prejudice-the-hellish-life-of-gaza-s-lgbtq-community-1.7403501.

36. "Between the Discourse of Opinion and the Discourse of Hatred and Incitement," alQaws, posted June 18, 2015, https://goo.gl/u4usFa.

37. Elhanan Miller, "Homophobic Op-Ed by Islamic Leader Raises Arab Israeli Ire," *The Times of Israel*, June 17, 2015, http://www.timesofisrael.com/homophobic-op-ed-by-islamic-leader-raises-arab-israeli-ire.

38. Ibid.

39. "Top Gaza News Agency Mocks Tel Aviv Pride Attendees with Homophobic Slurs," *The Tower*, June 9, 2016, http://www.thetower.org/3488-gaza-news-agency-mocks-tel-aviv-pride-attendees-with-homophobic-slurs.

40. James Kirchick, "Was Arafat Gay?," *Out*, July 29, 2007, http://www.out.com/entertainment/2007/07/29/was-arafat-gay.

41. Ibid.

42. Diaa Hadid and Majd Al Waheidi, "Hamas Commander, Accused of Theft and Gay Sex, Is Killed by His Own," *New York Times*, March 1, 2016, http://www .nytimes.com/2016/03/02/world/middleeast/hamas-commander-mahmoud-ishtiwi -killed-palestine.html.

43. "Palestine: Torture, Death of Hamas Detainee," Human Rights Watch, last modified February 15, 2016, https://www.hrw.org/news/2016/02/15/palestine-torture -death-hamas-detainee.

44. Ibid.

45. Aviram Zino, "'Beast Parade' Held in Jerusalem," *Ynet*, September 11, 2006, http://www.ynetnews.com/articles/0,7340,L-3326208,00.html.

46. Ibid.

47. Nigel O'Connor, "Gay Palestinians Are Being Blackmailed into Working as Informants," *Vice*, February 19, 2013, http://www.vice.com/en_uk/read/gay-palestin ians-are-being-blackmailed-into-working-as-informants.

48. Walaa Alqaisiya, "Decolonial Queering: The Politics of Being Queer in Pales-tine," *Journal of Palestine Studies* 47, no. 3 (Spring 2018): 29–44, https://doi.org/10.1525 /jps.2018.47.3.29.

49. Ibid., 34.

50. Further information in Kanaaneh, *Birthing the Nation*.

51. For example, see Mada al-Carmel, *Jadal*, no. 24, http://mada-research.org /en/2016/02/08/jadal-24-gender-sexuality.

52. "The Palestinian Gender Movement from the Identity Policy to the Quraysh," Quadita, last modified August 20, 2011, http://www.qadita.net/featured/queers-2.

53. Linah Alsaafin, "Though Small, Palestine's Queer Movement Has Big Vision," *Electronic Intidafa*, July 12, 2013, https://electronicintifada.net/content/though-small -palestines-queer-movement-has-big-vision/12607.

54. Jillian Kestler-D'Amours, "Sexuality and Gender Taboos Challenged by Haifa Project," *Electronic Intifada*, May 24, 2013, https://electronicintifada.net/content/sex uality-and-gender-taboos-challenged-haifa-project/12486.

55. Many of these materials can be found on the designated website for the proj-ect: www.ghanni.net.

56. Kestler-D'Amours, "Sexuality and Gender Taboos."

57. Ibid.

58. Ibid.

59. Ibid.

60. Ibid.

61. Debra Kamin, "Palestinian Gay Film Festival Breaks Down Barriers," *Vari-ety*, December 4, 2015, http://variety.com/2015/film/global/palestinian-kooz-queer -festival-opens-new-borders-1201652356.

62. Ibid.

63. Abdullah Hassan Erikat, "Coming Out as Grey," *This Week in Palestine*, March 30, 2015, http://thisweekinpalestine.com/coming-out-as-grey.

64. Ibid.

65. Ibid.

66. Ibid.

67. Abdullah Hassan Erikat, "'Will I Ever Not Be Haram?' Masculinity, Queerness and Visibility in Palestinian Culture," *Archer*, December 8, 2016, http://archer magazine.com.au/2016/12/will-ever-not-haram-masculinity-queerness-visibility-pal estinian-culture.

68. Ibid.

69. The discomfort with the term *informant* is not limited to this context; many anthropologists also express such concerns about this with regard to their respective interlocutors.

70. "Pinkwatching Kit," Pinkwatching Israel, last modified May 24, 2012, http://www.pinkwatchingisrael.com/portfolio/pinkwashing-kit.

71. Jason Ritchie, "How Do You Say 'Come Out of the Closet' in Arabic?: Queer Activism and the Politics of Visibility in Israel-Palestine," *GLQ: A Journal of Lesbian and Gay Studies* 16, no. 4 (2010): 569, https://doi.org/10.1215/10642684-2010-004.

72. Ibid., 562.

73. Ibid., 571.

74. Shafie, "Pinkwashing."

75. Haneen Maikey and Jason Ritchie, "Israel, Palestine, and Queers," *Monthly Review*, April 28, 2009, http://mrzine.monthlyreview.org/2009/mr280409.html.

76. Ritchie, "How Do You Say?," 570.

77. Ghaith Hilal, "Eight Questions Palestinian Queers Are Tired of Hearing," *Electronic Intifada*, November 27, 2013, https://electronicintifada.net/content /eight-questions-palestinian-queers-are-tired-hearing/12951.

78. "Queer Politics and Haneen Maikey," *We Are the Paper*, January 22, 2012, http://www.wearethepaper.org/5-ed-three/interview-with-haneen-maikey/.

79. Maikey and Ritchie, "Israel, Palestine, and Queers."

80. "Queer Politics and Haneen Maikey."

81. Noah Rankin, "Palestinian LGBT Activist Talks about Occupation," *Cornell Daily Sun*, October 23, 2013, https://issuu.com/cornellsun/docs/10-23-13_entire _issue_lo_res.

82. Heike Schotten and Haneen Maikey, "Queers Resisting Zionism: On Authority and Accountability beyond Homonationalism," *Jadaliyya*, October 10, 2012, http://www.jadaliyya.com/pages/index/7738/queers-resisting-zionism_on-authority-and -accounta.

83. Ibid.

84. "The US Embassy in Tel Aviv Continues to Be Complicit in Pinkwashing," Aswat, posted May 31, 2016, http://www.aswatgroup.org/en/article/us-embassy-tel -aviv-continues-be-complicit-pinkwashing.

85. For an example of a nuanced approach to representations of Palestinian citizens of Israel, see Rhoda Kanaaneh, *Surrounded: Palestinian Soldiers in the Israeli Military* (Stanford, CA: Stanford Press 2009).

86. Ritchie, "How Do You Say?," 560.

87. Tanya Habjouqa, "Jerusalem in Heels," photo collection, accessed October 1, 2019, http://habjouqa.photoshelter.com/gallery-image/Jerusalem-in-Heels/GoooouOJ TxsMmrAw/IooooeShiKoZh27A.

88. Pseudonyms

Chapter 2

1. "Gaza Could Become 'Uninhabitable' by 2020, UN Report Warns," *Haaretz*, September 2, 2015, https://www.haaretz.com/gaza-could-become-uninhabitable-by -2020-un-report-warns-1.5394133.

2. Sarah Schulman, *Conflict Is Not Abuse: Overstating Harm, Community Responsibility, and the Duty of Repair* (Vancouver, BC: Arsenal Pulp Press, 2016), 78.

3. Ibid.

4. James Kirchick, "Was Arafat Gay?," *Out*, July 29, 2007, http://www.out.com /entertainment/2007/07/29/was-arafat-gay.

5. Ibid.

6. That being said, marriage to a woman and fatherhood are not necessarily evidence of sexual orientation and/or preference.

7. Kirchick, "Was Arafat Gay?"

8. Zizo Abul Hawa, "As a gay Palestinian, I provided the 'other side' to Taglit-Birthright Israel groups. Now, I'm banned," Facebook, November 6, 2017, *Haaretz* video, 1:38, https://www.facebook.com/haaretzcom/videos/10155727999036341/.

9. Jayson Littman, "Birthright's Lesser-Known Rainbow Colors," *Haaretz*, August 16, 2012, https://www.haaretz.com/opinion/birthright-s-lesser-known-rainbow -colors-1.458681.

10. Jayson Littman, "How I 'Pink-Washed' My Way through Israel," *Jerusalem Post*, August 11, 2012, http://www.jpost.com/Opinion/Op-Ed-Contributors/How-I -pink-washed-my-way-through-Israel.

11. Ibid.

12. Ibid.

13. Ibid.

14. Ofer Matan, "A Gay Chabadnik, Lesbians Wearing Skullcaps and Hipsters Who Never Pray: Welcome to LGBTQ Birthright," *Haaretz*, June 19, 2015, http://www .haaretz.com/jewish/features/.premium-1.661976.

15. Ibid.

16. Ibid.

17. Ibid.

18. Ibid.

19. Ibid.

20. Ibid.

21. This also reflects Israel's denial of the "right of return" for Palestinian refugees and their descendants to their homes and ancestral lands in Israel/Palestine.

22. "Activist Speaks on Birthright during Israel Apartheid Week," *Daily Free Press*,

March 28, 2013, http://dailyfreepress.com/2013/03/28/palestinian-activist-speaks-on-birthright-during-israel-apartheid-week.

23. Zoë Schlanger, "Queers in the Holy Land: Choking on Blue and White Glitter on Gay Birthright," *Newsweek*, June 28, 2016, http://www.newsweek.com/queers-holy-land-choking-blue-and-white-glitter-gay-birthright-475503.

24. Ibid.

25. Raillan Brooks, "Double Jeopardy: Queer and Muslim in America," *Village Voice*, June 14, 2016, https://www.villagevoice.com/2016/06/14/double-jeopardy-queer-and-muslim-in-america/.

26. Ibid.

27. Tom Jones, "Pinkwashing Israeli Human Rights Violations in Palestine," *Muftah*, July 23, 2014, http://muftah.org/pinkwashing-israeli-human-rights-violations-palestine/#.V24MlPkrKUl.

28. Aeyal Gross, "Pinkwashing Debate/Gay Rights in Israel Are Being Appropriated for Propaganda Value," *Haaretz*, June 10, 2015, https://www.haaretz.com/opinion/.premium-1.660349.

29. Marc3pax, "Who you get in bed with—human rights, gay rights," June 23, 2011, YouTube video, 2:29, https://www.youtube.com/watch?v=vhmBbGFJleU.

30. Justin Elliot, "Pink-Washed: Gay Rights and the Mideast Conflict," *Salon*, July 2, 2011, http://www.salon.com/2011/07/02/pinkwashing_gaza_flotilla.

31. Ibid.

32. Ibid.

33. Jon Ronson, Lucy Greenwell, and Remy Lamont, "Finding Omer, the man accusing a free Gaza organisation of homophobia," posted by "Channel Flip," May 3, 2012, *Guardian* video, 9:48, https://www.theguardian.com/commentisfree/video/2012/may/03/jon-ronson-finding-omar-video.

34. Aviel Magnezi, "Mohammed Abu Khdeir's Killer: 'They Took Three of Ours, so Let's Take One of Theirs,'" *Ynet*, August 11, 2014, http://www.ynetnews.com/articles/0,7340,L-4557714,00.html.

35. Itamar Sharon, "Abu Khdeir Murder Suspect Gives Chilling Account of Killing," *Times of Israel*, August 12, 2014, http://www.timesofisrael.com/we-said-they-took-three-of-ours-lets-take-one-of-theirs.

36. Lizzie Dearden, "Mohammed Abu Khdeir Murder: Israeli Man Convicted of Burning Palestinian Teenager to Death in Revenge Killing," *Independent*, April 19, 2016, http://www.independent.co.uk/news/world/middle-east/mohammed-abu-khdeir-murder-israeli-man-convicted-of-burning-palestinian-teenager-to-death-in-revenge-a6991251.html.

37. Avi Issacharoff, "Palestinians: Slain Arab Teenager Was Burned Alive," *Times of Israel*, July 5, 2014, http://www.timesofisrael.com/palestinians-murdered-arab-teenager-was-burned-alive.

38. "Jerusalem Mayor 'Too Quick to Label Arab Boy's Death as Revenge," *Israel National News*, February 7, 2014, http://www.israelnationalnews.com/News/News.aspx/182432#.V24aUPkrKUl.

39. Mairav Zonszein, "'Jewish extremists' Arrested in Murder of Palestinian Teen in Jerusalem," +972 *Magazine*, July 6, 2014, http://972mag.com/jewish-extremists-ar rested-in-murder-of-palestinian-teen-in-jerusalem/93049.

40. Lisa Goldman, "Israeli police are exacerbating the violence with gag orders," +972 *Magazine*, July 5, 2014, http://972mag.com/israeli-police-are-exacerbating-the -violence-with-gag-orders/93034.

41. Shaked Spier, "After Abu Khdeir Murder, an Ugly Collision of Homophobia and Racism," +972 *Magazine*, July 27, 2014, http://972mag.com/after-abu-khdeir-mur der-an-ugly-collision-of-homophobia-and-racism/94465.

42. Ibid.

43. Ibid.

44. Lara Friedman, "A Blood Libel against All Palestinians," *Forward*, July 9, 2014, http://forward.com/opinion/israel/201752/a-blood-libel-against-all-palestinians.

45. Sigal Samuel, "The Pinkwashing of Mohammed Abu Khdeir," *Forward*, July 7, 2014, http://forward.com/opinion/israel/201531/the-pinkwashing-of-mohammed-abu -khdeir/.

46. Aeyal Gross, "How Pinkwashing Leaves Israel Feeling Squeaky Clean," *Haaretz*, July 9, 2014, https://www.haaretz.com/opinion/.premium-1.603731.

47. Ibid.

48. Aviram Zino, "'Beast Parade' Held in Jerusalem," *Ynet*, September 11, 2006, http://www.ynetnews.com/articles/0,7340,L-3326208,00.html.

49. Patrick Strickland, "LGBT Birthright: Israel's Latest Marketing Ploy?," edito- rial, *FourTwoNine*, March 4, 2013, https://www.haaretz.com/1.4985143.

50. Ami Kaufman, "MK Michaeli: Gays Need Therapy, Commit Suicide at Age 40," +972 *Magazine*, June 14, 2012, http://972mag.com/mk-anastasia-michaeli-gays-need -therapy-they-all-die-at-age-40/48294.

51. Judy Maltz, "In Their Own Words: What Some Israeli Politicians Really Think about Arabs and LGBTs," *Haaretz*, August 4, 2015, https://www.haaretz.com /israel-news/.premium-1.669500.

52. Ibid.

53. Ibid.

54. Ibid.

55. "Israeli MP Blames Quakes on Gays," *BBC News*, last modified February 20, 2008, http://news.bbc.co.uk/2/hi/middle_east/7255657.stm.

56. Rebecca Alpert and Katherine Franke, "Why We Boycotted the Equality Fo- rum: Gay Rights Became a Tool in Israel's Rebranding Campaign," *Gender and Sex- uality Law* (blog), May 11, 2012, http://blogs.law.columbia.edu/genderandsexualitylaw blog/2012/05/11/why-we-boycotted-the-equality-forum-gay-rights-became-a-tool-in -israels-rebranding-campaign.

57. Yair Ettinger, "Jerusalem Chief Rabbi Says Public Disgusted by Homosexu- ality," *Haaretz*, September 29, 2015, http://www.haaretz.com/israel-news/.premium -1.678089.

58. Ilan Lior, "Israel Refuses Asylum for Ghana Citizen Because 'She Chose to

Be a Lesbian,'" *Haaretz*, August 19, 2015, https://www.haaretz.com/israel-news/.pre mium-1.671833.

59. Danna Harman, "'No Such Thing as Jewish Terror' and More from the Poster Boy of Israel's Far Right," *Haaretz*, January 6, 2016, http://www.haaretz.com/israel -news/.premium-1.695866.

60. Yaakov Katz, "40% of IDF's Gay Soldiers Suffer Abuse," *Jerusalem Post*, August 16, 2011, http://www.jpost.com/Defense/40-percent-of-IDFs-gay-soldiers-suffer -abuse.

61. Alpert and Franke, "Why We Boycotted the Equality Forum."

62. Vered Lee, "Fighting AIDS Just Isn't Fashionable in Israel 2012," *Haaretz*, January 10, 2012, http://www.haaretz.com/fighting-aids-just-isn-t-fashionable-in-israel -2012-1.406380.

63. Ibid.

64. City Mouse Online, "Tel Aviv's Last Lesbian Bar Closes Its Doors after 14 Years," *Haaretz*, January 8, 2012, https://www.haaretz.com/israel-news/culture/tel -aviv-s-last-lesbian-bar-closes-its-doors-after-14-years-1.406139?date=1467009302105.

65. "Two Killed in Shooting at Tel Aviv Gay Center," *Haaretz*, August 1, 2009, http://www.haaretz.com/news/two-killed-in-shooting-at-tel-aviv-gay-center-1.281193.

66. Gross, "Squeaky Clean."

67. Dan Littauer, "Prosecutor: Shooter in Attack on Tel Aviv Youth Center Motivated by Anti-Gay Bias," *LGBTQ Nation*, July 8, 2013, http://www.lgbtqnation.com/2013/07 /prosecutor-shooter-in-attack-on-tel-aviv-youth-center-motivated-by-anti-gay-bias.

68. Yaniv Kubovich, "Group of Gay Men Assaulted by Young Attackers in South Tel Aviv," *Haaretz*, January 11, 2014, http://www.haaretz.com/israel-news /.premium-1.568054.

69. Yaniv Kubovich, "Transgender Woman after Attack: We're Assaulted Daily," *Haaretz*, January 7, 2014, http://www.haaretz.com/israel-news/.premium-1.567438.

70. Yaniv Kubovich, "11 Arrested Following Assault on Transgender Woman in Tel Aviv," *Haaretz*, January 5, 2014, http://www.haaretz.com/israel-news/.premium -1.567032?date=1467590955166.

71. Ibid.

72. Ido Efrati, "Half of Israel's Transgender Population Has Been Attacked, Study Shows," *Haaretz*, May 26, 2015, https://www.haaretz.com/israel-news/.premium -1.658091.

73. Ilan Lior, "Israel Actually Ranks Low in Tolerance of LGBT People, Survey Says," *Haaretz*, August 23, 2015, https://www.haaretz.com/israel-news/.premium -1.672505.

74. Shirly Seidler, "Israeli Deputy Education Minister Says Same-Sex Couples Aren't Families," *Haaretz*, February 12, 2014, http://www.haaretz.com/israel-news /.premium-1.573727.

75. Yarden Skop, "Israeli Schools Aren't Yet Reaching Out to Gay Kids, LGBT Leaders Say," *Haaretz*, January 21, 2014, http://www.haaretz.com/israel-news/.pre mium-1.569566.

76. Matan, "Welcome to LGBTQ Birthright."

77. Judy Maltz, "A Same-Sex Couple? Not in My Tel Aviv Apartment Building," *Haaretz*, June 9, 2014, http://www.haaretz.com/israel-news/.premium-1.597813.

78. Associated Press, "Rabbi's Remarks on Homosexuality Spark Protests in Jerusalem," *AP News*, November 20, 2016, https://apnews.com/6147ea791cf549959b42dc eb876dd44c/rabbis-remarks-homosexuality-spark-protests-jerusalem.

79. Itay Stern, "Israeli TV Authority Bans Advert for Backing Gay Marriage and Arabic Language," *Haaretz*, December 21, 2016, https://www.haaretz.com/israel-news /1.760525.

80. Haggai Matar, "Transgender Conscientious Objector Is Sent to Israeli Military Prison," *+972 Magazine*, March 30, 2016, http://972mag.com/transgender-consci entious-objector-is-sent-to-israeli-military-prison/118238.

81. Lizzie Dearden, "Transgender Teenager Jailed for Refusing Military Service in Israeli Defence Forces," *Independent*, March 30, 2016, http://www.independent .co.uk/news/world/middle-east/transgender-teenager-jailed-for-refusing-military -service-in-israeli-defence-forces-idf-west-bank-a6960541.html.

82. Liam Hoare, "Israel Won't Legalize Gay Marriage. Here's Why," *Slate*, November 21, 2013, http://www.slate.com/blogs/outward/2013/11/21/israel_won_t_legalize _gay_marriage_here_s_why.html.

83. Jonathan Lis, "Habayit Hayehudi: Yes to Civil Union, but Not for Gay Couples," *Haaretz*, November 5, 2013, http://www.haaretz.com/israel-news/.premium -1.556317.

84. Natasha Roth, "When Homophobia Becomes a Tool for Political Persecution," *+972 Magazine*, January 25, 2016, http://972mag.com/when-homophobia-becomes-a -tool-for-political-persecution/116255.

85. Ruth Preser, Hilal Amit, Evan Cohen, and Aviv Netter, "Israel's Gay Exodus?," *Al Jazeera English*, interview by Femi Oke and Malika Bilal, June 17, 2014, video, 35:52, http://stream.aljazeera.com/story/201406170004-0023844.

86. Jones, "Pinkwashing Israeli Human Rights Violations."

87. Hila Amit, "Why Do LGBT Israelis Leave the Country?," *+972 Magazine*, February 29, 2016, http://972mag.com/why-do-lgbt-israelis-leave-the-country/117497.

88. Dafna Arad, "Planned Concert by Popular Gay Israeli Singer Sparks Row in West Bank Settlement," *Haaretz*, September 19, 2016, http://www.haaretz.com/israel -news/.premium-1.742999.

89. Times of Israel Staff, "IDF Taps Chief Rabbi Who Once Seemed to Permit Wartime Rape," *Times of Israel*, July 12, 2016, http://www.timesofisrael.com/idf-taps -chief-rabbi-who-once-seemed-to-permit-wartime-rape.

90. Gili Cohen, "IDF's Chief Rabbi Appointee Believes Terrorists Are 'Animals' and Gays Are 'Sick,'" *Haaretz*, July 12, 2016, http://www.haaretz.com/israel-news /.premium-1.730532.

91. Yair Ettinger, "250 Israeli Rabbis Publicly Back Head of Pre-IDF Academy Who Called Gay People 'Perverts,'" *Haaretz*, July 20, 2016, http://www.haaretz.com /israel-news/1.732372.

92. Almog Ben Zikri, "Be'er Sheva Gay Pride Parade Canceled in Protest of Police Diverting Route," *Haaretz*, July 13, 2016, http://www.haaretz.com/israel-news/1.730756.

93. "Court-Backed Homophobia Canceled Be'er Sheva's Gay Pride Parade," editorial, *Haaretz*, Jul 15, 2016, http://www.haaretz.com/opinion/1.731089.

94. Almog Ben Zikri, "Southern Israeli City's First Pride Parade Draws 3,500 Participants; Knife-Wielding Haredi Man Arrested," *Haaretz*, June 23, 2017, https://www.haaretz.com/israel-news/1.797429.

95. Ibid.

96. "'Racist, Homophobe, Bully, Fascist': Sons of Israeli Leaders Trade Barbs on Facebook," *Haaretz*, August 2, 2017, https://www.haaretz.com/israel-news/1.804854.

97. Ibid.

98. Benjamin Butterworth, "Israel's Supreme Court Rules Same-Sex Marriage Is Not a Right," *PinkNews*, August 31, 2017, http://www.pinknews.co.uk/2017/08/31/breaking-israels-supreme-court-rules-same-sex-marriage-is-not-a-right.

99. Lee Yaron, "Israel Tells Top Court It Opposes Adoptions by Same-Sex Couples," *Haaretz*, July 16, 2017, https://www.haaretz.com/israel-news/1.801629.

100. Times of Israel Staff, "Government Will Not Allow Gay Couples to Adopt in Israel," *Times of Israel*, July 16, 2017, http://www.timesofisrael.com/government-will-not-allow-gay-couples-to-adopt-in-israel.

101. Aeyal Gross, "Israel Is Isolating the LGBT Community with Its Surrogacy and Adoption Laws," *Haaretz*, July 18, 2017, https://www.haaretz.com/opinion/.premium-1.801808.

102. "Ultra-Orthodox Lawmaker Ousted for Attending Nephew's Gay Wedding," *Forward*, September 13, 2017, http://forward.com/fast-forward/382578/ultra-orthodox-lawmaker-ousted-for-attending-nephews-gay-wedding.

103. Efrat Weiss, "Police Authorize Jerusalem Pride Parade," *Ynet*, June 14, 2007, http://www.ynetnews.com/articles/0,7340,L-3412574,00.html.

104. James Kirchick, "Pink Eye," *Tablet*, November 29, 2011, http://www.tabletmag.com/jewish-news-and-politics/84216/pink-eye.

105. Ibid.

106. Times of Israel Staff, "Police Okay Anti-Gay Protest during Jerusalem Pride March," *Times of Israel*, August 1, 2017, http://www.timesofisrael.com/police-okays-anti-gay-protest-during-jerusalem-pride-march.

107. Nir Hasson, "22,000 March in Jerusalem Pride Parade Jerusalem under Heavy Security," *Haaretz*, August 3, 2017, https://www.haaretz.com/israel-news/1.805071.

108. David-Elijah Nahmod, "It's Not Pinkwashing to Tell the Truth," *Times of Israel*, April 14, 2012, http://blogs.timesofisrael.com/its-not-pinkwashing-to-tell-the-truth.

109. Brian Whitaker, "Pinkwashing Israel," *Al-Bab*, June 17, 2010, http://www.al-bab.com/blog/2010/06/pinkwashing-israel.

110. Ibid.

111. Dan Littauer, "Israel to Lower Minimum Age Requirement for Gender Reassignment Surgery," *LGBTQ Nation*, May 15, 2014, http://www.lgbtqnation.com/2014/05/israel-to-lower-minimum-age-requirement-for-gender-reassignment-surgery.

112. Hoare, "Israel Won't Legalize Gay Marriage."

113. PinkNews Staff, "Israeli Attorney General Rules Gay Couples Can Jointly Adopt," *PinkNews*, February 11, 2008, http://www.pinknews.co.uk/2008/02/11/israeli -attorney-general-rules-gay-couples-can-jointly-adopt.

114. Lihi Ben Shitrit, "Photo Essay: Fighting Pinkwashing in Israel," *Carnegie Endowment for International Peace*, August 9, 2016, http://carnegieendowment.org /sada/64285.

115. "LGBT Rights," Association for Civil Rights in Israel, accessed October 1, 2019, http://www.acri.org.il/en/category/the-right-to-equality/lgbt-rights.

116. Jayson Littman, "The Case against Pinkwashing, or Why I'm Gay for Israel," *Queerty*, February 9, 2012, http://www.queerty.com/opinion-a-case-against-pink washing-or-why-im-gay-for-israel-20120209.

117. Dan Littauer, "More than One Thousand Rally in Tel Aviv to Protest Recent Anti-LGBT Violence," *LGBTQ Nation*, January 17, 2014, http://www.lgbtqnation .com/2014/01/more-than-one-thousand-rally-in-tel-aviv-to-protest-recent-anti-lgbt -violence.

118. Ibid.

119. Ilan Lior, "Tel Aviv to Extend LGBT Programs to Preschool, Elementary School Teachers," *Haaretz*, August 18, 2016, http://www.haaretz.com/israel-news /.premium-1.737177.

120. Ibid.

121. Katherine Franke, "The Greater Context of the Pinkwashing Debate," *Tikkun*, July 3, 2012, http://www.tikkun.org/nextgen/the-greater-context-of-the-pinkwashing -debate.

122. Jay Michaelson, "A 'Fight of the Century' over 'Pinkwashing' and Israel," *Forward*, May 15, 2015, https://forward.com/opinion/politics/308303/a-fight-among-lgbt -activists-over-israel/.

123. Jay Michaelson, "Pinkwashing Is Not Black and White," *Forward*, November 29, 2011, http://forward.com/opinion/israel/147026/pinkwashing-is-not-black-and -white.

124. Michaelson, "Fight of the Century."

125. Ibid.

126. Ibid.

127. Ibid.

128. Wendy Elisheva Somerson, "Widening the Frame: The Connections between Queer and Palestinian Liberation," *Truthout*, February 2, 2016, http://www .truth-out.org/opinion/item/34655-widening-the-frame-the-connections-between -queer-and-palestinian-liberation.

129. Ashley Bohrer, "Against the Pinkwashing of Israel," *Al-Jazeera*, August 9, 2014, http://www.aljazeera.com/indepth/opinion/2014/08/against-pinkwashing-israel -201489104543430313.html.

130. BBC News Staff, "Palestinian Gays Flee to Israel," *BBC News*, October 22, 2003, http://news.bbc.co.uk/2/hi/middle_east/3211772.stm.

131. Ibid.

132. Bohrer, "Against the Pinkwashing of Israel."

133. David Harris, "'Israel and 'Pinkwashing': What Was the *New York Times* Thinking?," *HuffPost*, last modified January 27, 2012, https://www.huffpost.com/entry /ny-times-sarah-schulman_b_1112171.

134. Milo Yiannopoulos, "This Week in Stupid: Queers for Palestine," *Breitbart*, August 1, 2014, https://www.breitbart.com/europe/2014/08/01/this-week-in-stupid -queers-for-palestine/.

135. Michaelson, "Pinkwashing Is Not Black and White."

136. James Kirchick, "Pink Eye," *Tablet*, November 29, 2011, https://www.tablet mag.com/jewish-news-and-politics/84216/pink-eye.

137. Queer West Bank Palestinians are more likely to be in hiding than queer Palestinian citizens of Israel, hence making their silencing even more prevalent. If there are fewer incidents of homophobic intrafamily violence among Palestinian citizens of Israel than among families in the Occupied Territories, one can make a case that we are not dealing with essentialized Palestinian homophobia but with the way homophobia is accelerated by poverty, hopelessness, and a political climate that has, in the Occupied Palestinian Territories (OPT), painted gay men as collaborators.

138. The fact that the vast majority of my queer Palestinian interlocutors requested that I not name them in this book reveals the extent to which they are not able to publicly respond to pinkwashing discourses in which their bodies and experiences are so centrally featured.

139. Jones, "Pinkwashing Israeli Human Rights Violations."

140. Ibid.

141. Ibid.

142. Nathan Guttman, "Israelis Win Asylum in U.S.—but Mostly Not for Politics," *Forward*, February 13, 2017, http://forward.com/news/israel/171224/israelis-win -asylum-in-us-but-mostly-not-for-pol.

143. Aviel Magnezi, "Committee: Palestinian Authority Does Not Persecute Gays," *Ynet*, December 31, 2014, https://www.ynetnews.com/articles/0,7340,L-4609594 ,00.html.

144. Michaelson, "Pinkwashing Is Not Black and White."

145. Kirchick, "Pink Eye."

146. Ibid.

147. Roberta P. Seid, "The Anti-Israel Lesbian Avenger," *Times of Israel*, August 1, 2013, https://blogs.timesofisrael.com/lgbt-and-israel-the-anti-israel-lesbian-avenger/.

148. Nahmod, "It's Not Pinkwashing to Tell the Truth."

149. Yossi Klein Halevi, "Refugee Status," *New Republic*, August 20, 2002, http:// www.glapn.org/sodomylaws/world/palestine/psnews008.htm.

150. Ibid.

151. Ibid.

152. Ibid.

153. Ibid.

154. Ibid.

155. Ibid.

156. Furthermore, it is possible to interpret Ganon's attempt to protect queer West Bank Palestinians in Israel by registering them with the police as poignant and as illustrating the limits of gay friendliness in Israel. How many Palestinians want to be registered with the Israeli police?

157. Sarah Schulman, "A Documentary Guide to 'Brand Israel' and the Art of Pinkwashing," *Mondoweiss*, November 30, 2011, http://mondoweiss.net/2011/11/a-doc umentary-guide-to-brand-israel-and-the-art-of-pinkwashing.

158. Michaelson, "Pinkwashing Is Not Black and White."

159. Littman, "The Case against Pinkwashing, or Why I'm Gay for Israel."

160. Tyler Lopez, "Why #Pinkwashing Insults Gays and Hurts Palestinians," *Slate*, June 17, 2014, https://slate.com/human-interest/2014/06/pinkwashing-and -homonationalism-discouraging-gay-travel-to-israel-hurts-palestinians.html.

161. Arthur Slepian, "An Inconvenient Truth: The Myths of Pinkwashing," *Tikkun*, July 3, 2012, https://www.tikkun.org/an-inconvenient-truth-the-myths-of-pink washing.

162. Ibid.

163. Ibid.

164. Ibid.

165. Ibid.

166. Jones, "Pinkwashing Israeli Human Rights Violations."

167. Alpert and Franke, "Why We Boycotted the Equality Forum."

168. Michaelson, "Pinkwashing Is Not Black and White."

169. Bohrer, "Against the Pinkwashing of Israel."

170. Lopez, "Why #Pinkwashing Insults Gays."

171. Kirchick, "Pink Eye."

172. Ishaan Tharoor, "Tel Aviv Mayor Links Terror Attack to Israeli Occupation of Palestinian Lands," *Washington Post*, June 10, 2016, https://www.washingtonpost .com/news/worldviews/wp/2016/06/10/tel-aviv-mayor-links-terror-attack-to-israeli -occupation-of-palestinian-lands.

173. Ibid.

174. Gayatri Chakravorty Spivak, "Can the Subaltern Speak?," in *Colonial Discourse and Post-Colonial Theory*, eds. P. Williams and L. Chrisman (New York: Columbia University Press, 1992), 66–111.

Chapter 3

1. Sarah Colborne, "Palestine Takes Center Stage at World Pride," *Mondoweiss*, July 11, 2012, http://mondoweiss.net/2012/07/palestine-takes-center-stage-at-world-pride.

2. Ibid.

3. "World Pride London 2012—No Pride in Israeli Apartheid—Gay Pride," posted by "NoPinkwashingUK," July 9, 2012, YouTube video, 3:03, https://www.youtube.com /watch?v=XHKyw7K5TJo.

4. It is important to note that pinkwashing has also been used by scholars to describe the practices of other countries such as the United States.

5. Natalie Kouri-Towe, "Solidarity at Risk: The Politics of Attachment in Transnational Queer Palestine Solidarity and Anti-Pinkwashing Activism" (PhD diss., University of Toronto, 2015), 89.

6. Andrew Robinson, "In Theory: Dialogism, Polyphony and Heteroglossia," *Ceasefire*, July 29, 2011, https://ceasefiremagazine.co.uk/in-theory-bakhtin-1/.

7. Ibid.

8. Ibid.

9. Ibid.

10. Ibid.

11. John Paul Lederach, "Conflict Transformation," in *Beyond Intractability*, eds. Guy Burgess and Heidi Burgess (Boulder: Conflict Information Consortium, October 2003), https://www.beyondintractability.org/essay/transformation/.

12. Ibid.

13. "Eliad Cohen," *A Wider Bridge*, accessed October 1, 2019, http://awiderbridge.org/eliad-cohen.

14. Ibid.

15. This is meant to further normalize the Israeli military and to grant it legitimacy in the eyes of primarily Western queer audiences. The acceptance of queer Israelis in the military is lauded as a signal of Israel's progressive politics and of Israel's need for self-defense. This praise comes without acknowledgment of the realities of the Palestinian occupation.

16. There is a sense among queer Israelis that Tel Aviv is such a hub also because of its secular inhabitants, whereas gay spaces are more fraught in other cities due to the presence of more religiously observant individuals.

17. "Tens of Thousands Celebrate Gay Pride in Tel Aviv," *Yahoo! News*, June 3, 2016, https://www.yahoo.com/news/tens-thousands-celebrate-gay-pride-tel-aviv-164649436.html.

18. Sarah Schulman, "Israel and Pinkwashing," *New York Times*, November 22, 2011, http://www.nytimes.com/2011/11/23/opinion/pinkwashing-and-israels-use-of-gays-as-a-messaging-tool.html.

19. Rina Rozenberg Kandel, "Foreign Tourists Flock to Tel Aviv for Gay Pride Parade," *Haaretz*, June 13, 2014, https://www.haaretz.com/israel-news/business/.premium-1.598508.

20. Israeli Defense Forces, "It's Pride Month. Did you know that the IDF treats all of its soldiers equally?," Facebook, June 11, 2012, https://www.facebook.com/idfonline/photos/a.250335824989295.62131.125249070831305/425165480839661.

21. Neetzan Zimmerman, "Israeli Military Celebrates Pride Month by Sharing 'Heartwarming' Facebook Photo of Gay Soldiers Holding Hands (UPDATE)," *Gawker*, June 12, 2012, http://gawker.com/5917730/israeli-military-celebrates-pride-month-by-sharing-heartwarming-facebook-photo-of-gay-soldiers-holding-hands.

22. Mitch Ginsburg, "Army's 'Gay Soldiers' Photo Was Staged, Is Misleading," *Times of Israel*, June 12, 2012, http://www.timesofisrael.com/idf-gay-soldiers-photo-is-misleading-military-source-says.

23. Mel Bezalel, "Gay Pride Being Used to Promote Israel Abroad," *Jerusalem Post*, June 7, 2009, http://www.jpost.com/Israel/Gay-pride-being-used-to-promote-Israel -abroad.

24. *Nakba* is the Arabic term, literally meaning "catastrophe," that Palestinians use to describe the 1948 birth of Israel in Palestine and the subsequent displacement of the Palestinian people.

25. Sarah Schulman, "A Documentary Guide to 'Brand Israel' and the Art of Pinkwashing," *Mondoweiss*, November 30, 2011, http://mondoweiss.net/2011/11/a-docu mentary-guide-to-brand-israel-and-the-art-of-pinkwashing.

26. Ibid.

27. Ibid.

28. "Apartheid Israel Is No Place for LGBT Leisure Tourism," Queers Against Is- raeli Apartheid, September 9, 2009, https://queersagainstapartheid.org/2009/09/09 /apartheid-israel-is-no-place-for-lgbt-leisure-tourism.

29. Sami is the pseudonym he used during the tour to protect his privacy.

30. See Sarah Schulman, *Israel/Palestine and the Queer International* (Durham, NC: Duke University Press, 2012).

31. Ibid., 23.

32. "Victory: IGLYO moves out of Israel!," BDS Movement, July 29, 2011, https:// bdsmovement.net/2011/victory-iglyo-moves-out-of-israel-2-7791.

33. "World LGBT Youth Leadership Summit—Tel Aviv," ILGA—International Lesbian, Gay, Bisexual, Trans and Intersex Association, October 12, 2011, http://ilga .org/world-lgbt-youth-leadership-summit-tel-aviv.

34. "About ISDEF," International Defense & HLS Expo, accessed October 1, 2019, https://www.isdefexpo.com/home/about-isdef-2.

35. Tanya Rubinstein, "Tel Aviv's Week of Pride and Militarism," +972 *Magazine*, June 1, 2017, https://972mag.com/tel-avivs-week-of-pride-and-militarism/127765.

36. Ibid.

37. "SHEFITA—Pink (Moran Kariv Remix)—Tel Aviv Pride official 2016," posted by "Municipality of Tel-Aviv-Yafo," May 20, 2016, YouTube video, 3:28, https://www .youtube.com/watch?v=oKn207E7ksI.

38. "SHEFITA—Pink [Aerosmith cover]—Tel Aviv Official Pinkwash 2016," posted by "Sahar M. Vardi," May 31, 2016, YouTube video, 1:40, https://www.youtube .com/watch?v=8dx1dGqJz5M.

39. Fady Khoury, "No Room for Palestinians at Tel Aviv Pride Parade," +972 *Mag- azine*, June 2, 2016, http://972mag.com/no-room-for-palestinians-at-tel-aviv-pride-pa rade/119740.

40. Fady Khoury, "Why I Won't Be Participating in Tel Aviv's Pride Parade," +972 *Magazine*, June 7, 2015, http://972mag.com/why-i-wont-be-participating-in-tel-avivs -pride-parade/107499.

41. See Dalit Baum, "Women in Black and Men in Pink: Protesting against the Is- raeli Occupation," *Journal for the Study of Race, Nation and Culture* 12, no. 5 (January 2007): 567–74, https://doi.org/10.1080/13504630600920274.

42. Yael Marom, "Ahead of Tel Aviv Pride, Queer Activists Bring the Occupa-

tion Home," +972 *Magazine*, June 3, 2016, http://972mag.com/ahead-of-tel-aviv-pride
-queer-activists-bring-the-occupation-home/119781.

43. "Pink Action against Homonationalism and Pinkwashing," *Femina Invicta* (blog), June 8, 2013, https://feminainvicta.com/2013/06/08/pink-action-against-homo nationalism-and-pinkwashing.

44. "Anti Pink-Wash Action—Pride Parade 2013," posted by "SocialTV," July 2, 2013, YouTube video, 3:24, https://youtu.be/VT6f9RIVcHM.

45. Shai Zamir, "Israeli Pride as Pinkwashing," *Tikun Olam* (blog), trans. Richard Silverstein and Dena Shunra, June 14, 2015, http://www.richardsilverstein.com /2015/06/14/israeli-pride-as-pinkwashing.

46. Ilan Lior, "Gay Activists May Transform Tel Aviv Pride Parade into Demonstration," *Haaretz*, April 18, 2016, https://www.haaretz.com/israel-news/.premium-1 .715151.

47. Yael Marom, "Did the Israeli Government Just Admit to 'Pinkwashing?,'" +972 *Magazine*, April 19, 2016, http://972mag.com/did-the-israeli-government-just-admit-to -pinkwashing/118691.

48. Jonathan Lis, "Ministers Reject Sexual Orientation Non-Discrimination Bill," *Haaretz*, June 15, 2015, http://www.haaretz.com/israel-news/.premium-1.661267.

49. Aeyal Gross, "Why the Israeli Government's Condemnation of Jerusalem Gay Pride Attack Is Hollow," *Haaretz*, July 31, 2015, http://www.haaretz.com/israel-news /.premium-1.668915.

50. Dawn Ennis, "Outrage Mounts after Israel Marks LGBT Rights Day by Vetoing LGBT Rights Bills," *Advocate*, February 29, 2016, http://www.advocate.com/world /2016/2/29/outrage-mounts-after-israel-marks-lgbt-rights-day-vetoing-lgbt-rights -bills.

51. Ibid.

52. Ibid.

53. Lahav Harkov, "Netanyahu Voices Support for Gay Rights on Knesset LGBT Day," *Jerusalem Post*, February 23, 2016, http://www.jpost.com/Israel-News /Netanyahu-voices-support-for-gay-rights-on-Knesset-LGBT-Day-445867.

54. Marom, "Did the Israeli Government Just Admit to Pinkwashing?"

55. Ibid.

56. Yael Marom, "LGBTQ Israelis Come Out against Occupation and Homophobia," +972 *Magazine*, June 5, 2017, https://972mag.com/lgbtq-israelis-come-out-against -occupation-and-homophobia/127863.

57. "StandWithUs Northwest Response to Seattle LGBTQ Commission's Refusal to Meet Israelis," StandWithUs, accessed October 1, 2019, https://www.standwithus .com/news/article.asp?id=2214.

58. Dominic Holden, "The LGBT Commission Apologizes for Canceling Meeting with Israeli Visitors," *The Stranger*, March 20, 2012, http://slog.thestranger.com /slog/archives/2012/03/20/the-lgbt-commissionisraelpalestine-mess.

59. "Reception for Israeli LGBT Leaders Canceled: Seattle Commission and Council Members Apologize," New Civil Rights Movement, April 29, 2014, http://

www.thenewcivilrightsmovement.com/reception_for_israeli_lgbt_leaders_canceled
_seattle_commission_and_council_members_apologize.

60. Phan Nguyen, "Northwest Pinkwashing Events Cancelled, StandWithUs's Record of Queer Exploitation Exposed," *Mondoweiss*, March 19, 2012, http://mondo weiss.net/2012/03/northwest-pinkwashing-events-cancelled-standwithuss-record-of -queer-exploitation-exposed.

61. "Reception for Israeli LGBT Leaders Canceled."

62. Nahmod, "It's Not Pinkwashing to Tell the Truth."

63. Dan Avery, "Seattle LGBT Commission Cancels Israeli Event after Complaint by Anti-Pinkwashing Activist," *Queerty*, March 16, 2012, http://www.queerty.com /seattle-lgbt-commission-cancels-israeli-event-after-complaint-by-anti-pinkwashing -activist-20120316.

64. Ibid.

65. "StandWithUs Northwest Response."

66. Nguyen, "Northwest Pinkwashing Events Cancelled."

67. Ibid.

68. Stefanie Fox, "Sponsors of Israeli Group Weren't Here for Open Dialogue," *Seattle Times*, March 26, 2016, http://old.seattletimes.com/html/opinion/2017845797 _guest27fox.html.

69. Zach Carstensen, "Gay Leaders from Israel Snubbed by Seattle LGBT Commission," *Seattle Times*, March 20, 2012, http://old.seattletimes.com/html/northwest voices/2017797429_isralets21.html.

70. Lornet Turnbull, letter to the editor, *Seattle Times*, March 16, 2012, http:// www.seattletimes.com/seattle-news/gay-leaders-from-israel-snubbed-by-seattles-gay -commission.

71. Holden, "LGBT Commission Apologizes for Canceling Meeting."

72. "Trailer: Pinkwashing Exposed: Seattle Fights Back!," posted by "Pinkwashing Exposed," October 2015, Vimeo video, 2:54, https://vimeo.com/125630192.

73. Alex Shams, "Seattle Mayor's Israel Trip Highlights Dangers of 'Pinkwashing,'" *Washington Blade*, June 12, 2015, http://www.washingtonblade.com/2015/06/12 /seattle-mayors-israel-trip-highlights-dangers-of-pinkwashing.

74. Ibid.

75. Eliana Rudee, "LGBTQ Group Shoots Itself in Both Feet by Criticizing Seattle Mayor's Trip to Israel," *Observer*, May 21, 2015, http://observer.com/2015/05 /lgbtq-group-shoots-itself-in-both-feet-by-criticizing-seattle-mayors-trip-to-israel.

76. Ibid.

77. Shams, "Trip Highlights Dangers of 'Pinkwashing.'"

78. Haaretz Staff, "Prime Minister's Office Hires Rightist Israel Advocacy Group for 1 Million Shekels," *Haaretz*, January 13, 2015, https://www.haaretz.com/israel -news/.premium-1.636953.

79. Nora Barrows-Friedman, "Israel's First Trans Officer Helps with Ethnic Cleansing," *Electronic Intifada*, April 12, 2017, https://electronicintifada.net/content /israels-first-trans-officer-helps-ethnic-cleansing/20171.

80. Ibid.

81. Naomi Zeveloff, "Meet Shachar Erez, Israel's First Transgender IDF Officer," *Forward*, April 3, 2017, http://forward.com/news/israel/367907/meet-shachar-erez-is raels-first-transgender-idf-officer.

82. Ibid.

83. Michael Lucas, "Michael Lucas Calls for Boycott of LGBT Center for Host-ing Anti-Semitic Event," *Cision*, February 22, 2011, http://www.prnewswire.com/news -releases/michael-lucas-calls-for-boycott-of-lgbt-center-for-hosting-anti-semitic -event-116669434.html.

84. Ibid.

85. Ibid.

86. Kelly Fong, "Lucas Talks Safe Sex, AIDS and Controversy," *Stanford Daily*, February 15, 2008, http://stanforddailyarchive.com/cgi-bin/stanford?a=d&d=stanford 20080215-01.1.3&e=-------en-20—1—txt-txIN-------.

87. Sadie Moran, "Save New York's LGBT Center! Don't Let Wealthy Bigots Shut Down Free Speech," petition, February 2011, http://www.ipetitions.com/petition/save nyclgbtcenter.

88. Steven Thrasher, "Gay Center Axes Israeli Apartheid Week Event after Boy-cott Threat by Porn Activist," *Village Voice*, February 23, 2011, http://www.village voice.com/news/gay-center-axes-israeli-apartheid-week-event-after-boycott-threat -by-porn-activist-6665496.

89. Mitchell Sunderland, "The Immigrant Who Conquered Porn and Became One of the Most Powerful Gay Men in New York," *Vice*, June 3, 2014, http://www.vice .com/read/body-of-an-american-0000320-v21n5.

90. Ibid.

91. Duncan Osborne, "LGBT Center Bars Sarah Schulman Reading," *Gay City News*, February 13, 2013, http://gaycitynews.nyc/lgbt-center-bars-sarah-schulman-reading.

92. Saeed Jones, "Queer Activist Sarah Schulman Accuses LGBT Center of 'a Weird Kind of Anti-Semitism,'" *Buzzfeed News*, February 14, 2013, https://www.buzzfeed .com/saeedjones/queer-activist-sarah-schulman-accuses-lgbt-center-of-a-weird.

93. Duncan Osborne, "Sarah Schulman Reads from 'Israel/Palestine' at Center," *Gay City News*, March 13, 2013, http://gaycitynews.nyc/sarah-schulman-reads-from -israel-palestine-at-center.

94. "Featured Nation: Israel," Equality Forum, accessed October 1, 2019, http:// www.equalityforum.com/Node/627.

95. Aeyal Gross, "Michael Oren Pinkwashes the Truth about Israel and Gay Pales-tinians," *Haaretz*, May 9, 2012, https://www.haaretz.com/opinion/michael-oren-pink washes-the-truth-about-israel-and-gay-palestinians-1.5220872.

96. Phan Nguyen, "After LGBT Forum, Oren Will Headline for Notorious Homo-phobic Pastor John Hagee," *Mondoweiss*, May 7, 2012, http://mondoweiss.net/2012/05 /after-lgbt-forum-next-stop-for-ambassador-oren-is-john-hagee-conference.

97. "(In)Equality Forum 2012," Pinkwatching Israel, March 13, 2012, http://www .pinkwatchingisrael.com/portfolio/inequality-forum-2012.

98. Rebecca Alpert and Katherine Franke, "Boycotting Equality Forum's Is-raeli Sponsorship," *Tikkun*, May 10, 2012, http://www.tikkun.org/nextgen/boycotting -equality-forums-israeli-sponsorship.

99. Benjamin Doherty, "Pro-BDS Columbia Prof's Gathering with Anti-BDS J-Street and Zionist LGBT Groups Stirs Controversy," *Electronic Intifada*, April 12, 2013, https://electronicintifada.net/blogs/benjamin-doherty/pro-bds-columbia-profs-gath ering-anti-bds-j-street-and-zionist-lgbt-groups.

100. Keshet, "We are appalled by JVP's disrupting of the LGBTQ youth con-tingent of the Celebrate Israel Parade, which included teens from Keshet and other LGBTQ Jewish organizations," Facebook, June 6, 2017, https://www.facebook.com /KeshetGLBTJews/photos/a.417063889122.193627.29766934122/10155634209244123.

101. Jay Michaelson, "Shame on You, Jewish Voice for Peace, for Targeting Pro-Israel Gays," *Forward*, June 6, 2017, http://forward.com/opinion/national/373902 /shame-on-you-jewish-voice-for-peace-for-targeting-gays-at-celebrate-israel.

102. Mordechai Levovitz, "JVP's Targeting of LGBTQ Youth Shows 'an Unbe-lievable Lack of Empathy,'" *Forward*, June 9, 2017, http://forward.com/scribe/374267 /jvps-targeting-of-lgbtq-youth-shows-an-unbelievable-lack-of-empathy.

103. Simone Somekh, "EXCLUSIVE: Jewish Voice for Peace 'Targeted' Gay Group at Celebrate Israel Parade," *Forward*, June 5, 2017, http://forward.com/scribe/373862 /jvp-targeted-queer-jewish-youth-at-israel-parade.

104. "'Jewish Voice for Peace' Infiltrators Sabotage At-Risk LGBTQ Jewish Youth at the Celebrate Israel Parade," Jewish Queer Youth, accessed October 1, 2019, http:// www.jqyouth.org/parade-statement.

105. Craig Willse, "No Apartheid in Our Name: LGBT Jewish Groups Block 'Celebrate Israel' Parade," *Truthout*, June 7, 2017, http://www.truth-out.org/opinion /item/40870-no-apartheid-in-our-name-lgbt-jewish-groups-block-celebrate-israel -parade.

106. Alissa Wise, "JVP: Reactions to Our Parade Protest Were 'Cruel,' 'Homo-phobic,' and 'Hyperbolic,'" *Forward*, June 7, 2017, http://forward.com/scribe/374055 /jvp-reactions-to-our-parade-protest-were-cruel-homophobic-and-hyperbolic.

107. Ibid.

108. Anna Fox, "I'm a Queer Jewish Student. Is My acceptance in Organized Jewish Communities Conditional?," *Jewschool*, June 14, 2017, https://jewschool.com /2017/06/79786/im-queer-jewish-student-acceptance-organized-jewish-communities -conditional.

109. "IfNotNow Stands with Queer Jews and against the Occupation," IfNotNow, June 8, 2017, https://medium.com/ifnotnoworg/ifnotnow-stands-with-queer-jews-and -against-the-occupation-16efcd33da1b.

110. Stephanie Skora, "Queer Jews Should Think Again before Celebrating Israel," +972 *Magazine*, June 18, 2017, https://972mag.com/queer-jews-should-think-again-be fore-celebrating-israel/128195.

111. See Bari Weiss, "I'm Glad the Dyke March Banned Jewish Stars," *New York Times*, June 27, 2017, https://www.nytimes.com/2017/06/27/opinion/im-glad-the-dyke

-march-banned-jewish-stars.html; Peter Holley, "Jewish Marchers Say They Were Kicked Out of a Rally for Inclusiveness Because of Their Beliefs," *Washington Post*, June 26, 2016, https://www.washingtonpost.com/news/acts-of-faith/wp/2017/06/26 /jewish-marchers-say-they-were-kicked-out-of-a-rally-for-inclusiveness-because-of -their-beliefs; Harriet Sinclair, "Gay Pride Marchers with Jewish Flags Told to Leave Chicago Parade," *Newsweek*, June 25, 2017, http://www.newsweek.com/gay-pride -marchers-jewish-flags-told-leave-chicago-parade-628879; Fox News Staff, "Women with Star of David Flags Told to Leave Chicago Gay Pride March," *Fox News*, June 25, 2017, http://www.foxnews.com/us/2017/06/25/women-with-star-david-flags-told-to -leave-chicago-gay-pride-march.html; Haaretz Staff, "Chicago 'Dyke March' Bans Jewish Pride Flags: 'They Made People Feel Unsafe,'" *Haaretz*, June 26, 2017, https:// www.haaretz.com/us-news/1.797650; Tracy Gilchrist, "Pride Flags Bearing Star of David Barred in Chicago Dyke March," *Advocate*, June 25, 2017, https://www.advocate .com/religion/2017/6/25/pride-flags-bearing-star-david-barred-chicago-dyke-march; Hilton Dresden, "Chicago Dyke March Asks Three People Carrying Flag with Star of David to Leave," *Out*, June 26, 2017, https://www.out.com/news-opinion/2017/6 /26/chicago-dyke-march-asks-three-people-carrying-flag-star-david-leave; and Liz Baudler, "Marchers, Police and Zionists Collide at SlutWalk," *Windy City Times*, August 12, 2017, http://www.windycitymediagroup.com/lgbt/Marchers-police-and-Zion ists-collide-at-SlutWalk/60071.html.

112. See "Chicago Jewish Voice for Peace Statement of Solidarity with Chicago Dyke March Collective," Jewish Voice for Peace, accessed October 1, 2019, https://docs .google.com/document/d/1VG2cPkufLCFVSv4DmvRbOSQnzMdUt7so8AlrQHcX SyA/pub; "Chicago Dyke March Official Statement on 2017 March and Solidarity with Palestine," Chicago Dyke March Collective, June 27, 2017, https://chicagodykemarch collective.org/2017/06/27/chicago-dyke-march-official-statement-on-2017-march-and -solidarity-with-palestine; and "Solidarity with Chicago Dyke March: It's Not Anti-semitic to Oppose Israel," No to Pinkwashing/No to Israeli Apartheid, July 21, 2017, http://www.nopinkwashing.org.uk/solidarity-with-chicago-dyke-march-its-not-anti semitic-to-oppose-israel.

113. "Zionist Activists Shunned at SlutWalk Chicago," *Forward*, August 13, 2017, http://forward.com/fast-forward/379811/zionist-activists-shunned-at-slutwalk-chicago.

114. Baudler, "Marchers, Police and Zionists Collide at SlutWalk."

Chapter 4

1. W. E. B. Du Bois, *The Souls of Black Folk* (Boston: Bedford Books, 1997), 155.

2. Ibid., 38.

3. Alex Tehranian, "Gay Man Criticizes Palestinian Society," *The Hoya*, October 22, 2004, https://www.thehoya.com/gay-man-criticizes-palestinian-society/.

4. Ibid.

5. Yossi Klein Halevi, "Refugee Status," *New Republic*, August 20, 2002, https:// newrepublic.com/article/66406/refugee-status.

6. Ibid.

7. Ibid.

8. Associated Press, "Palestinian Protesters Whitewash Rainbow Flag from West Bank Barrier," *Guardian*, June 30, 2015, https://www.theguardian.com/world/2015/jun/30/palestinian-protesters-whitewash-rainbow-flag-west-bank-barrier.

9. Ibid.

10. Daniel Ottoson, *State Sponsored Homophobia: A World Survey of Laws Prohibiting Same Sex Activity between Consenting Adults* (The International Lesbian, Gay, Bisexual, Trans and Intersex Association, 2010), 24, https://web.archive.org/web/20101122235101/http://old.ilga.org/Statehomophobia/ILGA_State_Sponsored_Homophobia_2010.pdf.

11. Trudy Ring, "WATCH: Gay Christian Palestinian Fears Death If Deported," *Advocate*, June 22, 2015, http://www.advocate.com/world/2015/06/22/watch-gay-christian-palestinian-fears-death-if-deported.

12. Laurie Segall, "Christian, Gay, Family Ties to Hamas: I'll Be Killed If I'm Deported," CNN, June 22, 2015, http://money.cnn.com/2015/06/22/news/economy/john-calvin-hamas-deported.

13. Ibid.

14. Dov Lieber, "Gay and Christian, a Scion of a Hamas Family Finally Finds Safety in US," *Times of Israel*, June 6, 2016, http://www.timesofisrael.com/gay-and-christian-a-scion-of-a-hamas-family-finally-finds-safety-in-us.

15. Yardena Schwartz, "Meet the Arab Woman Who Has Just Become the First Miss Trans Israel," *Time*, May 31, 2016, http://time.com/4352201/talleen-abu-hanna-first-miss-trans-israel.

16. Ibid.

17. Diaa Hadid, "A 'Seed of Hope' for Transgender People in Arab Communities," *New York Times*, July 29, 2016, http://www.nytimes.com/2016/07/30/world/middleeast/a-seed-of-hope-for-transgender-people-in-arab-communities.html.

18. Schwartz, "Meet the Arab Woman."

19. "Israeli Catholic Wins First 'Miss Trans Israel' Pageant," *Times of Israel*, May 27, 2016, http://www.timesofisrael.com/israeli-catholic-wins-first-miss-trans-israel-pageant.

20. Hadid, "A 'Seed of Hope.'"

21. "Meet Talleen Abu Hanna, Israel's Miss Trans Israel," posted by "Israel Speaks Arabic," September 21, 2016, Facebook video, 2:47, https://www.facebook.com/IsraelArabic/videos/1125091934194880.

22. "Israel's Christian-Arab Transgender Beauty Queen Opens Up: 'I'm Lucky to Be an Israeli,'" *Haaretz*, June 17, 2017, https://www.haaretz.com/israel-news/all-stories/1.796244.

23. Lihi Ben Shitrit, "Photo Essay: Fighting Pinkwashing in Israel," Carnegie Endowment for International Peace, August 9, 2016, http://carnegieendowment.org/sada/64285.

24. Diaa Hadid, "In Israeli City of Haifa, a Liberal Arab Culture Blossoms," *New York Times*, January 3, 2016, http://www.nytimes.com/2016/01/04/world/middleeast/in-israeli-city-of-haifa-a-liberal-palestinian-culture-blossoms.html.

25. Rajii Bathish, "Palestinian Writer Raji Bathish on the 'Conscious Decision

to Authoring Queer, Sexualized Texts," interview by Suneela Mubayi, trans. Suneela Mubayi, ArabLit, May 28, 2016, https://arablit.org/2016/05/28/palestinian-writer-raji -bathish-on-the-conscious-decision-to-authoring-queer-sexualized-texts/.

26. Hadid, "A Liberal Arab Culture Blossoms."

27. Ayed Fadel, "Good morning everyone," Facebook, January 4, 2016, https:// www.facebook.com/ayed.fadel/posts/10156343153705366.

28. Margaret Sullivan, "More Context Needed in Article on Haifa Culture," *New York Times*, January 8, 2016, http://publiceditor.blogs.nytimes.com/2016/01/08/more -context-needed-in-article-on-haifa-culture-2.

29. Ibid.

30. Ibid.

31. Ibid.

32. Margaret Sullivan, "Haifa, Part 2: Article's Author Responds to Complaints," *New York Times*, January 8, 2016, https://publiceditor.blogs.nytimes.com/2016/01/08 /haifa-part-2-articles-author-responds-to-complaints.

33. Ibid.

34. Kevin Naff, "Israel as 'Gay Heaven?' It's Complicated," *Times of Israel*, November 10, 2013, http://blogs.timesofisrael.com/israel-as-gay-heaven-its-complicated.

35. Ibid.

36. Jodi Rudoren, "Veterans of Elite Israeli Unit Refuse Reserve Duty, Citing Treatment of Palestinians," *New York Times*, September 12, 2014, http://www.nytimes .com/2014/09/13/world/middleeast/elite-israeli-officers-decry-treatment-of-palestin ians.html.

37. Ibid.

38. "Any Palestinian Is Exposed to Monitoring by the Israeli Big Brother," *Guardian*, September 12, 2014, https://www.theguardian.com/world/2014/sep/12/israeli-intel ligence-unit-testimonies.

39. Dahlia Scheindlin, "IDF's 'Start-Up Nation' Reservists Refuse to Serve the Occupation," +972 *Magazine*, September 12, 2014, http://972mag.com/idfs-start-up-na tion-reservists-refuse-to-serve-the-occupation/96636; Philip Weiss, "Israel Surveils and Blackmails Gay Palestinians to Make Them Informants," *Mondoweiss*, September 12, 2014, http://mondoweiss.net/2014/09/blackmails-palestinian-informants; Corey Robin, "Forget Pinkwashing; Israel Has a Lavender Scare," *Corey Robin* (blog), September 17, 2014, http://coreyrobin.com/2014/09/17/forget-pinkwashing-israel-has-a -lavender-scare.

40. "AlQaws Statement Re: Media Response to Israel's Blackmailing of Gay Palestinians," Al-Qaws, September 19, 2014, http://www.alqaws.org/articles/alQaws-State ment-re-media-response-to-Israels-blackmailing-of-gay-Palestinians.

41. "About Naomi," Naomi Klein, accessed October 1, 2019, http://www.naomi klein.org/meet-naomi.

42. John Greyson, "Open Letter to TIFF," accessed August 27, 2019, http://www .yorku.ca/greyzone/figtrees/docs/open_letter_to_TIFF.pdf.

43. Andy Levy-Ajzenkopf, "Brand Israel Set to Launch in GTA," *Canadian Jewish News*, August 20, 2008, http://www.cjnews.com/news/brand-israel-set-launch-gta.

44. "Toronto Declaration: No Celebration of Occupation," Toronto Declaration, September 2, 2009, http://torontodeclaration.blogspot.com.

45. Judy Rebick and John Greyson, "Courageous Film Maker John Greyson Pulls His Film from TIFF to Protest Their Spotlight on Tel Aviv," *Rabble*, August 29, 2009, http://rabble.ca/blogs/bloggers/judes/2009/08/courageous-film-maker-john-greyson-pulls-his-film-tiff-protest-their-sp.

46. Disability Justice, "Sins Invalid Pulls Film Out of Vancouver Queer Film Festival (VQFF) Due to Festival's Pinkwashing Ad," Tumblr, August 6, 2014, http://disability-justice.tumblr.com/post/94025105614/sins-invalid-pulls-film-out-of-vancouver-queer.

47. Philip Weiss, "Major Bay Area Arts Org Worked Closely with Israeli Consul General to Counter Protests," *Mondoweiss*, April 16, 2012, http://mondoweiss.net/2012/04/major-bay-area-arts-org-worked-closely-with-israeli-consul-general-to-counter-protests.

48. Toshio Meronek, "De-Pinkwashing Israel," *Truthout*, November 17, 2012, http://www.truth-out.org/news/item/12553-de-pinkwashing-israel.

49. Nirit Anderman, "Director of Opening Night Film in Tel Aviv LGBT Film Fest Boycotts Screening," *Haaretz*, May 28, 2017, https://www.haaretz.com/israel-news/1.792432.

50. Ibid.

51. GroundUp Staff, "SA Director Pulls Out of Tel Aviv International LGBT Film Festival," *GroundUp*, May 26, 2017, https://www.groundup.org.za/article/sa-director-pulls-out-tel-aviv-international-lgbt-film-festival.

52. Anderman, "Director of Opening Night Film."

53. Nadia Awad, "Forget the Hasbara, Israeli Army's Bombs Never Distinguish between Heterosexual and Queer Palestinians," *Mondoweiss*, March 3, 2011, http://mondoweiss.net/2011/03/forget-the-hasbara-israeli-army%E2%80%99s-bombs-never-distinguish-among-heterosexual-and-queer-palestinians.

54. Mitchell Sunderland, "The Immigrant Who Conquered Porn and Became One of the Most Powerful Gay Men in New York," *Vice*, June 3, 2014, http://www.vice.com/read/body-of-an-american-0000320-v21n5.

55. Ibid.

56. Ibid.

57. Debra Kamin, "A Zionist Porn Star Shows His Solidarity," *Times of Israel*, August 6, 2014, http://www.timesofisrael.com/a-zionist-porn-star-shows-his-solidarity.

58. "Michael Lucas Tells *Try State Magazine* all about INSIDE ISRAEL: Sometimes Politics and Porn Collide," *TryState Magazine*, November 2009, http://trystatemagazine.blogspot.com/2009/11/michael-lucas-tells-try-state-magazine.html.

59. Ella Taylor, "'Out in the Dark,' Where Nothing Is Black or White," NPR, September 26, 2013, http://www.npr.org/2013/09/26/224525632/out-in-the-dark-where-nothing-is-black-or-white.

60. Brady Forrest, "The Pinkwashing of 'Out in the Dark,'" *Mondoweiss*, September 24, 2014, http://mondoweiss.net/2014/09/pinkwashing-out-dark.

61. Ibid.

62. Nirit Anderman, "New Film Seeks to Show that Love Conquers All, Even the Israeli-Palestinian Conflict," *Haaretz*, March 8, 2013, http://www.haaretz.com/israel -news/new-film-seeks-to-show-that-love-conquers-all-even-the-israeli-palestinian -conflict.premium-1.508139.

63. Sigal Samuel, "'The Invisible Men' Accused of Pinkwashing," *Daily Beast*, December 11, 2012, http://www.thedailybeast.com/articles/2012/11/12/the-invisible-men -accused-of-pinkwashing.html.

64. "The Invisible Men," Journeyman Pictures, accessed October 1, 2019, https:// www.journeyman.tv/film/5538.

65. Queers Against Israeli Apartheid Vancouver, "Vancouver Queer Film Festival Urged to Come Out against Israeli Apartheid," BDS Movement, August 24, 2012, https:// bdsmovement.net/2012/vancouver-queer-film-festival-urged-to-come-out-against-is raeli-apartheid-9450.

66. Samuel, "'The Invisible Men' Accused of Pinkwashing."

67. Ibid.

68. "Yariv Mozer: What Does He Really Think about Palestinians and Israel?," posted by "katrap40," August 14, 2012, YouTube video, 5:56, https://youtu.be/XAkyxZ _hhDo.

69. "A Jerusalem Love Story," *Vox Tablet*, *Tablet Magazine*, interview by Daniel Estrin, February 12, 2013, podcast audio, http://www.tabletmag.com/podcasts/123927 /a-jerusalem-love-story.

70. Amira Hass, "Shin Bet Inquiry: Did the Israeli Slip His Gay Palestinian Lover into the Country Illegally?," *Haaretz*, May 28, 2012, http://www.haaretz.com/israel -news/shin-bet-inquiry-did-the-israeli-slip-his-gay-palestinian-lover-into-the-coun try-illegally.premium-1.432857.

71. Ibid.

72. Dana Weiler-Polak, "Gay Palestinian Seeks Residency in Israel on Humanitarian Grounds," *Haaretz*, September 29, 2010, http://www.haaretz.com/gay -palestinian-seeks-residency-in-israel-on-humanitarian-grounds-1.316274.

73. Ibid.

74. Rebecca Harrison, "Gay Palestinian Gets OK to Live with Israeli Lover," Reuters, March 25, 2008, http://uk.reuters.com/article/lifestyleMolt/idUKL25868658200 80325.

75. Itay Hod, "Gay Palestinians In Israel: The 'Invisible Men,'" *Daily Beast*, August 13, 2014, http://www.thedailybeast.com/articles/2014/08/13/gay-palestinians-in -israel-the-invisible-men.html.

76. Dana Weiler-Polak, "Gay Palestinian Seeks Residency in Israel."

77. *Zero Degrees of Separation*, directed by Elle Flanders (2005; Montréal, QC: Canadian Heritage Department, National Film Board of Canada), DVD.

78. Colleen Jancovic and Nadia Awad, "Queer/Palestinian Cinema: A Critical Conversation on Palestinian Queer and Women's Filmmaking," *Camera Obscura* 27, no. 2 (September 2012): 140, https://doi.org/10.1215/02705346-1597231.

79. Ibid.

80. Omar Kholeif, "Queering Palestine: Piercing Eytan Fox's Imagined Bubble with Sharif Waked's Chic Point," *Camera Obscura* 27, no. 2 (September 2012): 158, https://doi.org/10.1215/02705346-1597249.

81. Gil Z. Hochberg, "'Check Me Out': Queer Encounters in Sharif Waked's Chic Point: Fashion for Israeli Checkpoints," *GLQ: A Journal of Gay and Lesbian Studies* 16, no. 4 (October 2010): 581, https://doi.org/10.1215/10642684-2010-005.

82. Ibid., 580.

83. Ibid., 591.

84. Fady Khoury, "No Room for Palestinians at Tel Aviv Pride Parade," trans. Tal Haran, +972 *Magazine*, June 2, 2016, http://972mag.com/no-room-for-palestinians-at-tel-aviv-pride-parade/119740.

85. Fadi Daem, Facebook, May 28, 2016, https://www.facebook.com/photo.php?fbid=10154227921026477&set=a.10150359818316477.401548.564336476&type=3&theater.

86. Khoury, "No Room for Palestinians."

87. "AlQaws' Opinion Piece about the Documentary 'Oriented,'" Al-Qaws, November 17, 2015, http://www.alqaws.org/news/alQaws-Opinion-Piece-about-the-Documentary-Oriented-?category_id=0.

88. Ibid.

89. Jake Witzenfeld, "Oriented: 'We Are Palestine, We Are Queer, We Are Here!,'" *Palestine Square*, interview by Khelil Bouarrouj, February 16, 2016, https://palestinesquare.com/2016/02/16/oriented-we-are-palestine-we-are-queer-we-are-here.

90. Jake Witzenfeld and Khader Abu-Seif, "In Conversation with Jake Witzenfeld and Khader Abu-Seif of Oriented," *Out*, interview by James McDonald, July 6, 2017, http://www.out.com/interviews/2015/7/06/conversation-jake-witzenfeld-and-khader-abu-seif-oriented.

91. Khader Abu-Seif, "'We're Fighting Two Fights Here': Being Gay and Palestinian in Israel," *Vice*, interview by Matthew Schultz, November 29, 2015, https://broadly.vice.com/en_us/article/were-fighting-two-fights-here-being-gay-and-palestinian-in-israel.

92. Khader Abu-Seif, "Here's What LGBT Life in the Middle East Is Really Like," *GOOD*, interview by Yasha Wallin, July 31, 2016, https://www.good.is/features/lgbt-life-middle-east.

93. Suze Olbrich, "What's Life Like for Gay Palestinians?," *Dazed*, June 4, 2015, http://www.dazeddigital.com/artsandculture/article/24777/1/what-s-life-like-for-gay-palestinians.

94. Suze Olbrich, "Oriented: The Film That's Redefining What It Means to Be Gay, Arab and Living in Israel," *Telegraph*, October 4, 2016, http://www.telegraph.co.uk/on-demand/2016/10/04/oriented-the-film-thats-redefining-what-it-means-to-be-gay-arab.

95. The delegates, in alphabetical order, were Katherine Franke (director, Center for Gender and Sexuality Law, Columbia University), Barbara Hammer (award-winning independent filmmaker), Richard Kim (executive director, *The Nation* magazine), Rabbi Sharon Kleinbaum (senior rabbi, Bet Simchat Torah, the LGBT syn-

agogue), Tom Leger (publisher, *prettyqueer.com*), Troy Masters (founder and publisher, *Gay City News*), Tim McCarthy (core faculty and director, Human Rights and Social Movements Program, Carr Center for Human Rights Policy, Harvard Kennedy School), Darnell Moore (project manager, Hetrick-Martin Institute's New School Development Project in Newark, New Jersey; and visiting scholar, Center for the Study of Gender and Sexuality at New York University), Vani Natarajan (humanities and area studies librarian, Barnard College), Pauline Park (chair, New York Association for Gender Rights Advocacy), Jasbir Puar (associate professor of Women's and Gender Studies, Rutgers University, and board member, Audre Lorde Project), Roya Rastegar (independent film curator and visiting fellow, Center for the Study of Women, University of California, Los Angeles), Dean Spade (assistant professor, Seattle University School of Law; and founder, Sylvia Rivera Law Project), Kendall Thomas (director, Center for the Study of Law and Culture, Columbia University), Lisa Weiner-Mahfuz (coordinator, Roots Coalition: Queer People of Color Network), and Juliet Wildoff (primary care physician, Callen/Lorde LGBT Community Health Services).

96. The Birthright Unplugged program was designed as a counter to the Birthright Israel program, which provides young Jewish North Americans with free trips to Israel that are ideologically aligned with the Israeli state. Birthright Unplugged no longer exists.

97. Sa'ed Atshan and Darnell Moore, "Reciprocal Solidarity: Where the Black and Palestinian Queer Struggles Meet," *Biography* 37, no. 2 (Spring 2014): 680–705, https://doi.org/10.1353/bio.2014.0033.

98. Guy Shalev, "A Doctor's Testimony: Medical Neutrality and the Visibility of Palestinian Grievances in Jewish-Israeli Publics," *Culture, Medicine, and Psychiatry* 40, no. 2 (June 2016): 247, https://doi.org/10.1007/s11013-015-9470-7.

99. "The Queer Arab Imaginary," posted by "CLAGS: The Center for LGBTQ Studies," July 6, 2013, YouTube video, 1:17:02, from a panel during the CLAGS Homonationalism and Pinkwashing Conference at The Graduate Center, CUNY, New York City, April 10–11, 2013, https://www.youtube.com/watch?v=9u5g2wG6H6c.

100. "Jasbir Puar—Keynote from the Homonationalism and Pinkwashing Conference," posted by "CLAGS: The Center for LGBTQ Studies," July 19, 2013, YouTube video, 1:49:31, from the keynote during the CLAGS Homonationalism and Pinkwashing Conference at The Graduate Center, CUNY, New York City, April 10–11, 2013, https://youtu.be/3S1eEL8ElDo.

Chapter 5

1. Joseph A. Massad, *Desiring Arabs* (Chicago: University of Chicago Press, 2007); and Joseph A. Massad, "Re-Orienting Desire: The Gay International and the Arab World," *Public Culture* 14, no. 2 (Spring 2002): 361–85, https://doi.org/10.1215/08992363 -14-2-361.

2. Gil Z. Hochberg, "Introduction: Israelis, Palestinians, Queers: Points of Departure," *GLQ: A Journal of Gay and Lesbian Studies* 16, no. 4 (October 2010): 515, https://doi.org/10.1215/10642684-2010-001.

3. Ibid., 506.

4. Ibid.

5. Lama Abu-Odeh, "That Thing that You Do: Comment on Joseph Massad's 'Empire of Sexuality,'" *Al-Akhbar*, March 25, 2013, http://english.al-akhbar.com/node /15350.

6. Ibid.

7. Félix Éwanjé-Épée and Stella Magliani-Belkacem, "The Empire of Sexuality: An Interview with Joseph Massad," *Jadaliyya*, March 5, 2013, http://www.jadaliyya .com/pages/index/10461/.

8. The Queen Boat incident occurred in 2001 when Egyptian police raided a floating gay nightclub in Cairo, leading to the arrest of fifty-two men.

9. Joseph A. Massad, *Islam in Liberalism* (Chicago: University of Chicago Press, 2016), 271.

10. Michel Foucault, "Nietzsche, Genealogy, History," in *Hommage a Jean Hyppolite* (Paris: Presses Universitaires de France, 1971), 79.

11. Ibid, 80.

12. S. Taha, "Joseph Massad: An Occidentalist's Other Subjects/Victims," *Arab Leftist* (blog), posted April 21, 2013, http://arableftist.blogspot.com/2013/04/joseph -massad-occidentalists-other_21.html.

13. Ibid.

14. Ibid.

15. Ibid.

16. Ibid.

17. Edward Said, *Orientalism* (London: Penguin Books 1978), 300–301.

18. Massad, *Islam in Liberalism*, 271.

19. Ibid.

20. Ibid.

21. Hochberg, "Introduction," 506–7.

22. Abu-Odeh, "That Thing that You Do."

23. Ibid.

24. Ibid.

25. Gil Z. Hochberg, "Check Me Out: Queer Encounters in Sharif Waked's Chic Point: Fashion for Israeli Checkpoints," *GLQ: A Journal of Gay and Lesbian Studies* 16, no. 4 (October 2010): 580, https://doi.org/10.1215/10642684-2010-005.

26. Abu-Odeh, "That Thing that You Do."

27. Ibid.

28. Hochberg, "Introduction," 507.

29. Éwanjé-Épée and Magliani-Belkacem, "Empire of Sexuality."

30. Brian Whitaker, review of *Desiring Arabs*, by Joseph Massad, *Al-Bab*, http:// al-bab.com/distorting-desire.

31. Natalie Kouri-Towe, "Solidarity at Risk: The Politics of Attachment in Transnational Queer Palestine Solidarity and Anti-Pinkwashing Activism" (PhD diss., University of Toronto, 2015), 89.

32. Jasbir Puar and Maya Mikdashi, "Pinkwatching and Pinkwashing: Interpen-

etration and Its Discontents," *Jadaliyya*, August 9, 2012, http://www.jadaliyya.com/pages/index/6774/pinkwatching-and-pinkwashing_interpenetration-and-.

33. Ibid.

34. Ibid.

35. Ibid.

36. Ibid.

37. Ibid.

38. Ibid.

39. Ibid.

40. Ibid.

41. Ibid.

42. Ibid.

43. Heike Schotten and Haneen Maikey, "Queers Resisting Zionism: On Authority and Accountability beyond Homonationalism," *Jadaliyya*, October 10, 2012, http://www.jadaliyya.com/pages/index/7738/queers-resisting-zionism_on-authority-and-accounta.

44. Ibid.

45. *Jadaliyya* did the same that year with an academic article critiquing DAM, a Palestinian hip-hop group, for one of their feminist music videos. *Jadaliyya* allowed DAM to publish a response, but it was accompanied by the rejoinder from the academic authors (Lila Abu-Lughod and Maya Mikdashi).

46. Jasbir Puar and Maya Mikdashi, "On Positionality and Not Naming Names: A Rejoinder to the Response by Maikey and Schotten," *Jadaliyya*, October 10, 2012, http://www.jadaliyya.com/pages/index/7792/on-positionality-and-not-naming-names_a-rejoinder-.

47. Éwanjé-Épée and Magliani-Belkacem, "Empire of Sexuality."

48. Puar and Mikdashi, "On Positionality and Not Naming Names."

49. Ibid.

50. Kouri-Towe, "Solidarity at Risk," 58.

51. Ibid., 59.

52. Ibid.

53. Ibid., 60.

54. Puar and Mikdashi, "Pinkwatching and Pinkwashing."

55. Schotten and Maikey, "Queers Resisting Zionism."

56. Ibid.

57. Ibid.

58. Ibid.

59. Ibid.

60. Puar and Mikdashi, "Pinkwatching and Pinkwashing."

61. Éwanjé-Épée and Magliani-Belkacem, "Empire of Sexuality."

62. Whitaker, review of *Desiring Arabs*.

Conclusion

1. Personal communication with Farha Ghannam, October 17, 2019.

2. See Rashid Khalidi, *Palestinian Identity: The Construction of Modern National Consciousness* (New York: Columbia University Press, 1997).

3. José E. Muñoz, *Disidentification: Queers of Color and the Performance of Politics* (Minneapolis: University of Minnesota Press, 1999), 25.

4. José E. Muñoz, *Cruising Utopia: The Then and There of Queer Futurity* (New York: NYU Press, 2009), 38.

5. Ibid., 114.

6. Ibid., 49.

7. Ibid., 114.

8. For example, see Jason Ritchie, "How Do You Say 'Come Out of the Closet' in Arabic? Queer Activism and the Politics of Visibility in Israel-Palestine," *GLQ: A Journal of Lesbian and Gay Studies* 16, no. 4 (2010): 557–76, https://doi.org/10.1215/1064 2684-2010-004.

Index

Printed in the USA
CPSIA information can be obtained
at www.ICGtesting.com
LVHW041129231023
761865LV00005B/130